Angela Thirkell
Portrait of a Lady Novelist

Margot Strickland

Margot Strickland

Chicago 1996

D1569005

Other books by Margot Strickland
The Byron Women
Moura Lympany - Her Autobiography

First published in 1977 by
Gerald Duckworth & Co. Ltd
The Old Piano Factory
43 Gloucester Crescent, London NW1

© 1977 by Margot Strickland

ISBN 0 7156 1124 0

Second printing 1996
Angela Thirkell Society
North American Branch

To

Simon

and

Diana

Printed in the USA by

Morris Publishing
3212 E. Hwy 30 • Kearney, NE 68847
800-650-7888

Contents

Cover illustration: Angela McInnes.
Oil painting by the Hon. John Collier.
National Gallery of Victoria, Melbourne

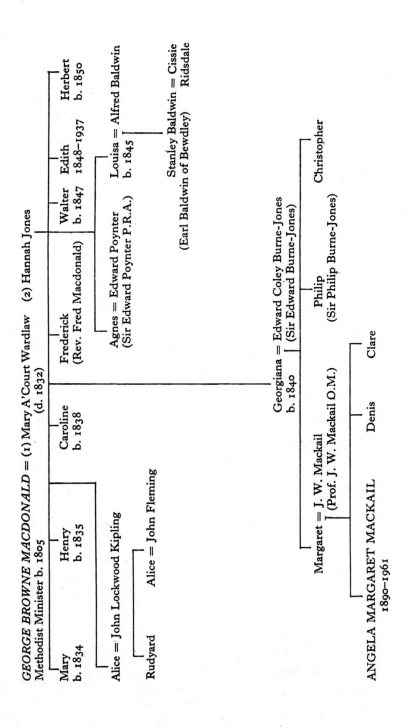

GEORGE BROWNE MACDONALD = (1) Mary A'Court Wardlaw   (2) Hannah Jones
Methodist Minister b. 1805   (d. 1832)

Mary   Henry   Caroline   Frederick   Agnes = Edward Poynter   Walter   Edith   Herbert
b. 1834   b. 1835   b. 1838   (Rev. Fred Macdonald)   (Sir Edward Poynter P.R.A.)   b. 1847   1848–1937   b. 1850

Alice = John Lockwood Kipling   Louisa = Alfred Baldwin
                                                                                                 b. 1845

        Alice = John Fleming   Stanley Baldwin = Cissie
                                                                                                 (Earl Baldwin of Bewdley)   Ridsdale

Rudyard

                                    Georgiana = Edward Coley Burne-Jones
                                    b. 1840   (Sir Edward Burne-Jones)

                                                Philip   Christopher
                                                (Sir Philip Burne-Jones)

Margaret = J. W. Mackail   Denis   Clare
           (Prof. J. W. Mackail O.M.)

ANGELA MARGARET MACKAIL
1890–1961

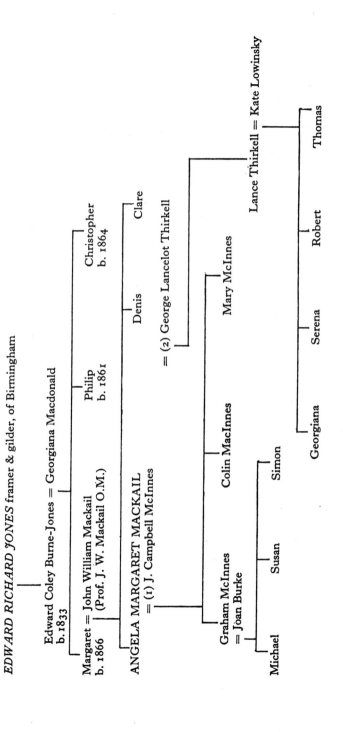

EDWARD RICHARD JONES framer & gilder, of Birmingham

Edward Coley Burne-Jones = Georgiana Macdonald
b. 1833

Margaret = John William Mackail
b. 1866   (Prof. J. W. Mackail O.M.)

Philip
b. 1861

Christopher
b. 1864

Denis

Clare

ANGELA MARGARET MACKAIL
= (1) J. Campbell McInnes

= (2) George Lancelot Thirkell

Graham McInnes
= Jöan Burke

Colin MacInnes

Mary McInnes

Lance Thirkell = Kate Lowinsky

Michael

Susan

Simon

Georgiana

Serena

Robert

Thomas

This is all a fairy-tale, and ...you are not
to believe a word of it, even if it is true.
Charles Kingsley, *The Water Babies*

Preface

Angela Thirkell wrote middle-class novels for middle-brow tastes. They were novels about well-mannered families who were living in a society increasingly threatened with extinction. As novels, they were neither vulgar nor lewd, nor profound, but they were read all over the world; readers outside England found them a valuable guide to the nuances of English social life.

Most of the novels are set in the imaginary county of 'Barsetshire', around the cathedral city of Barchester. When I first began to read them I was in Africa, and later I came to live in a village in Hertfordshire, five miles from the cathedral city of St Albans. I found that they were an inside account of what was to me the outside reality; I had only to walk down the High Street of Wheathampstead to find an illustration of the text.

When I began my quest for Angela Thirkell I found that the mere mention of her name aroused strong feelings. The novels were either detested with a quite alarming vehemence, or adored with the fervour of discipleship. To engage with the novels and their creator was to enter into a love-hate relationship with Angela Thirkell and oneself, England and the English, and one's kinsmen overseas. Imperceptibly, I became 'counsel for the defence' of a woman of tenacity and courage who won my respect and affection.

There are few contemporary women authors who are called 'lady-novelists', as Angela Thirkell was in her day. The term now has a pejorative ring. Egalitarianism and mass-marketing have crushed the middle-class middle-brow English novel almost out of existence. The people Angela Thirkell wrote about went out of fashion, as Angela Thirkell herself did, and the society revolving round an English cathedral city and its attendant villages lost a valuable chronicler. She and they have, in a sense, gone to earth. Yet the same sort of people are still there—clergymen and their families, the district nurse, the gentleman farmer, the doctor's wife, the gardener, the squire, and the charitable wives, widows and spinsters who make up country society. Has the literary genre become extinct? Whether it has or not, the Thirkell novels continue to be read.

I should not have been able to write this account of Angela Thirkell if Mr Lance Thirkell had not put his family papers at my disposal. To him, and to his wife, Kate, who showed me every kindness, I am greatly indebted.

Mr Hamish Hamilton, Angela Thirkell's publisher, allowed me to rake over the Thirkell-Hamilton archive, and forbore with me in spite of the dust I was stirring. To him I wish to express my gratitude.

I must also warmly thank the following persons for hospitality on my 'Mrs Thirkell' quest, for information, and for the loan of letters: Miss Enid Bagnold, Dr D. S. Bailey, Miss Effie Barker, Mrs Margaret Bird, Mr Vincent Brome, Mrs Sunnie Carr, Miss Dorothy Collins, Lady Diana Cooper, Dorita Lady Clutterbuck, Mr R. G. Davis-Poynter, Canon Peter Dennis, Commander Charles Drage, Mr James Fergusson, Mrs Penelope Fitzgerald, Miss Joyce Grenfell, Professor Gordon C. Haight, Miss Margery Hirschfeld, Mr Christopher Hollis, Lady Lorna Howard, Lady Mary Lyon, the Earl of Lytton, Mrs Joan McInnes, Lady Mander, Dame Daphne du Maurier, Mr Stephen Mitchell, Mr Raymond Mortimer, Mr John Grey Murray, Miss Carola Oman, Miss Louise Orr, Miss Catherine Paton, Mr Stanley Parker, Mrs P. Reynolds, Mr & Mrs Julian Ridsdale, Mr Ian Robertson, Mr John Symonds, Professor Kathleen Tillotson, Susan Lady Tweedsmuir, Mr Arthur Wooller, Miss Joan Waldegrave, and Mrs M. Wyn-Reeves.

I am grateful also to the staffs of the following libraries for their co-operation: the Humanities Research Center, the University of Texas; the University of Athens, Georgia; the National Library of Australia at Canberra; Ramsbottom Library, Lancashire; the Library of the Royal College of Music; the Metropolitan Toronto Library Board Music Library, Toronto; St Paul's Girls' School, London; Kensington Central Library; the Army Records Centre, Ministry of Defence; and Houghton Library, Harvard, Mass.

Lemsford, Hertfordshire.   M.S.
March 1977

Prologue
Birtley House, Bramley

In the autumn of 1960, an elderly lady with china-blue eyes, cool judgment and a sharp tongue, lay dying of a rare blood disease in a nursing-home in Surrey.

The private room she occupied was expensive, but the greater part of the fees was paid by her insurance company. Although her income was considerable and she was to leave over £80,000, she was obsessed by a fear of poverty. In addition, she was inconsolably lonely.

She was one of the most dependable and successful authors of her age; she had produced a novel a year for the previous thirty years. But now her publisher was beginning to receive enquiring and even anxious letters about the failure of his latest catalogue to announce the new 'Angela Thirkell'.

She was nearly seventy-one. When writing to Margaret Bird, who had been typing her work for a decade, she had taken to signing herself 'Old Mrs Thirkell', and later 'Very Old Mrs Thirkell'.

Her last novel had been a predictable success. Her American publisher, Borzoi, an imprint of Knopf, had inserted the following advertisement about her:

> Tomorrow, at her home in England,
> ANGELA THIRKELL
> will celebrate her seventieth birthday.
> As her American publishers since 1937,
> all of us at the Borzoi salute an
> indomitable and gifted lady, whose
> works across the years have won her the
> loyal devotion of tens of thousands
> of readers in this country.

And Knopf announced her new novel:

> Angela Thirkell does it again in

'Love at All Ages'
her *thirtieth* novel
$4.50 at better bookstores everywhere.

A photograph of the celebrated authoress wearing her amused and most ladylike expression accompanied the advertisement.

Early in January, Blanche Knopf received the good news from Mrs Thirkell that she had begun work on a new novel: 'Thirkell 1961' or 'T 1961'. And in reply to what must have been an unusually revealing letter, she wrote: 'I think you are right. The men easily get the better of it *always*. I have discovered this and even abetted it.'

Mrs Thirkell would never have 'abetted' it, for she did not subscribe to the theory of masculine superiority, nor had she ever succumbed to male domination. At worst, the sex wars she had engaged in had ended with no clear winner.

Blanche Knopf continued: 'I like the idea of your *Trooper to the Southern Cross*.* That must have been quite a book, particularly if you told all.' *Trooper to the Southern Cross* was the story of Angela Thirkell's journey on a troopship to Australia at the end of the First World War accompanied by her new husband and her two young sons by a previous marriage. 'I cannot believe you have written thirty books.† Well, I hope for many, many more but you must keep on writing.'

But Mrs Thirkell in her Surrey nursing-home was unhappily brooding on her inability to continue 'T 1961'. And for some time now her many friends and acquaintances had been worried about her. Her prodigious memory, from which flowed a stream of quotations, was failing. She frequently forgot appointments and would even reappear for an appointment which she had already kept.

Real people around her grew vague, and characters from her childhood and even from her omnivorous reading began to take over: the novel her illness had interrupted consisted largely of quotations from the authors she had loved from her youth—Dickens, Thackeray, and Browning predominating.‡

---

* Published in 1934 under the pseudonym Leslie Parker.

† Angela Thirkell had forgotten the number of books she had published —thirty-five.

‡ *Threescore and Ten*, Angela Thirkell's thirty-fifth book, was completed by C. A. Lejeune.

I

Angela Margaret Mackail

'Mrs Thirkell' was baptized Angela Margaret, the eldest child of Dr
and Mrs Mackail of Kensington. She was born 30 January 1890. Her
father was a civil servant, her mother the only daughter of Edward
Burne-Jones, the painter. When Angela was a little girl, her grandfather, Burne-Jones, and his wife, Georgiana, were well-known
members of a circle of English painters, musicians, writers, actors and
politicians. The ethereally pretty Georgiana was the prototype of all
the females in her husband's canvases—those young women who exhibited the haunting expression which came to be known as 'the Burne-
Jones look'.

Angela was an imperious, strong-willed, demanding child. She
usually managed, even from an early age, to be the centre of attention.
Children, declared Dr Mackail, with all the wisdom of a classical
scholar, should not be physically disciplined but reasoned out of their
bad behaviour. But Angela—so the story goes—shocked him into the
action he deprecated by publicly slapping her father's face. Dr Mackail
gave his young daughter a severe spanking.

One of her childhood friends was W. Graham Robertson, author of
a successful play for children called *Pinkie and the Fairies* in which
Ellen Terry played a leading part. He wrote in a book of reminiscences
that Angela between the ages of 4 and 9 was the most terrifying female
he had ever met.

To her grandfather who doted on her, she could do no wrong. He
gave her a copy of *Old Celtic Romances* and wrote in it, 'I wonder if my
little Angela would like this book—I can't tell a bit—but *she* can't tell
unless I give it to her—so I had better give it to her and if she doesn't
like it she can throw it away—or give it to the maid to light the fire with
of a morning—but whatever she does—bless her. And as for me, I am
her obedient Bapapa.'

The punishment she disliked most was being made to stand in a
particular corner of an upstairs room. To help her endure it, 'Bapapa'
painted on the walls a picture of a water-mill and a peacock perched on
a tree. He also painted on her bedroom wall, beside the window, an

angel in the act of drawing back the curtain. It looked, in the morning, as if the angel had let light into the room.

Burne-Jones was the son of a carver and gilder in Birmingham. He and his father lived above the shop. His mother died at his birth and all he knew of her was the grave in the churchyard, to which his weeping father would take him every Sunday. It is a touching Victorian picture —the man, with tears in his eyes, holding the little boy by the hand, as they stand before the grave. The loss of his mother, together with the Welsh strain in his inheritance, helps to explain his melancholy temperament, and the 'neurosis' of his later years. As a young man he felt destined for the church—his father had ambitions for him in this direction—and he even wished to found a monastic order, but he soon discovered that he was drawn more to the aesthetic qualities of High Anglicanism than to its doctrines. He required constant reassurance and a great deal of attention.

In 1860, at the age of 27, he married Georgiana Macdonald. They lived at Fulham in a large old house, now demolished, called The Grange, which had been occupied in the previous century by Samuel Richardson. At the Grange Richardson had written *Pamela* and Samuel Johnson had visited him there. To The Grange in Burne-Jones's day came artists and writers—George Eliot, Beatrix Potter, Alma Tadema, Henry James, Ellen Terry, James Barrie, Sarah Bernhardt, Oscar Wilde, Aubrey Beardsley, John Ruskin, William Morris. The list seems endless. The Prince and Princess of Wales called. And among the distinguished visitors would sometimes be found Angela, Burne-Jones's little granddaughter, who always sat at his right hand at the luncheon table. 'For thirty years,' wrote Angela, 'the house was filled with hopes, work, love and the intercourse of many friends.'

When Angela was 6, William Morris died. All she remembered of him was 'the aggressive mop of white hair', but he had been the greatest single influence on her father's life. The two men met at Oxford; Burne-Jones was still thinking of entering the church, and was reading vaguely to that end. He left Oxford without taking a degree, and entered the workshop of Dante Gabriel Rossetti as an apprentice. Later he founded with Morris a company called Morris and Co., for the designing of furniture, textiles, books and stained glass. Morris was an upper-class bohemian and socialist; Burne-Jones was neither. Morris liked clever women; Burne-Jones detested them, probably because he was afraid of them. 'None of your Girton girls for me,' he declared. But he shared Morris's ideal of beauty.

Georgiana's father, George Browne Macdonald, was a Methodist minister. There were many children—well-read, sharp-tongued, good-looking and clever children. They had no settled home and moved about the midland and northern counties of England, where their father had two- or three-year appointments.

George Macdonald gave one tenth of his income to charity, wrote tracts and collected books—the children had plenty of books to read. One of his works bore the unusual title of *An Apology for the Disuse of Alcoholic Drink*, 1841. A son, Frederick, became a Methodist preacher like his father and was much in demand for his eloquence. He lectured in America and Australia, and wrote several books, including an autobiography, *As A Tale That is Told*.

The children of George Browne Macdonald were brought up frugally. On one occasion, probably as a lesson in humility, they were given mouse pie to eat. One of the daughters cooked it herself; it was a dish which poor people sometimes ate, and the Macdonald children ate it.

Georgiana was not the only Macdonald sister to marry a remarkable man. Her sister Agnes married Edward Poynter, who became President of the Royal Academy. Louisa married Alfred Baldwin, a Shropshire ironmaster; they became the parents of Stanley Baldwin. Alice Macdonald married John Lockwood Kipling, a museum curator in India, and their son was Rudyard Kipling. Though greatly admired by William Morris, Edith Macdonald remained a spinster. Unlike her sisters, she retained a north-country accent all her life. Her favourite adjective was 'gradely'. She had a sense of humour and took pride in her Scottish ancestry. Her great-niece Angela remembered her sitting up in bed wearing a ginger wig and writing the family chronicles, *Annals of the Macdonald Family*. Her sharp tongue was so feared that 'subjects likely to be perilous to family concord' were avoided.

Georgiana was proud of her husband, his work and the company he kept. 'I felt in the presence of a new religion,' she wrote, summing up her reaction. Among Burne-Jones's expanding circle of friends were the painters of the Pre-Raphaelite Brotherhood: Rossetti, Holman Hunt, and others.

To Burne-Jones, Georgiana was a 'holy thing'; he worshipped her. At the same time, he said that a painter ought not to marry, as the responsibility was too great. The two main sources of his inspiration were Dante's *Divine Comedy* and the Arthurian legends, in which women were exalted. Georgiana soon found that her husband was regarding her not as a real woman but as a *femme inspiratrice*, a role

which she found hard to sustain, especially after becoming a mother. In
the over-heated atmosphere of the Pre-Raphaelite Brotherhood, Ned,
as she called him, began to meet, and certainly to observe, other
women, who filled him with longing. As far as is known, he did not
keep mistresses or have affairs; these 'other women' merely played a
part in his fantasy life. Georgiana read to him while he worked, and
when he became famous she shielded him from the excessive demands
of society. But in spite of their unquestioned devotion to one another
Georgiana could still describe Ned as 'the pang of my life'. The pedestal
on which she had been placed had isolated her and she blamed her own
undemonstrative temperament. She confided in George Eliot whose
passionate response was, 'Ah! say I love you to those you love. The
eternal silence is long enough to be silent in.'

Georgiana made good use of the little set of wood-engraving tools
Burne-Jones gave her on their marriage. With them, she cut many of
her husband's designs. He praised her work: 'There is just the proper
quality of echo in it.' In coloured wools she stitched miles of undulating
patterns for The Grange. She also played the piano and sang.

The Garden Studio at The Grange was like a chapel. The walls
were lined with dream-like luminous paintings and their cumulative
effect was suffocating. The visitor felt that he was in a cloister. 'Every
single picture was deliberately romantic in subject as well as treatment.
The influence of that studio—one I was very slow to shake off—was
to make me look away from, instead of into life, for beauty,' wrote
Lady Cynthia Asquith, who sat for Burne-Jones. Angela was an
impressionable child and she was profoundly affected by her grandfather's dream-world.

Three children were born to Edward and Georgiana: Philip,
Christopher (who died in infancy) and Margaret. The surviving son,
whose godfathers were Ruskin, Rossetti, and Henry James, was sensitive and nervous, but he was sent, in emulation of William Morris, to
Marlborough, an experience from which he never recovered. The only
daughter was educated at home. She was a lonely child and pined for
the company of other girls of her own age. One wet afternoon when she
was confined indoors, her brother's godfather called. 'Mr Ruskin took
little Margaret into the drawing-room and played with her at jumping
over piles of books that he piled up on the floor.'

When Margaret grew up, she frequently took her mother's place in
the studio. She read aloud to her father the entire works of Thackeray,
and more than once. She was also her father's favourite model and posed

for the figure and features of the sleeping princess in the hauntingly beautiful paintings known as the 'Briar Rose Series'. The Sleeping Beauty is an allegory of a sexually unawakened woman. Burne-Jones called his daughter his 'bright blue little Margot'. Among other presents he gave her a moonstone and seriously expressed the hope—he was not being ironic—'that she might never know love, and stay with me'. When she was thirteen years old, she accompanied her parents to Oxford, where Burne-Jones received the honorary degree of Doctor of Civil Law. Following the ceremony, the winner of the Newdigate Prize recited his winning poem. He was John William Mackail, a brilliant Dante scholar who had graduated from the University of Edinburgh at the age of sixteen. The tall young man with the strikingly classic profile was introduced to the Burne-Jones family and he was soon a regular visitor to The Grange.

Swinburne, with the unthinking sentimentality of his middle age, called Margaret Burne-Jones a 'little country violet with blue eyes and long lashes, as good and sweet as can be'. Mackail, who was at the start of a notable career, was soon in love with her and when he later proposed to her he was accepted. Burne-Jones was furious. He felt betrayed and his openly-displayed jealousy distressed his family and friends.

When Jack was twenty-nine and Margaret twenty, they were married in the church on the green in the middle of the village of Rottingdean in Sussex, before the stained-glass windows designed by the bride's father, and dedicated to his wife and daughter. Margaret wore a dress of grey silk and lace and a feathered hat. After the wedding, which was conducted with the minimum of pomp and attended by only eleven people, the newly-married pair walked across the green and within a few minutes reached North End House, the country home of the bride's parents.

Margaret was particularly fond of music; she played the piano and the harp and sang prettily. As a wedding-present, Burne-Jones gave her a clavichord made by Carl Dolmetsch, bearing a sentimental Latin inscription; he decorated it with a picture of a maiden encumbered with lilies, leading a dragon on a silk rope. The tamed dragon, one would like to speculate, was Burne-Jones.

Some time later Dr and Mrs Mackail travelled to Italy. While at Venice, John—or Jack, as he was generally known—made a cryptic note in his diary; a few weeks later Margaret Mackail's pregnancy was confirmed.

The following year, 1890, their daughter Angela was born.

Burne-Jones was called Angelo after the Italian master Fra Angelico: hence Angela. Graham Robertson commented that he liked the name, 'but it always turns its owner into a perfect devil'. Her parents' friend, Sir James Barrie, was her godfather.

Burne-Jones spoilt her. Gladstone also spoiled his granddaughter. The painter and Prime Minister were friends and would argue as to who spoilt his granddaughter the more. 'But you,' Burne-Jones reportedly said, 'don't take her breakfast up to bed of a morning.' The child did not altogether care for her grandfather's overpowering attention. He wrote of her, 'She is a haughty-looking person, with an expression mostly of indignant surprise', and when she was three years old, he signed one of his many adoring notes to her, 'your humble grandpapa'.

Margaret Mackail, or 'Maany', was of a stature usually described as 'petite'. In her father's paintings it was not easy to tell the difference between her and her mother. This may have been the fault of Burne-Jones. Not a few of the women whose portraits he painted complained that he had transformed them into his ideal and that to their friends and family they were unrecognizable. Margaret was a kind of second-generation copy of her mother; and although she married a man of distinction, she regretted that she had been unable to continue the role that her father had designed for her, namely that of a romantic heroine. Jack's position as a civil servant, compared with that of the celebrated painter who was idolized by innumerable women, seemed rather prosaic.

Margaret cultivated an elaborate taste in dress. She was only five feet tall and her costumes were unsuitable for such a small woman. She draped herself in voluminous gowns, hung herself with beads, and wore immense hats trimmed with flora and fauna in such quantities that in later years they frightened her grandsons.

By contrast, Jack Mackail was very tall. He spoke softly and with a Scottish accent. He would rise early and write in his study before going off to his day's work at the Ministry of Education; he resumed his writing in the evening, and maintained an astonishing output of translations, criticism and biography, his life of William Morris being his best-known work.

His colleagues at Oxford had expected him to continue with an academic career. Instead he chose to become an administrator, but he never ceased to regret the decision. In 1905, when Angela was 15, he was appointed to the Chair of Poetry at Oxford, and travelled to the university by train to give the required number of lectures during the five years' tenure of the post. When the greater prize of the Mastership of Balliol was offered to him, he passionately wanted to accept. It would have meant living in Oxford, and the thought of this delighted him; but it did not appeal to his wife, and a battle of wills ensued. Margaret, who had a reputation for reticence, even lost her temper, and Dr Mackail declined the post. He continued to live in Kensington and to go to the Ministry of Education, and hid his disappointment under his usual quiet courtesy.

Angela lived with her parents in a pretty terraced house facing Kensington Square. The address was 27 Young Street. A few doors away Thackeray had written *Vanity Fair*. No 27 was owned by the author's daughter, Lady Ritchie, who described the area as 'quiet and unpretending'. It was mostly inhabited by gentlefolk. No 41, on the opposide side of the square, had been Margaret Mackail's birthplace. A flamboyant if not bohemian element was supplied to the neighbourhood by the presence of the actress Mrs Patrick Campbell, who lived nearby and was known to the young Angela as 'Aunty Stella'. Angela's sensible pinafores were sometimes, to her joy, replaced by the glamorous silk and gold thread pinafores cast off by the actress's daughter.

In one respect the choice of 27 Young Street was unfortunate, for next door was the Greyhound public house. The noise from the customers was frequently raucous and went on till late at night. Angela was not worried. On the contrary she rather enjoyed it, finding it both comforting and stimulating. There were times when she wistfully wished to join in the fun that seemed to be going on next door.

The little old house dated from the reign of James II. Margaret Mackail disliked the lack of privacy and abhorred lace curtains; the glass in the parlour windows which looked on to the street were replaced by 'bull's eye' panes. The interior was furnished with Morris furniture and of course Burne-Jones's work was everywhere displayed.

The house was run with a Scottish frugality that bordered on the mean. Meals were dull and unimaginative. Margaret Mackail's servants did not find her a sympathetic employer, and there were frequent changes of staff.

Dr and Mrs Mackail adhered to the late-Victorian habit of distrusting any display of emotion, grave or gay. Their marriage held together, but they did not indulge in little gestures of affection, nor did they speak fondly to each other. Undemonstrativeness was a virtue they were proud of.

Georgiana and Margaret were living embodiments of 'the Burne-

Jones look'—cavernous vivid blue eyes set in an almost triangular face. Angela's facial features were similar and 'Bapapa' used her as a model too. But the rest of her was different. She was built like an Amazon, extremely tall, with legs like columns and feet which were large and masculine. 'Angela never walked into a room,' recalled a contemporary; 'she stumped in.' She was also very bossy. At Rottingdean by the sea, where a colony of their friends and relatives gathered for long holidays, Angela was referred to by other children as 'AKB'—Angela Knows Best.

One of their favourite games was dressing up, and a trunk was kept for the purpose, filled with old evening frocks and discarded costumes. Angela always had the first choice. Despite her unpopularity, the children usually obeyed her, and she was their self-appointed leader.

Artists rise or fall through society; they are taken up, or not taken up, by wealthy and fashionable people who set the taste of the time. Mrs Prinsep of Little Holland House, Melbury Road, Kensington, was one such patroness of the arts in mid-Victorian England. She gave G. F. Watts a studio in her house and drove off his young wife, Ellen Terry. Rossetti was a frequent visitor to her salon and he introduced Burne-Jones. It was inevitable that Burne-Jones should find his way to Little Holland House, for he was elegant and charming and his brand of romanticism was catching on fast in industrial England.

Among Burne-Jones's patrons were several politicians. William Graham, a Scottish Member of Parliament, was one of the earliest. Burne-Jones dined at his table several times a week and fell platonically in love with his daughter. Arthur Balfour, later to be Prime Minister, was another. The houses of these and other statesmen were hung with Burne-Jones's work. Once Balfour took him to Wiltshire to meet his Private Secretary and great friend, Percy Scawen Wyndham, a direct descendant of the great Earl of Egremont who, a century earlier, had discovered and encouraged Turner. The friendship that sprang up between the Wyndhams and the Burne-Joneses was an important strand in Angela Thirkell's development as a novelist. Clouds was one of the houses, and the Wyndhams were one of the families, which supplied her with the raw material for her art. Mrs Wyndham's daughters, Lady Wemyss and Lady Glenconner, were friends of Margaret Mackail, and Lady Wemyss's daughter Cynthia, later Lady Cynthia Asquith, and Lady Glenconner's son Stephen Tennant, were life-long friends of Angela.

Clouds gave the occupants the sensation of being above the earth. The interior 'was light, airy and spacious, a perfect setting.' The house, like William Morris's own, was designed by Philip Webb, and the entire interior decoration, furniture and hangings were designed by Morris and Co.; Burne-Jones supplied the pictures. Percy Scawen Wyndham allowed all the artists a free hand.

Other families were also competing for the work of Burne-Jones. He was invited to castles, manors and mansions all over the country, and the tedium and anxiety, as well as the excitement, of country-house visiting became part of his daily life. But he soon grew tired of being lionized, for he was never quite at his ease with great families or their servants. Success exhausted him and inevitably made his artist friends jealous; Rossetti and William Morris even quarrelled with him at times. 'I cut old friends when they fit no more,' Burne-Jones wrote. 'I can't wear the clothes I had when I was a child'.

Ten years before Angela was born, Georgiana Burne-Jones, walking across the Sussex downs from Brighton, came across a small empty cottage which faced the green; behind it the black sails of Rottingdean windmill slowly turned. She found the cottage and the village delightful and was soon in love with them; Burne-Jones bought the cottage for her—and for himself too. London life, even as far out as Hammersmith, was relentlessly social, and he was in need of a retreat. They improved and extended it until it was twice the size, painted it a gleaming white, and called it North End House; it became a second home to them, and later, to the Mackails. North End House was full of nooks and crannies; Morris filled it with his uncomfortably rigid furniture, and his fabric designs were everywhere.

By 1883 Rottingdean was established as a holiday centre, and the four Macdonald sisters gathered there regularly with their families; there were Baldwins and Poynters and Kiplings and Burne-Joneses all over the place. The Wyndhams pedalled to Rottingdean from Petworth Place. The community at Rottingdean became a permanent settlement, an artistic, social and political enclave. Two preparatory schools for boys were founded in the area. There were nannies for the innumerable children and they were succeeded by French and German governesses. It was an ambience in which reverence for the arts flourished.

The governesses were cultured women. 'They sang Mendlessohn duets all over the downs,' recalled Angela. Angela had a good voice herself and it was improved by the regular singing lessons which she took with an elderly Spaniard at Finchley who had taught the famous

Jenny Lind. The families and friends made choirs and sang part-songs. Someone played the piano, another the cello, a third the violin; trios, quartets and quintets were formed. It was a world relatively untouched by outsiders and entirely self-sufficient.

Another diversion, in London and the country, was acting. Often the plays performed in the private houses were written by leading dramatists, and everyone took part. Sir Gerald du Maurier played in Barrie's *The Greedy Dwarf*, and in another Barrie play, *The Little White Bird*, Angela and her sister Clare were among the cast.

When in London, Angela and her brother and sister were taken to Kensington Gardens to play. It was here that Barrie met the five Llewellyn Davies boys whose mother was the beautiful Sylvia du Maurier. Barrie told them stories, and one of the boys, Peter, gave him the idea of a play about a little boy who never grew up: Peter Pan. In the original draft of *Peter Pan*, the full name of Wendy, the leading lady, was Wendy Moira Angela Darling, in tribute to his little god-daughter Angela Mackail.*

Apart from Clouds, The Grange, and North End House, Angela's childhood holidays were spent sometimes at Wilsford Manor, Lake, near Salisbury, and at Stanway, Winchcombe, near Cheltenham— houses where Lady Wemyss and Lady Glenconner were the châtelaines. But there were times when she visited less exalted homes. Dr Mackail's only sister, Nan, had married a country doctor whose general practice was in the then rural village of Uxbridge in Middlesex. The house was called St Andrews, and when she stayed with her aunt and uncle there she saw a quite different aspect of provincial life. She watched medicines being compounded and pills counted out in the dispensary attached to the house. She would accompany her Uncle John on his rounds and return to eat a frugal meal.

Angela recalled that Elizabeth Gaskell's background had been a provincial doctor's family, and that her best-loved book 'had no plot at all but that of etiquette in a small provincial town'. In a letter to Ruskin, Mrs Gaskell had confessed that it was the only book of hers which she could re-read with enjoyment, 'taking her back as it did to the scenes of her childhood'.

On her third birthday, Angela's mother began to teach her to read, and she was soon devouring the printed word. In later life she could not remember a time when she was unable to read. Daily, usually after

---

* Angela du Maurier believed she owed her Christian name to Angela Mackail.

dinner, her father and mother read aloud to each other. The habit had been established by Burne-Jones at Oxford when he and his fellow undergraduate William Morris had together read Dante, Keats and other favourite authors. Reading aloud became a cherished ritual in the household, and nothing was allowed to interfere with it. Angela's father taught her to care for books and their bindings, showing her how to feed the leather covers with lanolin applied gently with the tips of the fingers. Later she wrote that ink was like alcohol to her and that she got drunk on words. She re-read the books she loved most, many of them written by authors who were personal friends of her parents and grandparents: Dickens, Trollope, Mrs Gaskell, George Eliot, Charles and Henry Kingsley, William and Mary de Morgan, Thackeray, Meredith, George Macdonald (who wrote children's books and was a Chelsea neighbour, not the George Macdonald who was her great-grandfather).

When she was eleven she fell ill with chicken-pox and the doctor who attended her advised against her straining her eyes; her mother began reading Trollope's *Barchester Towers* aloud to her. On her recovery she finished it by herself and went on to read Trollope's other works. But at this tender age her mind was more impressed by myth and legend, the subject of many of her father's pictures. Her inner world was a magical one: She was that beautiful maiden in mortal danger; the knight on his white charger was hastening from his castle to her rescue . . . To a stranger, even perhaps sometimes to her parents, she was a fat little girl with a disagreeable expression. At the age of 4 she had suffered agonies of jealousy at the birth of her brother Denis. Two years later came her sister Clare. Neither had her robust constitution, and neither was able to resist her domination. And she was, after all, the eldest.

The Kensington of Angela's childhood was garlanded with flowers in May and jolly with street-musicians all the year round. Winter brought the welcome drama of muffling fogs and the fun of ice-skating on the Serpentine. As night fell, the friendly lamp-lighter made his rounds and the street was lit up with the soft glow of gas-lamps. Almost everyone travelled in the exciting horse-drawn omnibus. To Angela, Kensington was an enchanting place and she only saw its beauty.

One of Burne-Jones's last commissions was to design the sets and costumes for *Pelléas and Mélisande*, the English translation of which had been made by Dr Mackail. The leading lady was their friend and neighbour Mrs Patrick Campbell, and the first night was in the late spring of 1898. Burne-Jones was not there to see it for he had died in his sleep a week before. Angela was 8 years old.

Burne-Jones's death brought a great change in her life. The Mackail family moved west from Young Street to the more sedate Pembroke Gardens. No 6 was a double-fronted house with a grandiose Italianate portico. The high-ceilinged rooms were cold, and the narrow stairs were covered with dark green linoleum. The happy days with Burne-Jones were over. It was as if a heavy curtain had fallen on her life, shutting out the gaiety and colour that had characterized The Grange.

Scarborough, on the Yorkshire coast, had become a fashionable resort since the Prince and Princess of Wales had stayed there in 1871. Georgiana and Edward Burne-Jones, with their friends George Lewes and George Eliot, took a house one summer at Whitby, a few miles further up the coast. In 1901, the Mackails spent the summer at Scarborough and the Mackail children played with the Thompson children. Sylvia Thompson was a special friend of Angela. One very hot summer when Sylvia had been a guest of the Mackails at Rottingdean, Angela had written to Sylvia's mother, 'I *wish* Sylvia could stay longer than the 18th because I do love her so.' And she had decorated her letter with a drawing of the children on the beach in the sunshine. Sylvia too was to grow up to be a novelist. They played their favourite game of dressing up. Angela divested herself of the Edwardian frilled pinafore she usually wore and put on a long robe and an embroidered bolero which she found in her mother's room. She confined her hair under a bright kerchief, attached big brass curtain rings to her ears, hung many strings of jangling beads round her neck, and carried a fan. She loved to dress as a gypsy. One of the children borrowed a guitar and a photograph was taken of them all.

All the children at Rottingdean were naturally creative; they acted, painted, sang, wrote stories and poems. During Angela's childhood, her cousin Rudyard Kipling was a familiar figure to her and she grew up in the shadow of his great fame. While his parents had been in India, he had stayed for part of the time with his uncle, Edward Burne-Jones. 'Uncle Ned' was the model for the Lama in *Kim*. Kipling would try out his tales on the children while they ran at his heels over the Sussex downs. One winter evening, Angela spent hours copying out her poems for her beloved cousin Josephine, Kipling's gentle and fair-haired daughter, who died at the tender age of six. With unusual diffidence, Angela asked Cousin Ruddy to look at her poetry. He did so, told her that her handwriting was like 'sick spiders in an ink-pot' and cursorily dismissed them. It was not deliberate unkindness on his part, but his rejection of her verses was one of the wounds that never healed. 'I sank into a state of dejection,' she wrote; she remembered it with bitterness. In other ways he was kind; he gave them his signature for the children to swap at school for stamps or chocolate, for his autograph was valuable currency. During the summer months Rottingdean was almost impassable from the admirers who thronged the little village in the hope of a glimpse of the great author.

The village did not altogether relish its growing celebrity; neither did it welcome the political views of the artists who had come to live there. 'We were the greatest radicals of the day,' recalled Julian Ridsdale, whose parents also had a house at Rottingdean. During the South African War, Georgiana Burne-Jones retired to Rottingdean and, freed from her husband's restraint, was militantly progressive and entirely sympathetic towards the Boers. When peace was declared, she spent days stitching angrily at a large blue cloth—a banner, which she hung out of the window. The normally phlegmatic villagers were transformed into a threatening mob that surrounded North End House. Rudyard Kipling, who had, of course, espoused the British cause, crossed the Green and managed to pacify them. The blue banner with its message, WE HAVE KILLED AND TAKEN POSSESSION, was withdrawn.

Angela's formal education began early. She attended the Froebel Institute at Kensington, of which Claud Montefiore, a leader of the Jewish community in London, was one of the governors. Although it was nominally Anglican, all the children, whether Catholics, Protestants or Jews, received the same religious instruction and partook of all the hymns. Philip Burne-Jones's studio in Manresa Road was not far away, and sometimes, on her way home from school in the afternoons, Angela would drop in on her melancholy Uncle Phil. He called her 'Aglet' and was flattered by her interest in his work in progress.

Most of the children from the Froebel went on to St Paul's School in Hammersmith. Angela, at 14, was one of the original fifty-four pupils at St Paul's. The great opening by the Princess of Wales was marked by much ceremony, and Angela was singled out to write an account of it for the school magazine. The St Paul's girls wore a tunic made of rather coarse material known as a 'djibbah'. Angela's djibbah was different—of fine Egyptian cotton, which she girdled with a thin leather thong. Her brown hair descended in a plait down her back.

She had one distinct advantage over most of the pupils; she knew

French and German, for she had had French and German governesses. On the other hand, she was hopeless at arithmetic. 'I never could do it at all,' she said. She copied the work of a friend, who was good at arithmetic, and the friend, who was no good at French, copied hers, for quite a long time before they were found out. Angela developed a crush on the Science mistress who had 'a large pink face and *very* scanty fair hair'. Every Tuesday, Angela gave her a bunch of flowers. It is hardly surprising that Angela, with her literary background and temperament—her literary 'genius' did not manifest itself until much later—should have won the prize for literature several times during her time at St Paul's.

One of her stories, published in the school magazine, was *The Thrush and the Owl*. 'If a fairy sees too much of the world she becomes earth-struck . . . and then does not care for Fairyland any longer, and goes and lives on its very edge, always longing to pass over into the world but never being able to do so.' This echoed Burne-Jones's belief that his dream-world was more real to him than the world around him. In *The Thrush and the Owl* the following revealing passage occurs: ' "I have got to look for a prince whom my fairy godmother wishes me to marry, and I cannot find him in fairyland." "That is all right then," said the thrush cheerfully. "I have not seen a prince, but if you go on you will probably find one." "Thank you," said the Princess, and went away.'

One of her prize-winning essays was 'The Respective Merits of Cricket, Hockey and Baseball'. Angela was said to be brilliant at games, but she did not make a good team member. The teaching of games to girls at this time was uncommon, and the controversy, games versus study, raged in the pages of the school magazine. Angela was in favour of both.

Her other activities included music, she took piano lessons from a Mrs Norman O'Neill, who, it was said, was paid a guinea a term more than another music teacher at the school because she had been a pupil of Clara Schumann. When Angela was in her teens, she fell in love with the strange novels of Henry Kingsley and found that she could read them and practise the piano at the same time, deceiving her mother in the room upstairs. She played regularly at school concerts, but on the whole she preferred literature to music.

Bending over books gave her round shoulders, and to straighten her up, her mother bought an iron brace, in which Angela was fastened every day. It had the desired effect, and she carried herself perfectly.

When Angela was in the sixth form, her sister Clare won a scholar-ship to St Paul's. Clare too wore her long hair hanging down her back in a single plait. But the contrast between the sisters was a subject for comment. Clare was slender, small and retiring. She was also musical, but she wished to study painting.

In January 1901, the Serpentine in Hyde Park was frozen over for several weeks. Every day it was covered with brightly-clad skating figures. During the previous year, every family in the land had argued whether the new century began on 1 January 1900 or 1 January 1901. On 18 January the Court Circular announced that her Imperial Majesty Queen Victoria was seriously ill. On 2 February, at Osborne House in the Isle of Wight, the old Queen, surrounded by members of her family, quietly died. The Queen had seemed indestructible; now she was gone and the ascendancy of Britain entered a new and less confident phase. In August of the same year, the coronation of King Edward VII took place amid general rejoicing.

The Countess of Wemyss and her sister Lady Glenconner were two of the greatest beauties of the day. Kipling's father, John Lockwood Kipling, or 'Mr Kipperling' as the Wyndham children called him, taught them to paint, model in clay, and read the best literature. When they were older, and vibrantly lovely, John Singer Sargent, the portraitist then most in vogue, painted them with their sister, and the picture was exhibited at Burlington House. The Prince of Wales admired it unreservedly and called it *The Three Graces*.

Ettie, Lady Desborough, in writing to Margaret Mackail, gives us a glimpse of the Countess of Wemyss while she was still a girl. 'I first knew her at Brocket*—she was engaged to Hugo, and I was a little younger, a schoolgirl of 15—I fell in love with her then and there and forever.' A later picture of her comes from Alice 'Trix' Kipling: 'Oh do you remember how she flashed into The Grange in a yellow ball dress in 1881—or was it '82—with the smallest waist in the world and the most lovely dark eyes? I think that was the first time I ever saw her—and I was called in from the garden—very plump and pink to find a Shakespeare quotation.' Lady Wemyss was not only famous for her beauty and her love of literature; she was also famously kind-hearted to all the artists she met. With her tact, humour and genuine kindness, she was able to help artists and writers feel more at ease in polite company, when success caught them unprepared for Society.

The death of Burne-Jones in 1898 did not bring the cordial relationship between the patricians and the artists to a halt. That year Lady

* Brocket Hall, Hertfordshire, then in the possession of Earl Cowper.

Elcho (later Countess of Wemyss) took her children to the Royal Academy Summer Exhibition at Burlington House to see Sir Philip Burne-Jones's portrait of their father, Lord Elcho. The patronage continued.

The relationship between the artist and his patron was a delicate one. No rules were overtly stated, and the relationship differed of course from artist to artist. Turner had been an exception to the rule—he broke all rules: while staying at Petworth Place as the guest of Lord Egremont, he locked his door against all comers and got on with his work, and his Lordship had to knock and wait for the invitation before entering. The artists who worked for the Wyndham and Wemyss families were only in the tradition of the seventeenth and eighteenth centuries, superior servants, and there were undercurrents of hostility. Lesser members of the family, and particularly the staff, sometimes adopted an attitude of condescension towards the artists, whom they tended to regard as parasites or interlopers.

Margaret Mackail grew up with feelings of reverence towards all the members of the great families who had brought her father fame and fortune and the distinction of a baronetcy. Even the youngest and most diffident of the young scions whom she met at Lady Wemyss's inspired her with awe. She and her husband Jack were returning one day from a visit to Clouds when, to her surprise and delight, the Honourable Yvo Charteris, then aged eighteen, deigned—as it seemed to them—to share his railway carriage with them. Dr Mackail had a similar attitude. He regarded Hugo Charteris, Lord Elcho, then in his early twenties, as a figure superior by far to the common run of mankind, including himself—the noble Lord was haloed, and from his eyes 'shone a gleaming glory' which was so powerful that anyone in his presence would be 'shamed out of an intention to misbehave'.

Angela was very much aware of the position of her parents in relation to these aristocrats. It was apparent to her that invitations were dependent on her parents' proper show of deference. They had to entertain as well: sing for their supper. Angela was merely the artist's granddaughter; and she felt her position to be a little anomalous, if not precarious, and resented the servility that was expected of her. On the contrary, she felt herself to be, as the famous artist's granddaughter, not a whit inferior to these noble lords and ladies. 'I'm not a servant,' she declared sulkily as a young girl when she was asked to hand round the cakes.

Angela and her sister were frequent visitors to the National Gallery in Trafalgar Square, where they painstakingly copied their favourite masterpieces. A guard was posted to watch them, for recently a suffragette had slashed Velasquez's *Rokeby Venus* across the buttocks, on the grounds that the painting was degrading to women.

Angela had no clear idea of what she wanted to do when she left school. Her sister was determined to go to the Slade. Many of the sisters' contemporaries nursed academic ambitions, aiming to go to Newnham or Girton. At that time, entry to the women's colleges did not depend on intellectual ability. In addition to German and French, Angela had acquired a certain amount of Greek and Latin and had even begun to learn Russian. But although she was precociously clever, she did not aspire to an academic life.

The house at Pembroke Gardens was almost a museum, filled with books, pictures, sculpture: heads and busts of Homer, Virgil, Dante and other great men of antiquity. Current affairs, whether imperial, foreign or local, was hardly a subject for discussion in the Mackail household. It was the past with all its glories that was talked about. Amazingly, the condition-of-England question, which had preoccupied Dickens and other eminent Victorians, was ignored.

With her extraordinary memory, Angela retained quotations she heard at her father's dinner table; they came in useful later, when she delivered them with aplomb. Elderly clerics, academics and other gentlemen were entertained and amused by her and she, for her part, was flattered by their attention. Gilbert Murray was a great friend of her father's, and when she was 14 he gave her a present of Newbolt's *Froissart in Britain*. She was the favourite of an elderly clergyman, a Canon of Norwich cathedral called Augustus Jessop, known to the family as 'the Patriarch', who had written several books about East Anglia. From his rectory in Scarning, he wrote her a number of affectionate letters. 'Do you know what "ye" stands for? . . . I'll tell you! There used to be in ye English alphabet a letter which stood for "th" and they called it ye thorn letter and it was written almost exactly as Y is written now, and so "ye" spelt "the" was never pronounced "ye" as some foolish people suppose.' Canon Jessop thought little of the Poet Laureate, Alfred Austin. 'I know a little maiden,' he told his wife, 'who could write much better stuff than that any day', and he sent Angela, who was then only ten, some of Austin's work. 'Rubbish', he called it. 'You may do better.'

On New Year's Day, 1903, the three Mackail children received a letter from a neighbour at 2 Bolton Gardens of whom they were especially fond. She thanked them for their Christmas letter. 'I have been quite stupid with a bad cold,' she wrote. 'When I am not sneezing, I am busy drawing a little squirrel.' The paper was covered with delightful pen-and-ink sketches of her pet squirrels Twinkleberry and Nutkin, which she kept in a cage. 'I don't think either of them are as nice as my little rabbit, but I daresay I shall make a book about them before next Christmas, so goodbye till then and all good wishes for a Happy New Year.' Her name was Beatrix Potter.

By the time Angela was in her teens, she had absorbed a great deal of literature, Tennyson and Browning being her favourite poets. On leaving St Paul's she went for six months to Paris, where she stayed at a pension kept by an elderly schoolmistress who had taught French at Kensington High School. There she spoke French daily and took up dressmaking. Her fingers were deft and she was developing a sense of style, becoming adept at fashioning her own clothes. She walked about Paris alone and observed that she did not attract admiring glances. 'The nearest to it was two men on the grands boulevards . . . one of whom said to the other "*voila une grosse fille*".' The comment was fair, for she was tall and well-built, with a fine bust. Her waist was not as small as she wished and she spent hours trying to lace it tighter, but it never measured less than twenty-two inches.

The following year she went for several months to Gotha in Germany, where she was similarly occupied in reading and speaking the language, but her extra-curricular activities were centred on music. She grew to love Schubert and Wagner, Schumann and Beethoven and Brahms.

She had acquired a great deal of grace and poise, but at five feet ten inches she was a little too tall and towered over most of the young men she met. She had a small shapely head and her hair was pinned up, revealing the extent of her throat, so that she became known as 'swan-neck'. She was an acknowledged beauty. Among Burne-Jones's effects was a striking costume, worn for his painting of Sidonia von Bork*, a legendary Pomeranian noblewoman of great beauty who was executed as a witch in 1620. Angela dressed herself up as the sorceress for the painter Neville Lytton†. At musical evenings in Kensington, and at friends' country houses, she sang the French and German songs

---

* In the Tate Gallery. Wilhelm Meinhof's *Sidonia the Sorceress* was translated by Lady Wilde. The costume derived from Giulio Romano's *Portrait of Isabela d'Este* at Hampton Court.

† Later 3rd Earl of Lytton.

she had learned abroad, playing her own accompaniment at the piano. She was a radiant young woman, and it was said there was something dauntless about her.

One of the earliest productions in England of *Peer Gynt* took place in the spacious garden of Aubrey House, the London house of the Alexander family on Campden Hill. Two of the guests were Angela and her sister Clare. When they arrived they were told, 'You've got to act. Seven people have failed us . . .' Angela sat under a mushroom and pretended to be a troll, and listened to Grieg's incidental music.

She found that she had vague aspirations to be a writer, and she bought a typewriter, wrote stories and typed them out slowly; but she had little to say, and writing was not so easy as she thought. Her father and mother discouraged her. Margaret Mackail hoped that her beautiful and accomplished daughter would make a fashionable marriage, and it was not necessary for her to be a writer or to have any other profession.

Angela adored dancing and dressing-up. To Lady Debenham's costume party in Kensington she went dressed as a Circassian slave, with many gold coins sewn on her violet gauze dress tinkling as she danced. Her grandfather's old friend Lawrence Alma Tadema took her to *Hedda Gabler*, which made a great impression on her; but she thought Hedda too hard and unyielding, and she did not care for the play's unhappy ending. She failed to understand Hedda, whose attitude to men affronted her romantic outlook. Like her parents, she had no sympathy with the feminist movement.

One of the most memorable parties that she attended at this time was given by William de Morgan and his sister Mary, in 1909, at The Vale. William was a designer and potter; several rooms in the Kensington house of the artist Lord Leighton were covered with his exotically beautiful tiles. Mary wrote fairy stories, one collection of which she dedicated to the Mackail children. 'As one walked along the King's Road, nearly opposite Paulton Square one came to a small crossing guarded by an unpretentious wooden gate; curiously rural in appearance and suggestive of being the entry to some derelict field.' This cul-de-sac led to the quaint house, shrouded in creepers, of the de Morgans. The party was a 'house-cooling' one, for the Vale was about to fall to the developers. The whole neighbourhood seemed to have been invited, including some Chelsea pensioners in their red coats. The trees sparkled with fairy-lamps, and there was music, singing and dancing in the flower-scented gardens as darkness fell. 'It was like a dream-party,' said Angela.

2

James Campbell McInnes

Near Bury in Lancashire lies the village of Ramsbottom, most of whose inhabitants in the mid-nineteenth century and later were workers in the cotton mills. Holcome Brook was a hamlet on the outskirts of the village; it consisted of a few rows of grimy back-to-back cottages, a church, a manor house, and a public house. In one of these cottages, in 1874, Margaret McInnes gave birth to a son, James. Her husband was an engraver called Archibald McInnes who etched the designs which patterned the fabric that was manufactured in the mill. The McInnes family had lived in Lancashire for some years, but they were proud of their Scottish ancestry. The name Campbell occurred in the father's family. James McInnes's mother's maiden name was Gallacher; she may have been one of the girls who left Ireland during the potato famine, for many Irish families during the 1840s settled in Lancashire and became mill-workers. There was soon a thriving Catholic community there, and when Margaret McInnes registered her son's birth, she signed the certificate with a cross. A few years later she gave birth to a daughter, whom she named Margaret.

A small school had been established in Ramsbottom. The scholars, thirty boys, sat on two long benches at either side of the fireplace and rested their slates on their knees. For most of them, their lessons were the prelude to work at the mill.

There were two or three families of gentlefolk in Holcombe and Ramsbottom. One of these was a Mr Thomas Aitken and his wife, May, who occupied the manor house, Holcombe Hall,* and owned the mill.

People in Ramsbottom made their own music; there was usually a piano in the parlour, and songs were sung to the children. James learned to sing his father's Scottish airs. He was tall, and remarkably handsome, with black hair, a pale complexion, large dark eyes and a baritone voice of unusual power. When he was twenty, Mrs Aitken sent for him, and told him that his voice should be trained. She knew of a singing teacher in Bury. Mrs Aitken paid for the lessons; and once a week James walked

* Later Aitken Memorial Hospital, now a training centre for Moslem priests.

the five miles to Bury, had his lesson, and walked back.

The northern counties of England are famous for their choral tradition, music festivals being an integral part of north-country working-class life. A singer can rise to fame through the local church choir and the various singing competitions which take place throughout the year. Manchester was not far away from Ramsbottom, and in Manchester in 1857 Charles Hallé had established the famous orchestra which still bears his name. James justified Mrs Aitken's faith in him. He won many awards, and made many important friends in the singing world, such as Derek Oldham from Accrington and Maggie Teyte from Wolverhampton. Everybody who heard him was convinced that his voice was quite extraordinary, and he was urged to try for a scholarship at the Royal College of Music in London, where he could train to become a professional singer.

The new premises of the Royal College were in Prince Consort Road in Kensington, behind the great dome of the recently-built Albert Hall. The entrance was flanked by life-size marble statues of the Prince and Princess of Wales, who had performed the opening ceremony. Chattering students went in and out, carrying their instruments. Competition for places was strong and James was understandably nervous. He felt shy, out of place, and conscious of his north-country accent.

Once he began singing, however, his confidence reasserted itself and he made a good impression on his examiners. A few weeks later, after he had returned to Ramsbottom, the letter which he had been impatiently awaiting, arrived. The Royal College offered him a place, but not a scholarship.

The fees were twelve guineas a year and he would have to pay for his lodgings. His family were poor. Of course, Mrs Aitken agreed to pay the fees. Lodgings were arranged for him at 44 Hamfrith Road, Stratford East, which meant a long journey on the omnibus every day. Thus James McInnes, at 21, began his studies at the Royal College of Music in 1895. In addition to singing, he learnt the piano. He changed his lodgings to Forest Hill, and from there to Brixton.

James left the Royal College of Music just before Christmas 1897, without sitting for the leave-taking examination. The following year he was in Paris, armed with introductions and now calling himself J. Campbell McInnes. His new teacher was the famous Belgian baritone Jacques Bouhy who trained many well-known singers. Bouhy and McInnes took to each other immediately. Bouhy's speciality was the development and refinement of phrasing, though it was said that he neglected the important matter of breathing exercises and breath control, both fundamental to the preservation of the voice. Under Bouhy, McInnes's interpretations acquired a European refinement that they had hitherto lacked. He broadened his range and made his London debut in 1899.

In the autumn of 1901 he was singing at the Massingberd's festival at Gunby, attended by the young tenor Gervase Elwes and his beautiful wife, Lady Winefride. Both remarked on the improvement in James's technique. Lady Winefride said that James was an excellent advertisement for Bouhy.

In other directions too, James was fast making a reputation, and he was a frequent recitalist in London drawing-rooms and country houses. The earthy quality of the country airs he had learned as a boy was what moved his hearers most. These airs were in dialect, and his 'northern forthrightness of style' gave them an intimacy rare in English concert soloists.

James was eager to learn new songs and willing to try difficult parts in modern music. British composers of new music for the voice, such as Ralph Vaughan-Williams, who at that time was not at all well known, were dependent on singers of established reputation to get a hearing, and singers with delicate voices took risks with these 'difficult' modern works. One of Vaughan-Williams's friends wrote to the composer, 'You are every bit as wicked as most composers of your time in expecting human larynxes to adapt themselves to impossible feats and to stretch or contract their vocal chords to notes not in their registers.' Vaughan-Williams was warned that he would drive his soloists to the throat specialist and that he should be prepared to pay the specialist's bill.

By 1903 Campbell McInnes was regularly including songs by Vaughan-Williams in his recitals at the St James's Hall and Bechstein Hall. He was now studying under William Shakespeare, author of *Plain Words on Singing*, and Charles Santley, a fellow-northerner who was knighted in 1907. In the autumn of 1910, the first performance of Vaughan-Williams's 'A Sea Symphony' took place in Leeds; his wife Adeline had written that he was 'completely absorbed in the terrors of his first really big work', and now its moment of sound had come. James McInnes was to sing the baritone solos and was, himself, if not in a state of terror, certainly very nervous. The rehearsals had not gone smoothly. Insufficient time had been allowed for McInnes to master the unfamiliar music, and the orchestra was under-rehearsed. While they waited in the wings McInnes said jocularly to the composer, who was conducting the work, 'If I stop, you'll go on, won't you?' This hint of a possible break-down on McInnes's part shocked Vaughan-Williams.

'A Sea Symphony' opened with the triumphant phrase 'Behold the Sea Itself', sung fortissimo by the choir. Adeline recalled that her husband was nearly blown off the rostrum by the noise. Afterwards, he did not feel that the performance had been a good one, but it was a triumphant success. It went on to Bristol, Oxford, Cambridge, and finally, London, in all of which cities it was acclaimed.

Vaughan-Williams lived in an old country house near Dorking, in which a music festival was held annually. There James sang more of Vaughan-Williams's compositions. The composer's family were gregarious and hospitable and their house was open to all their musical colleagues. Among their circle of friends was Angela's sister Clare, in whom the love of music was only secondary to her love of painting. She met James McInnes, and was soon a fervent member of his personal entourage.

Early in 1911, Vaughan-Williams received a commission to compose a new work for the Worcester Festival. He had in mind to set to music a number of poems by George Herbert, to be called 'Five Mystical Songs' for baritone solo, choir and orchestra. Clare and a party of friends went to Worcester to hear the first performance. The occasion was for her an unforgettable one and she was profoundly moved. Vaughan-Williams himself reminded her of a piece of medieval sculpture. The entire performance was 'one of unearthly beauty'. James was heaped with adulation.

Another young composer who was also becoming known among serious music lovers was a former music-master at Radley College, George Butterworth. McInnes's success in the genre of country ballads made him a natural choice for Butterworth's musical settings of Housman's 'A Shropshire Lad', which he was able to infuse with a quality of grandeur. Of one of the songs, 'Ploughing', a critic wrote that McInnes's performance was altogether 'too outspoken, too elemental'. But on the whole, he won only praise. 'A singer with soul.' There was about his singing 'a terrible beauty'. 'It was like coming face to face with nature.' With the Butterworth songs, McInnes was at the peak of his career.

On 17 February 1911, Bach's St Matthew Passion, with full orchestral accompaniment, was performed in Westminster Abbey. Among the soloists were Rhoda von Glehn, Gervase Elwes, and James

Campbell McInnes. It was an important cultural and devotional event. *The Times* wrote, 'Mr Campbell McInnes sang the part of the Saviour with dignity . . . unfortunately he was a little out of tune in the beautiful *arioso* . . . so that the supreme repose of the movement was broken.'

The leader of the Conservative Party, Arthur Balfour, who had a passion for music, was in the Abbey that night, and it was he who suggested to Lady Wemyss's sister, Lady Glenconner, that she should invite James to Wilsford Manor to entertain her guests during a house-party week-end, at which he, Balfour, was going to be present.

At the time James was in his late thirties. He was still very handsome; women called him *très male*, which is a little surprising, since he was perfumed and pomaded, wore rings on his fingers, and adopted a theatrical style of dress. With his six feet four inches, his black mane—it waved luxuriantly back from an olive complexion—and his eyes which were as eloquent as the lyrics he sang, he made frequent conquests, of whom Clare was said to have been one. He imbued the oratorios and lieder which composed his repertoire, with passion—a rare quality in singers trained in the austere English choral tradition.

James was unmarried, though he had had many opportunities to make a good marriage and was pursued by quite a few young women of good family. Behind the large black moustache was a temperament which found men as attractive as women, and by 1911 he had developed a more or less permanent relationship with a composer called Graham Peel, who was McInnes's junior by five years. They shared a north-country background, for Peel had been born near Manchester, but in other respects they were entirely different.

Peel belonged to a family of wealthy cotton-manufacturers, and was slight of build, delicate of feature and, flaxen-haired. He had been educated at Harrow and Oxford, and after taking his degree had stayed on at Oxford to study musical composition. The insipid ballads he wrote himself enjoyed a certain popularity, but when they were sung by McInnes they were infused with passion. Musically they were inferior to other compositions that McInnes sang and they did not add to his reputation. His partnership with Peel, however, was useful to him. Life in London even for a well-known singer, was expensive, and McInnes had developed extravagant tastes. The two men lived together in Cavendish Road, St John's Wood. Peel had considerable private means, while McInnes was entirely dependent on his voice for his living.

McInnes was at a point in his career that could not be carried much further unless he was determined and ambitious, but he was neither. He needed to consolidate his reputation, but he was lazy and too fond of drinking; his father, it was depressing for him to remember, had been a drunkard. He remained a singer endowed with a magnificent voice, and he relied on this natural gift.

At the Wilsford house-party during March 1911, both Angela and Clare were guests. Angela was already a practised flirt. She longed to break away from the excessive refinement of her Mackail upbringing. She was uninterested in the polite young men of good breeding whom she normally met and to whom she was expected to respond in a lady-like way. McInnes had a savage quality about him which she found absolutely thrilling. For his part, he was attracted to clever, strong-minded women. Every time he made a conquest among educated women, his sense of inferiority, which arose out of his constant aware-ness of his humble origin, was assuaged.

His reputation as a philanderer was an added attraction to Angela— at that time a high-spirited virgin. She found herself fascinated by his 'heroic' looks, his marvellous voice, and his femininity; to her, he was like an ancient god, half male, half female. James, for his part, was drawn to this Amazonian beauty. Their acquaintance soon erupted into passion, and their engagement was straightway made known, though it was not announced in the newspapers.

The older members of Angela's family disapproved of the engage-ment. Graham Peel was dismayed. He had just published a new song, 'Wind of the Western Sea', a setting of Tennyson's lullaby. Its recep-tion was encouraging and he hoped for further success in partnership with McInnes. He urged James not to go through with the marriage. Knowing James's temperament, he warned him that it would have disastrous consequences.

The marriage was hastily arranged six weeks after the couple had first met; there was no time for any elaborate ceremony at Rottingdean, traditionally the scene of weddings in the family. The original date, the last week in May, was advanced to 5 May, and a special licence was obtained.

During the brief engagement, James called at the Mackail house to take his betrothed to hear him sing at the Bechstein Hall in Wigmore Street (later the Wigmore Hall). The unhappy younger sister watched Angela walk down the stairs, a dazzling sight in an emerald green silk dress.

At the recital James sang a group of Schubert's loveliest songs, 'with all his usual taste', reported the critic of the *Daily Telegraph*. The critic particularly praised the song by Graham Peel, and commented, 'How ill-founded is the complaint of vocalists that they cannot find English songs which are worthy of places in ambitious programmes.'

Canon Jessop sent his congratulations from his Norfolk rectory— 'my old heart that is palpitating at ye blessed news will get quiet bye and bye . . . May you feel lofty and exalted aspirations.'

The couple were married in the recently-built church of St Philip in the Earl's Court Road, round the corner from the parental home in Pembroke Gardens. Only thirteen people were present. Margaret McInnes, the bridegroom's sister, Denis Mackail, and Lady Burne-Jones signed the register. Several older members of the family were shocked that the ceremony should take place on a Friday. The following day a bare announcement appeared in *The Times*.

> The marriage took place yesterday at St Philip's Church, Kensington, of Mr J. Campbell McInnes and Miss Angela Margaret Mackail, daughter of Dr J. W. Mackail, of 6, Pembroke Gardens, W., formerly Professor of Poetry at Oxford.

Dr Mackail had omitted from this notice his wife's name, and there was no mention of the bridegroom's parents, or his address. The absence of these details was scarcely compensated for by the information which most people who knew the family were familiar with, that Dr Mackail was formerly Professor of Poetry at Oxford.

The newly-married couple rented a pretty house at 108 Church Street, Kensington, a short walk from Pembroke Gardens. Angela entered her new life with enthusiasm.

Angela's wedding day, 5 May 1911, coincided with the start of the Season. The annual Royal Academy Dinner was presided over that night by Sir Edward Poynter, Angela's uncle by marriage. An important guest was Rudyard Kipling. Also present was the Prime Minister, H. H. Asquith, whose second son had married Lady Wemyss's daughter Cynthia Charteris. During the week of Angela's marriage, Lady Cynthia gave birth to a son at her mother's London house in Cadogan Square, and Queen Mary drove out into the bright sunshine with Princess Mary by her side. The Queen's tall toque was smothered in full-blown pink roses and swathed with tulle veiling; it signalled that the Court was no longer in mourning for Edward VII, who had died the previous spring. Stands for the Coronation of George V were being erected around Westminster Abbey, and the King's cousin, Kaiser Wilhelm, had already arrived in London for the great event. The press reported that he was in every way delighted with the warmth of the welcome accorded to him by the British people. He attended the unveiling of the grandiose Memorial to Prince Albert in Kensington Gardens. The proposal to erect another, smaller monument in Kensington Gardens—to Peter Pan—was meeting with opposition; the authorities considered that it would be a dangerous precedent. It was said that to obtain a key to the Gardens, which Barrie tried to do, was more difficult than to be granted a baronetcy. Popular sentiment, however, overruled the objections.

A few days after the official resumption of gaiety, their Majesties held the first court of their reign. It was preceded by an announcement that hobble skirts were considered dangerous and would not be permitted at court.

The Coronation Season promised to be glittering. All the notables of the day crowded in splendid array at the Royal Opera House, Covent Garden, to hear Melba sing. The ladies wore tiaras, furs and feathers, and every degree of finery. The Royal Family was in the royal box. Angela and James, who knew Melba as a fellow professional, were among the audience. Angela wore a dress of brilliant blue *peau de soie* girdled with silver and blue aigrettes in her upswept hair.

At the Savoy an even more glittering event took place—a costume ball in aid of the Middlesex Hospital, at which Angela's uncle, Philip Burne-Jones, helped Prince Alexander of Teck, the new Queen's brother, make the awards. Lady Diana Manners, costumed with breathtaking dramatic brilliance as a Velasquez Infanta, was presented with the first ladies' prize of a handsome chain and pendant of diamonds containing nearly four hundred stones and valued at two hundred and fifty guineas. Angela's long fine hair was plaited into braids, a golden fillet wound round her forehead, and her statuesque figure draped in robes girdled with gold, she was ideally costumed as Brünnhilde, and was enormously admired. When, after the ball, Philip Burne-Jones painted Lady Diana Manners in the Velasquez costume, the result was disappointing. He had not his father's master touch.

A minor news item about the exchange of telegrams between the Postmaster Generals of England and Australia was hardly noticed, eclipsed by the glamour of the Coronation festivities. The Australian message read: 'Pleased that today Australia has penny postage with

Motherland. Trust it will tend to draw closer the bonds of kinship.'

In the *Daily Chronicle* a lively correspondence was started on the subject of corporal punishment, 'Sir . . . it is a great mistake to do away with the time-honoured punishment of the birch,' wrote two Etonians. 'In an age when this nation is becoming all too soft and flabby, let Eton at least try to harden off her sons . . . that part of the anatomy selected for birching at Eton is singularly free from chilblains.'

But in the rest of the country all was not well. In Llanelly in Wales, the railwaymen came out on strike. The strike soon became nationwide. Without horses, people could not get from A to B. There was rioting in Llanelly, and the Home Secretary, Mr Winston Churchill, sent troops to restore order. Fifty thousand soldiers tried to maintain communications in the rest of the country. For May, the weather was unusually hot and tempers around Llanelly exploded. *The Illustrated London News* published drawings of the conflict and added this account:

> A number of bayonet charges were made against the rioters . . .
> Several members of the crowd were injured . . . A young man
> sitting on a garden wall fell back into the garden, shot dead, and
> almost immediately afterwards others fell at the same spot . . . The
> rioting was begun again after nightfall and ended even more
> tragically.

In the House of Commons, the Home Secretary defended his decision to send troops to Wales. 'It was necessary to use the military forces of the Crown with the utmost promptitude . . . The Llanelly rioters . . . wrought, in their drunken frenzy, more havoc to life and limb, shed more blood, and produced more serious injury among themselves, than all the 50,000 soldiers who have been employed on strike duty all over the country.' He exonerated the strikers themselves from blame.

In Russia during the same month of May an aeroplane surprised some peasants, who fled, thinking it a monstrous bird.

On the last day of May, James McInnes gave his usual monthly recital at the Bechstein Hall. He sang Schubert's 'Frühlingslaube' and Brahms's 'Magyarisch' and 'Ständchen', followed by songs by Vaughan-Williams and Graham Peel.

The Times and the *Daily Telegraph* ignored this concert. Instead, *The Times* devoted a column to an afternoon recital by a completely unknown soprano.

Early in 1912, Angela gave birth to a son. He was named Graham after Graham Peel. The composer had ceased to write songs for his friend to sing, but he stood godfather to James's son.

Music was now the dominant influence in Angela's life. She accompanied James to all his musical engagements up and down the country and translated German and French songs into English for him. En route to a festival in Manchester, she found herself in Knutsford, Cheshire, the town in which Mrs Gaskell had spent her childhood and round which she had written *Cranford*. Angela wrote of this visit, 'I knew it was Cranford, but when you are young as I was then and your whole life is suddenly bound up with music, Manchester and a concert have more importance than a little town that has been in a book.'

They were still invited for week-ends at country houses, but now they went more often to Bournemouth, where Graham Peel had a house.

After two years of married life, Angela was still content. George Wyndham, whose son Percy had just become engaged, reported in a letter to Mrs Mackail, 'Angela recommends marriage, [she] still holds the record for time; but for complete initiative and independence of action, Percy ties with her. He saw Diana for the first time out hunting, on January 24th, made a point of seeing her on foot on the Wednesday following, and was accepted that day fortnight.'

1914 became known to fashionable society women as 'the wild tango year', in spite of terrible events that were fast approaching. Angela had given up dancing for the time; she was pregnant again. The McInnes family had moved to the other side of Kensington High Street, to the Little Boltons, south of the Cromwell Road; it was more suitable for children than the busy thoroughfare that Church Street was becoming, and there were some pretty gardens nearby.

On 28 June, in the town of Sarajevo, the heir to the thrones of Austria and Hungary, Archduke Francis Ferdinand, and his wife were assassinated by a Serbian called Gavrilo Princip. Uncomprehending Europe was suddenly at war.

In Kensington life went on much as usual. Mrs Mackail attended one of the summer garden parties on Campden Hill. Angela was unwilling to be left out of anything. Mrs Mackail told a friend, 'Angela is about to have a baby in the next ten minutes but she's determined to come.' She made a striking entrance, for she had spent the morning dressmaking. She was draped in a frock of Chinese blue *crêpe de chine* and had improvised a little black hat trimmed with a nodding scarlet ostrich feather. The painter John Collier was present; he admired Angela's ensemble and implored her to sit for him. Angela promised to do so after the birth of her baby.

At the end of July Mrs Patrick Campbell was in the final rehearsals of a new play by Bernard Shaw, *Pygmalion*. Denis Mackail, who had embarked on a career as a stage designer, had devised the scenery. The play created a sensation, and 'Not bloody likely!' uttered by Eliza Dolittle echoed around London. But by the middle of the summer all Europe was holding its breath and on 16 August the British Expeditionary Force landed in France. During that month, Angela's second son, Colin McInnes, was born. And in due course, she kept her promise to Collier. Wearing her blue *crêpe de chine* frock and the hat with the scarlet feather, she arrived at his studio for the portrait sitting.

Kipling's only son fell in France, at the age of 18. In the autumn of 1914, Denis Mackail attempted to enlist, but at that time the Army was not short of recruits and he was rejected on medical grounds. He had always been rather delicate. Margaret Mackail wrote her cousin a letter of sympathy, and in it expressed the regret that her son Denis had been prevented from fighting. 'Yours is the greater loss,' came the grimly patriotic rejoinder. Percy Wyndham also fell. The youngest and most beautiful Charteris boy, Yvo, quickly followed. And after him, his eldest brother, Hugo, Lord Elcho. Then the two sons of Lady Glenconner. The young composer George Butterworth too. The terrible toll continued.

The famous and enormously successful American painter John Singer Sargent, whose portraits dominated the Royal Academy during the years of the new century, was in London again. He was stimulated by the personalities and features of the English upper classes. It was said that he 'excelled with women of pronounced character'. His greatest triumph was the group portrait of the famous sisters *nées* Wyndham: Mrs Adeane, Lady Glenconner, and the Countess of Wemyss, sitting in a dark drawing-room furnished by William Morris. The painting was such a success that it was followed by clamorous portrait commissions from both sides of the Atlantic. To keep up with the demand, Sargent began sketching portraits in charcoal. He spent his mornings doing them very quickly for a fee of fifty pounds, no small sum in those days.

Sargent drew Lady Cynthia Asquith in the presence of a tempestuous Mrs Patrick Campbell, who behaved so badly that she had to be asked to leave the studio, and he sketched Lady Cynthia's brother Hugo and his fiancée Lady Violet Manners. He also drew Lady Winefride Elwes, and Thackeray's sister, Lady Ritchie, wearing a frilled cap. And he sketched the delicate profile of a young Scottish girl, Lady Elizabeth Bowes-Lyon.

Angela sat for Sargent in his studio at 31 Tite Street, Chelsea; but by this time the celebrated artist was nearly 60, bored with painting portraits, and had even come to hate his facility. Angela was a woman of 'pronounced character', and his sketch of her was one of his most successful. Everybody remarked upon it. He had exactly captured Angela's pride and vulnerability: her swan-neck was elongated, her mouth tremulous; there was a fearless gaze in her eyes. Angela invited Henry James, now a naturalized Englishman, to see the drawing. He had known her grandfather and had himself sat to Sargent. 'I will, with pleasure, undertake to be in some sort of condition to come to you at 5,' he replied.

Angela and James had now been married for three years. James was forty and his career had begun to decline. In the circumstances of the war, not so many people wanted to listen to oratorio and lieder, and he was frequently without an engagement. A different kind of song was heard, of which 'Keep the Home Fires Burning', written by Ivor Novello, was the most popular. James tried to augment his income by taking pupils, but he had little taste for teaching: he lacked patience and was essentially a performer. Bored and idle, he began drinking again and was soon in debt. Angela was appalled at what was happening to her husband but seemed powerless to prevent his apparent drift downhill.

Angela had an allowance from her father, which was enough to pay for a staff of three—a cook, a parlourmaid and a nursemaid—and she would inherit quite a considerable sum of money from her grandmother, Lady Burne-Jones, now settled at Rottingdean.

'Marriage,' remarked Angela some years later, 'is not a cure for alcoholism.' When James was drunk, he turned 'his worship of her into something from the memory of which her mind shudderingly withdrew'. The quotation is from one of Angela's novels (*O, These Men, These Men!*), not a letter. James, in his cups, was a bore, and his resentment, especially of Angela's family, rose to the surface. He sneered at her mother's well-bred airs and at her father's scholarship. And Angela, of course, got the worst of it. He even beat her and then disappeared for days on end. A character in one of her novels remarked, 'That's the woman who was such a soft fool that she couldn't stop her husband drinking.' She grew resigned or, as she said in the same novel, she fell into 'stupefied resignation'.

The war intensified some aspects of social life in England. Working parties of ladies assembled for good causes. *Our Home*, a popular weekly, described how the Misses Hargrove of Sandown in the Isle of Wight had initiated the pastime of sandbag-making, an activity which was hard on their delicate hands.

Through the columns of the same journal, Lady Hamilton, one of the daughters of the Dowager Lady Muir of Deanston, appealed for gifts of cotton khaki shirts, socks, writing pads, Woodbine cigarettes, condensed milk and sweets: they were destined for 'her husband's soldiers fighting in the Dardanelles Straits', and were to be sent to her at 1 Hyde Park Gate.

Wounded Tommies in their hospital blue were laughing and singing in Hyde Park among the well-tended flowerbeds, thankful to be away from the horror of the war. The eleven-year-old Crown Prince of Italy joined his father in the trenches, and according to the report he showed no sign of fear.

During the summer of 1916 the McInnes family—Angela, James, the two boys and a nursemaid—went to Rottingdean. Georgiana Burne-Jones was now a frail old lady and received her visitors in her room on the first floor sitting up in a small lace-draped bed which resembled a child's cot.

They slept in the room which had been Angela's as a child. The angel her grandfather had painted for her on the wall was still there. It was on this visit that Angela discovered that she was pregnant for the third time. One morning during this holiday at Rottingdean, James was absent from the breakfast-table. Angela explained that he had slept badly and was feeling tired. The truth of the matter was that he'd come in drunk, woken her up, created a scene. They had spent most of the night quarrelling and bickering. From all accounts his rages were frightening.

The marriage was breaking-up. Her romantic vision of him had crumbled away. For his part, he too was disappointed. The adoring girl he had fallen in love with had been replaced by a distant, critical young woman. In her words, her only protection was 'a kind of cold and dispassionate, almost brutal, aloofness'.

In September she accompanied him to Edinburgh, where he had a singing engagement at the Usher Hall. He drank heavily on the train, and when they arrived at the Royal Caledonian Hotel he made a scene with the reception clerk. In their room he picked up a suitcase and threw it at her. No one knows what was upsetting him. Next day he had sufficiently recovered to get through the recital, and together they returned to Kensington.

In the autumn of 1916, James found a new pupil, an attractive young woman with a promising voice. Soon, it was rumoured that they were lovers.

At Little Boltons on 30 March 1917, Angela gave birth to a daughter, Mary; and in a downstairs room, her husband James dallied with his pupil. He left the house with her and did not return for some days.

James McInnes sang, drank and fornicated; he was least successful at the drinking. It was said of him, 'He just can't touch it. One glass— even of sherry—and he is off and away into some private world of his own. He really doesn't know where he is . . . Campbell has to be protected from himself . . . and other people have to be protected from him . . . [he] has the most terrifying temper when roused; a black unreasoning Celtic rage.' These remarks were made to his son Graham who added, 'My father suddenly disappeared after one or two scenes of towering violence.'

The break happened in the middle of May 1917. In an amazingly calm mood, Angela telephoned her parents and simply asked them to come and take her and the children away. The news soon spread throughout the Royal Borough of Kensington. The Mackails were ultra-respectable, and the scandal of their daughter's broken marriage and of the drunken behaviour of their son-in-law enlivened conversation. In Cadogan Square on 18 May, Lady Wemyss, her daughter Lady Cynthia, and Mrs Patrick Campbell, now 'disfiguringly fat', discussed in great detail over luncheon the latest gossip from the Mackail-McInnes sector. And when they had exhausted that subject, the famous actress, who was on her way to give a poetry reading to soldiers in hospital, rehearsed some of the poems, reducing her audience of two to tears. Afterwards Lady Cynthia wrote in her diary, 'Conversation with Mama . . . She told me of the terrible Campbell McInnes melodrama. He has become a raging drunkard and she is going to divorce him. She has just been packed off to Clouds with her baby.'

After a few days James returned; he seemed to be enormously surprised to find the house empty and all the signs that Angela had packed up and gone, taking of course the children with her. He concluded that she had fled to Rottingdean. He hurried down there, full of guilt, surprising Angela's uncle, Philip Burne-Jones, who had not expected this visit.

Philip declined to tell him where Angela was. James pleaded, threatened and finally hit him. Philip was a small man but he was not a coward. Lady Cynthia wrote in her diary, 'Poor, tiny little Phil had a ghastly struggle at Rottingdean and Phil actually downed him.' Angela was terrified when she heard about this and fled from Clouds to Stanway in Gloucestershire to be the guest of her mother's friend Lady Wemyss. 'It was unbearably hot,' wrote Lady Cynthia in her diary. 'Angela McInnes is a pathetic refugee here; a singing husband having brought her an ordeal of misery, she has now decided to divorce him.'

Lady Wemyss, who was in her early fifties, offered Angela understanding and endless sympathy. The atmosphere of Stanway gradually soothed Angela.

In the late Middle Ages, built on holy ground, Stanway House had been the summer residence of successive Abbots of Tewkesbury. It was acquired through marriage by the Wemyss family in the eighteenth century. It was approached through villages of honey-coloured stone and was almost hidden between the contours of the embracing Cotswold hills. The beautiful sixteenth-century gate-house, said to have been designed by Inigo Jones, suddenly came into view round a bend. The house itself was gabled and mullioned, and built and roofed of the golden stone. It invoked intense adoration among all the people who lived and visited there.

The life of Stanway was leisurely, and Angela had little to do. She sat in the great oriel window. Through the amber diamond panes, round which clambered roses, the courtyard was tinted gold. Lady Cynthia likened it to 'a vast honeycomb of stored sunshine'.

On Sundays Angela attended mattins with Lady Wemyss at the little church, which was reached through the courtyard by its own connecting door. The ancient gravestones were encrusted with centuries-old lichen, amber with age.

The family had been cruelly bereaved by the war. The heir, Lord Elcho, was dead; and so was his younger brother, Yvo Charteris. Furthermore, the condition of Lady Cynthia's son John was distressing; in later years his problem would be diagnosed as autism. Lady Cynthia wrote in her diary: 'Mamma and I took her five-year-old son for a walk with John in the Sling after tea. I wept tears of anguish over poor John—it is so tantalizing seeing that other boy'. The 'other boy' was Graham McInnes, and he had his problems too: at Stanway he hit his mother on the head with a silver teapot.

James McInnes was now 48. In 1917, men were desperately needed in the Army. He joined the Royal Flying Corps at the end of May and in August applied for a commission as an Equipment Officer. He was stationed at Henley-on-Thames.

> Our children are sleeping, and calm is the night
> As the crime of the Hun who loves not the light
> Spreads terror. To whom do we turn in our plight?
> Britain's airmen!
> (from a poem by Miss Lyle Thomas)

Dr Mackail had never liked his son-in-law, and he was not surprised that the marriage had fallen apart. Cousin Stanley Baldwin, a rising statesman and a very wealthy man, was consulted, and he suggested Ellis Hume-Williams, K.C., M.P., as an advocate. Further, he offered Angela, who had little money of her own, a loan to pay for the cost of the case. Hume-Williams, who lived in Kensington, was Conservative Member of Parliament for a division of Nottingham.

On 19 November 1917, while James McInnes was in the Royal Flying Corps, the case opened in the High Court by Temple Bar. 'Mrs Angela McInnes . . . prayed for divorce from James McInnes, a professional singer, on the grounds of cruelty and adultery. The respondent by his answer denied the charges, but the suit was now undefended.' James had wanted to contest the suit; by divorce he would lose too much—not only his wife, but his children and his share of the monies Angela was due to inherit on the death of her mother and grandmother. And he discovered, to his surprise, that he was very much in love with Angela.

His marriage, which had lasted six years, had provided him with comfortable circumstances. He was persuaded that it would be futile to defend the case, for the evidence against him was overwhelming. If it is to be believed, he had turned satyr; he had locked himself and the nursemaid into the dining-room and raped her, and afterwards boasted of the deed to Angela, crying, 'She belongs to me body and soul!' The tearful nursemaid had confirmed it all. Angela had arranged for the girl to go back home to her mother, with a month's wages. The nursemaid gave evidence, and so did Angela's doctor, who declared that Angela's health, and even her life, had been in danger.

The report in the *Weekly Dispatch* of Sunday 8 November 1917
bore the headline: WIFE'S LIFE OF HORROR. *The Times*
quoted Mr Justice Hill's remark: 'Her husband evidently behaved like
a drunken beast.' A decree nisi was granted and Angela was given the
custody of her three children. Costs were awarded against James, but it
is unlikely that he ever paid them.

For a woman of those days, being divorced was something of a
disgrace, even for the innocent party. In Angela's case, it was said that
she had provoked James's cruelty towards her. Her character was dis-
sected and blame apportioned: she was 'too proud'; she had tried to
reform James and what man of spirit would stand for that?

Angela with her three children disrupted the household at Pembroke
Gardens. The furniture and belongings from the home at the Little
Boltons were put in store, apart from some pieces which helped to
furnish the rooms on the nursery floor of her parents' house where she
and the children's quarters were.

Further tragedy was to come. The baby, Mary, had never been
strong. The winter of 1917–18 was unusually cold and long; after
Christmas there were weeks of below-freezing temperatures and the
large house in Kensington was not adequately heated. Mary developed
pneumonia and died a month before her first birthday. Blame for the
baby's death was heaped upon James.

The family proceeded to Rottingdean for the funeral. The child was
buried beside the church wall, which bore a memorial tablet to Burne-
Jones. Angela returned to Kensington, to a life which she described as
that of being 'neither wife nor maid'. She was a penniless divorcee with
two small sons to bring up. Graham and Colin were attending the
Froebel Institute, the fees for which were paid by Dr Mackail. He also
paid for a nanny. The crisis was over but the future looked bleak.
Angela felt immense gratitude to her parents, but it was tempered by
guilt. Dr Mackail exuded a patience and resignation which made
Angela feel 'that she was seven years old and in disgrace'. What should
she do now? She had lost her independence and her home; she had
neither training nor education to enable her to earn her own living. She
could re-marry, of course; she was still under thirty. But it was tragically apparent that the war had left tens of thousands of widows everywhere and most of them would never marry again.

One early summer afternoon in 1918, the two little boys—Graham
was six, Colin four—were out with their nanny, walking along Kensington High Street, when suddenly a tall man in uniform loomed up

before them. Graham recognized his father and greeted him excitedly. The nanny was upset by the stranger and attempted to hurry away. But the boy wanted to stay with his father. There was a scuffle. When they arrived back at Pembroke Gardens, Graham burst out with the news. Angela explained: 'Dadda was like Reuben and I had to send him away.' Reuben was the drunken coachman in *Black Beauty* who caused the horse in his care to go lame. Later Angela was to write: 'There are natures that can be generous and forgiving under slights, neglect, privation, but if once terrified, physically or mentally, the wound to their inner self, the degradation of the immortal being, is such that they will never seek revenge, nor speak bitter words, but their lives will run frozen over the black depths where past cruelties lie.' She never spoke directly of James McInnes again.

3
George Lancelot Thirkell

Britain asked Australia for 7,000 men a month, and Australia sent them—to the beaches of Gallipoli and the trenches of France. Among the men of the Australian Imperial Forces who rode to war was a 23-year-old Tasmanian engineer called George Lancelot Allnut Thirkell.

In April 1915, the Australians landed at Anzac Cove. As an engineer, George's job did not begin until the hand-to-hand fighting had cleared the ground ahead. On the deck of the destroyer *Bacchante*, George watched the action through field-glasses. The Australians with fixed bayonets charged the Turks. 'It was as though one was looking into the stage from the Royal box in a theatre,' Captain Thirkell wrote.

Later, when he saw the casualties, he was less entertained. The hospital ships were soon full and the warships had to take on the wounded. 'It drizzled with rain—and large loads of wounded were brought alongside the ship. We were ill-equipped to deal with them ... there was not a single complaint, nor do I remember any moaning. Never shall I forget the warm sickly smell of that lacerated mass of wounded humanity.'

The shell fire was coming mostly from a fort called Gaba Têpe. The *Bacchante* trained its guns upon it; the ship's gunners hit the fort time and again and even penetrated the hole from which the Turkish fire came, but unavailingly. It was uncanny. The fort was impregnable. The *Bacchante* had to pull up its anchor and withdraw to a safer distance.

On the morning of 28 April sufficient headway had been made to permit the engineers to land. The work of consolidating the position was done under constant heavy fire—again from the fort Gaba Têpe. The donkeys and mules carried the heavy equipment ashore. On 2 May, a week after the initial landing, the Brigade Commanders and Battalion Commanders decided to reconnoitre the fort and landed a party of men on the beach immediately below it.

The fort was built on a natural promontory, described as a miniature

Gibraltar. The Turkish forces had been entrenched there for years. The whole area was in fact honeycombed with well-concealed and well-constructed trenches. In addition, there were observation posts looking in all directions. This natural vantage point, both for defence and offence, had defeated the Greeks who had tried to land there during the Graeco-Turkish war of 1913. The Australians, with George Thirkell among them, succeeded where the Greeks had failed.

For some miles round the point, the water was unusually clear. Entirely submerged were rolls of Turkish barbed wire, stronger than the English variety and with the barbs closer together. During the preliminary reconnaissance the dark shadows in the clear water were dismissed as seaweed.

The party chosen for the hazardous, if not lunatic, enterprise on 3 May 1915 consisted of 100 men of the 11th Battalion under Captain R. L. Leane. George Thirkell was then a lieutenant in charge of 10 engineers. They were landed in rowing boats at 3.30 a.m., and shortly afterwards firing broke out from all parts of the fort. There was virtually no shelter and many of the men were killed at once. Captain Leane ordered a withdrawal. 'To extricate even the unwounded from such a place was an ugly problem and the withdrawal of the wounded offered greater difficulties still,' wrote George Thirkell. The men remained on the beachhead for three hours, where they were under constant fire before being rescued by the Royal Navy. George Thirkell was wounded in the right leg and shortly afterwards he found himself a patient at Dundee Royal Infirmary.

In the county of Forfarshire in Scotland, a 15-year-old girl spent much of her time bicycling round the grounds of her home. The war had dislocated family life. Her older brothers were fighting in France. One of them had been killed in the battle of Loos. Her elder sister was a nurse in London. Part of the house had been turned into a hospital for the war wounded, and she greatly enjoyed the company of the soldiers. She played cards with them, wrote letters for them, and in the evenings joined her mother in singing songs for them. And the men joined in the singing.

The girl was Lady Elizabeth Bowes-Lyon, the daughter of the 14th Earl of Strathmore, and the house was Glamis Castle, the most famous and impressive building in Scotland.

With its battlements, moat, pepperpot turrets, and pinnacles, it ful-filled a child's dream of a castle. It stood off the Kirriemuir-Dundee road in the vale of Strathmore, five hundred miles north of London, and had been in the Strathmore family for over five hundred years. In 1372, the records say, it had been leased to the Lyon family for the rent of 'one red falcon to be delivered yearly on the feast of Pentecost'.

The young Walter Scott stayed there in 1793, overawed by the massive walls hung with medieval armour, and the gloomy vaults, scenes of ancient crimes. Malcolm III, King of Scotland, had been murdered there. The story of Glamis Castle is one of crimes, punishments, hauntings. There was more than one ghost at Glamis. As Walter Scott lay in the tartan-hung four-poster bed in one of the castle's rooms, he reflected that this place was 'too far from the living and somewhat too near the dead'.

When George Thirkell was well enough to be discharged from Dundee Royal Infirmary, he was met by Lady Strathmore, who took him, and probably a few other soldiers too, to Glamis Castle, ten miles away.

His first glimpse of Glamis enthralled him.

Entrance to the Castle was through a small doorway surrounded by lions incised in the stonework. High up on the surface of the turret wall was the dial of the castle clock.

Captain Thirkell was led up a twisting stair built into the 14-feet-thick wall to the apartment where the family lived.

The Strathmore family provided every comfort for the men in their care. The soldiers' dining-room was in the crypt, a cylindrical chamber, the walls of which were hung with relics of the castle's past—battle-axes, swords, cuirasses, and the stuffed heads of noble animals. Whole suits of armour stood about amid the occasional stuffed bear rampant.

The large dining-room used by the family had been converted into a ward for seventeen beds. The men played billiards in a room hung with old tapestries. The leather-bound books in the library, mainly in Latin, were at their disposal. The lion emblem abounded; nut-crackers, door-stops, and mud-scrapers were all lion-embellished—letter-boxes and door-handles too. The huge open fireplaces with logs burning in the grate, round which the men sat during the evenings, were guarded on either side by great gilt lions, and lions embellished the fire-irons in the open hearth. A special treat was a visit to Dundee to watch the 'moving pictures', which were shown to the accompaniment of a tinkling piano.

George Thirkell was described at the time as a 'handsome captain with dark brown hair and freckles in the irises of his eyes', whose voice had a 'strange twangy lilt'. The Strathmore family found him charming. When he was sufficiently recovered and the time came for him to say goodbye—he was returning to the front—Lady Strathmore invited him to spend his leaves at Glamis and drove him to the station. And during the next two years he did return to Glamis, several times.

It seems that something in the nature of a friendship sprang up between Lady Elizabeth and Captain Thirkell. At 17 she was in the full flower of her girlish beauty—her grey eyes were set in a complexion like a wild rose, round which curled tendrils of dark hair. In the sunshine, seated in wicker basket chairs on the castle terrace, they took each other's photographs with her box camera. And while he was away at the front, she wrote to him, and sent him their photographs.

In 1917, George Thirkell was posted to a training depot on Salisbury Plain near Amesbury in Wiltshire. Not far away was Wilsford Manor.

A house can play an important part in a person's life. Wilsford Manor had certainly played a vital role in Angela's life; for there she had met her husband James, from whom she was now divorced. It is possible, even likely, that when she and her two sons were invited by Pamela, Lady Glenconner, to spend a few weeks there during the summer of 1918, she had hopes of meeting her second husband. If she had such hopes or fantasy, it was surprisingly fulfilled, for in the drawing-room there at this time, she was introduced to Captain Thirkell who, with some of his fellow Australians, had been invited round to tea.

He, for his part, saw a beautiful young woman. Her vivid blue eyes, melancholy in repose, were brightened by the animation of her conversation. Her long brown hair was coiled and twined about the small shapely head, two dark wings falling on either side of her forehead. She wore a severely-cut dark frock softened by creamy lace at the breast. The fashion of the day reflected the nation's mood of mourning. George Thirkell's second name was Lancelot, and Angela seemed to him the very embodiment of Queen Guinevere.

Angela had learned something of Australia from the novels of Henry Kingsley, who had suffered a five-year exile in Australia. She had also read Anthony Trollope's autobiography and his Australian books. Trollope had spent some time in Australia and Tasmania.

George Thirkell had never read either of these writers. He could, however, tell her about Tasmania at first hand: of how an ancestor of his had gone there to manage a farm, and how his father had pioneered a new road through previously uncharted territory, a feat which had earned him the honorary Fellowship of the Royal Geographical Society. Hobart, Tasmania's capital city, had been built with the labour of convicts, but it was a rich land, and a country of opportunity. George made Australia and Tasmania sound most exciting.

During Angela's stay at Wilsford Manor, they saw each other almost every day. He brought her flowers, gave chocolates to her boys, and played games with them. They called him 'Thirk'. The young lovers walked along the banks of the river Avon which flowed through the grounds of the Manor. It was an ideal summer background to a romantic courtship.

Angela's family were astounded that their daughter should embark upon another hasty marriage. Her first marriage had failed and the Mackails had borne with Scottish stoicism the distressing publicity, with all its sordid details, of their daughter's divorce. Was this second marriage also going to turn out to be a misalliance? A million young men from Britain had been slaughtered and there was a multitude of bereaved women. Angela owned no property and was encumbered with two sons; yet in spite of the fierce competition she had found a new husband within a year of her divorce. It was a solution to her present problems and the boys' future.

The peace that the Bolsheviks made with Germany at Brest-Litovsk in December 1917 took Russia out of the war and enabled the Germans to mount a great spring offensive which brought General Ludendorff's army, after it had broken through the British and French lines, to within forty miles of Paris. Sir James Barrie, who must have been regarded by newspaper editors as a kind of oracle, was asked if Paris would fall. He replied, 'The Allies will get to Berlin.' The Allies did not march through Berlin, but the German offensive was broken and the God of War went over to the Entente.

The first intimation that the Armistice had been declared was the sight of a little Paris midinette running down the deserted rue de la Paix calling out gaily. It was 11 November 1918. All the people of Paris immediately poured out into the streets and the great squares were soon filled with people surging with joy. A British military band played triumphantly in the Place de la Concorde, and when night fell Kaiser Wilhelm II was burnt there in effigy, instead of being hanged in reality in Whitehall, as had been promised to the great British public by a popular British newspaper. Behind the euphoria was a grave shortage of food and fuel, especially in Germany.

The following spring, Sir James Barrie in Versailles quietly celebrated the fulfilment of his prophecy that the Allies would win the war.
He attended the Peace conference, which ended in a treaty that led
speedily and directly to the Second World War. Kipling and Shaw were
also in France at the time.

Dr Mackail wrote, 'This war will be a legend for the whole human
race, like the war of Troy . . . Perhaps these two wars will be the only
ones remembered thousands of years hence, and all that will be remembered of them will be their heroisms.'

Immediately after the Armistice, George Thirkell was demobilised
and moved into 6 Pembroke Gardens. And on 13 December, he and
Angela were married at Kensington Town Hall. For the occasion,
Angela wore a mole-velvet coat trimmed with chinchilla collar and cuffs
and the new-style cloche hat. They set off for a touring honey-moon.

Their first stop was Oxford, where they stayed at the Mitre. Angela
gloried in her knowledge of the city, its history, and its associations with
her father and grandfather. And George beamed with reflected glory.
Before meeting Angela, he had never heard of any of her famous
relatives, apart from Rudyard Kipling.

'Oxford looks very heavenly', Angela wrote to her mother-in-law in
Tasmania; she sent her a stream of picture postcards. The weather was
cold and Angela's complexion glowed pink. 'D'you know, Angela,
you're quite a good-looking girl,' said George.

Angela's Oxford friends were impressed by George. He was a few
years younger than Angela, several inches shorter, and with a serious
modest manner.

From Oxford they drove to Stratford-on-Avon, where they stayed
and called on the novelist Marie Corelli, who had been a friend of
Burne-Jones. Then on to Warwick, where George wished to see the
castle. Next stop, Kenilworth. They made a special trip to Birmingham
so that Angela could show George the stained-glass windows that
Burne-Jones had designed for one of the churches there. He was duly
impressed. She was disappointed that there were no picture-postcards of
them to send to her mother-in-law.

The honeymoon over and back in London, Angela guided her
husband round London. He was thrilled by the Tower and the Crown
Jewels and sent a postcard to Tasmania that day. The boys, who were
beginning to call him 'Dad', were taken to Derry and Toms' big store,
where that year's special Christmas attraction for children was a ride in
a 'zeppelin'.

In George's mind was a scheme to start his own business in Australia, where he was convinced that a prosperous future awaited him. He had grown up among an adventurous people whose forbears had made their fortunes fast, mostly from land speculation, gold-digging and trading. With a strong-minded and inspiring woman beside him, he felt he could not fail.

Early in the new year George travelled to the north of England. He spent four days in Newcastle and was shown over the Armstrong-Whitworth engineering works and ship-building yards. He went to Darlington to see the Firth steel works. He needed further training in metallurgy, and he was offered a job by the research laboratories of the Brown, Firth Steel Co. at Darlington under the scheme of providing ex-soldiers with work known as 'non-military employment'.

Early in 1919, Angela and the boys went to South Yorkshire. They found homely lodgings with a Mr and Mrs Isitt at a house called Sunny-side in the small village of Totley, near Grindleford, on the outskirts of Sheffield, where they had the use of two bedrooms and a parlour and Mrs Isitt did the cooking.

Angela enjoyed life in Yorkshire. 'It is no longer fashionable,' declared *The Gentlewoman*, 'not to know how to cook a potato ... even a woman of such masculine genius as Madame Curie is an adept at domestic matters.' Angela, for the first time in her life, began to learn to cook.

During her first year of marriage to George Thirkell she was very happy. She recalled a saying of her grandfather's that honeymoons should always be spent in Yorkshire. There was a closeness and a candour among Yorkshire folk that was lacking in the more sophisticated people in the south. Angela was herself frank and forthright.

She loved the wild romantic moors which surrounded the cluster of stone-built cottages at Totley. The summer was hot, but up on the moors there was always a breeze. She and the boys went for long tramps and picnicked among the gorse and bilberries. In the late summer they picked the fruit, and Mrs Isitt showed Angela how to cook a bilberry pie and make a summer pudding. The fruit stained their teeth and lips blue. She took the boys to see the Burne-Jones windows in St James's church,* Brighouse, near Bradford.

Now and again one of George's army friends came to see him and they relived their war experiences. Angela was bored by their con-

* Now demolished. The Burne-Jones windows are in a museum in Bradford.

versation and on these occasions went to bed early. George worked hard at the steel works and in his spare time studied metallurgy. By the autumn he had an impressive list of qualifications.

Christmas at Pembroke Gardens 1919 was disrupted by the preparations for Angela's imminent departure for Australia. There were Mackails and Poynters in Australia, twigs of the branches in Britain. Angela wrote to Cousin Ruddy, expressing apprehension at the prospect of living among strangers, and asked him for introductions. He answered discouragingly, from Bateman's at Burwash, Sussex: 'With Australia, I have had nothing to do for some thirty years.' But he told her that Australia was 'an easy and a friendly land where all the world is willing to help, and I think your boys will enjoy the new life tremendously'. He wished her good fortune and, knowing her love of books, added this piece of advice: '*You'll* have to discover the literature of that land. When I was there it was only just beginning to find itself.'

Angela's furniture was crated. It included a grandfather clock, the cane-sided rocking cradle which Morris had made for her mother and in which she had slept as a child, her roll-top desk, the Morris chairs. Curtains, covers, carpets too. Her pictures were assembled. The John Collier portrait, the charcoal by Sargent, the Burne-Jones works, and a pair of Dürer etchings, *Melancolia* and *The Knight, Death and the Devil*. George commented that just as nice things could be bought in the emporium in Sydney. Hundreds of books, among which was the little set of Shakespeare that Burne-Jones had had specially bound for Angela in white vellum enclosed in a white vellum case. He had written to his 'darling Angela':

With this letter comes a set of little volumes which I know you will love to have, and keep for my sake—the print is clear and the words are glorious and the volumes easy and light for a little maiden to hold. So from time to time, but never too much at a time, live inside them and be happy.

And among the personal baggage was the typewriter she had acquired in her teens with thoughts of becoming a writer.

Early in January 1920 they were given berths on a troopship which was soon departing. Angela reacted to the news with a flood of tears. She wept for several hours and George was unable to console her. The passages were cancelled. When it came to the point she was unable to bear the thought of leaving her family, her home, England. George promised her that they would not stay in Australia indefinitely. He would work hard, make a lot of money and bring her back to England.

The packing continued and they waited for berths on another ship. Angela was delighted when, as an alternative to a troopship crowded with returning Australian soldiers, they were offered berths on a liner. George reacted differently. Life aboard a liner would involve him in a certain formality. He protested that he would have to dress for dinner and 'all that sissy stuff'. He told Angela that a troopship would be more fun and that she would have his friends' wives for company. After an argument, the passages on the liner were rejected.

Angela said farewell to all her friends and family. They went to Rottingdean to say goodbye to Lady Burne-Jones, who was very distressed. Both women thought that they were unlikely to see each other again.

Angela had engaged a young woman called Mabel Baden as a nursery governess for the two boys, in spite of George's protest that it was not the custom in Australia for young families such as theirs to employ nursery governesses. Australian women looked after their own children, cleaned their own houses, and did their own cooking. But Angela had her own way. Mabel Baden's status was that of general maid, a 'mother's help'. The boys called her 'Nursie'. She was, recalled Graham McInnes, 'a refined and prim young woman' from north-west London.

4

'Trooper to the Southern Cross'

Paddington Station at 6.30 on a January morning in 1920 was crowded with men in uniform, women in tears, kit-bags and luggage piled everywhere. It reminded George of the days when he was returning to France and the trenches. The only difference was the absence of rifles. Colin and Graham ran about wildly, and were repeatedly lost, and found.

The train was crowded with Diggers, singing away in the compartments and corridors. Officers and their families had reserved seats in the first-class carriages.

They travelled all day. When they arrived in Devonport, the port of embarkation, it was dark again, and raining too. On the tender going out to the waiting ship, the sea was very rough. Angela behaved stoically, but Mabel Baden was terrified by the tender's violent swaying and actually vomited over Angela's fur coat.

They were told that among their fellow passengers on board the *Friedrichsruh* were a number of prisoners—Australian deserters who had spent most of the war in gaol. Several of them were reputedly murderers, 'just about the scum of the A.I.F.'

The *Friedrichsruh* was an old coal-burning vessel which, as part of the German reparations, had been handed over to the British. The Germans, who were not devoid of a sense of humour, played the following practical joke on the victors: they had disconnected the entire plumbing system and re-connected it so that the hot water pipes discharged cold water, the cold water pipes dispensed sewage, and the lavatories flushed boiling water. Posteriors were scalded. And the practical joke was not confined to the ship's plumbing. Graham McInnes suffered an electric shock from a bell-push.

The Germans apart, there was no refrigeration on board and the ship was 'dry'. The troops were furious.

The Thirkells' quarters were in two- and three-berth cabins on the stifling lower deck. Angela and George shared one, the two boys and Mabel Baden another. The Diggers were below them, and the 'convicts' at the very bottom of the ship.

For the first time Angela found herself among Australians. There were eight hundred Diggers on board, sprawled all over the lower decks. The officers and their wives on the upper deck were within sight and sound and smell of the Diggers below. As the wife of an Australian, there was a whole new vocabulary to learn—later called 'Strine': 'wowser', 'bonzer', 'cobber', 'stoushed', 'good-oh', etc. On board she met again George's friend Gerald Carr, who had also married an Englishwoman—a nurse from Lincolnshire, called Sunnie. She was more practical than Angela. Both women agreed that they greatly disliked their husbands' habit of introducing them as 'Mrs Carr' and 'Mrs Thirkell' instead of as 'my wife'.

The Diggers made Mabel Baden's life a misery. When they heard Graham and Colin McInnes address her as 'Nursie' they called out to her to put them to bed too. As soon as the ship began to roll, Mabel was sea-sick again and she spent much of the voyage wretchedly ill.

The two boys were in a floating paradise and they ran wild. Their language soon included most of the Diggers' colourful expletives. Colin was discovered tipping all the deck chairs overboard. They locked the lavatory doors on the inside and crawled out underneath the doors, and they climbed partitions to look at ladies lying in their baths. Neither Angela nor George could control them.

The journey took nine weeks. Gradually the weather changed from fog and rain to semi-tropical heat. The ship did not call at Gibraltar or Malta, but staggered on to Port Said with incredible slowness.

As is usual on long voyages, committees were formed to organize sports tournaments and other diversions. Angela was prominent on the committee.

As the *Friedrichsruh* steamed through the Suez Canal, George pointed out to Angela the very spot where he and the 3rd Field Company of Australian Engineers had built a temporary bridge over the Canal. To Angela the Canal 'curved away over the edge of the world'. Once through it and into the Red Sea, the romantic moment that George had promised her arrived. 'I saw what many will say you don't see till you are in the Red Sea, but that is just want of observation, namely, the Southern Cross.' It reassured her; and for the first time she felt that her, and her sons', destinies must lie in that hemisphere. With George Thirkell, Australia would indeed be a land of promise.

But soon troubles began to harass the passengers aboard the *Friedrichsruh*.

The ship had not taken on at Port Said sufficient supplies for the babies. There was a chronic shortage of fruit and milk. The lack of refrigeration meant that the fresh meat rapidly became unsavoury or unsafe to eat. The soaring temperatures became insupportable. The Thirkells were in a badly ventilated inside cabin and soon they were sleeping with the doors open, and later they carried their mattresses out into the passage-ways in a fruitless quest for air. Electric fans were scarce and constantly being pilfered. The passengers, Diggers and crew grew tired of one another. Tempers were frayed and even a missionary became violent.

The traditional fancy-dress dance was to take place the night before the ship was due to berth at Colombo. Women on board were heavily outnumbered, and only the ladies and the Diggers were invited. George, who disliked dancing and dressing up and preferred to spend the evening playing cards with his friends, was relieved that his presence wasn't required.

Angela dressed herself up in a long dress, hung herself with beads, fastened on long earrings, and tied a scarf round her head. Realizing that the Diggers' hands would get hot and sweaty, 'the gypsy' completed her ensemble by adding a pair of white silk elbow-length gloves. She danced tirelessly and with great enjoyment. Mabel, on the other hand, who had also dressed up, assumed an air of obstinate refinement, and refused to dance with anyone lower than sergeant. As the evening wore on, the men removed their jackets, and to her dismay she could no longer distinguish their rank.

The following day at Colombo, George, the boys and a number of friends they had made on the ship went ashore together. Angela was fascinated by the bazaar. George bought her knick-knacks made of tortoiseshell and jade and a silk scarf. They had dinner in a hotel. The long journey was nearly over, but not the alarums. The Diggers had also gone ashore. They spent the day drinking and by the evening had started to riot. Angela and company were surprised when suddenly the staff ran into the dining-room and began to close the window-shutters. Outside, the natives had disappeared from the streets. Rickshaws were abandoned, and the fare, if there was one, had made off. The tide of Australian soldiery was approaching. 'Australia's native weapon', the bottle, was being brandished. Bottles and heads were broken. The bazaar was in flames. Rumour reached the ship that the passengers beleaguered in the hotel had all been murdered. The captain ordered boats to be sent out in the hope that the Diggers could be persuaded to

come back. George and the other men in the hotel took charge. The
Diggers were slowly herded towards the quay-side. 'Men and bullocks
are much the same once you get them on the move', George told
Angela the next day. 'Keep them going and don't let them straggle.'

Once on board the *Friedrichsruh* the Diggers would not be contained, and the following day they were using the tins of food as
ammunition in the fights which had broken out everywhere. Much of
the food was lost overboard.

As the ship steamed towards Fremantle, the only food left for the
children was cornflour, biscuits and tinned milk. Measles broke out
and quarantine was ordered. Angela and Sunnie Carr were recruited to
help nurse the sick children. Drinking water had to be rationed. In
addition, the ship developed engine trouble and began to go round in
circles. It seemed unlikely that it could reach Fremantle and distress
signals were sent out. Ironically, the liner which came to its aid was the
ship which George Thirkell had refused to travel on. Angela gazed at
the sleek white liner and ardently wished she were aboard it. But the
engine-trouble on the *Friedrichsruh* was put right in time. There wasn't
much farther to go.

And all the while, over six weeks, the prisoners had been confined in
the bowels of the ship, in conditions which reminded them of the
journey their forebears had made in convict-ships a century earlier. The
night before the ship was due into Fremantle, they broke out of their
cells, armed themselves with belts and bottles, and raided the crew's
quarters. The Diggers, who had been bored ever since their exploits at
Colombo, were spoiling for just such a fight. The officers and crew
were fighting the Diggers and the prisoners were fighting both groups,
or could it have been that the officers and crew were fighting the
Diggers and prisoners? At the height of it all the lights failed and the
fighting continued in the darkness.

George Thirkell left Angela in their cabin. When he returned
several hours later, Angela, sitting up on her bunk, levelled a water-
pistol; for a moment he looked, with his battle-scars, like a convict.

The following morning Fremantle was sighted, and a few days later
the ship reached Perth. The Thirkells and the Carrs hired a car and
drove up into the hills.

The first sight of Australia fascinated Angela. All her senses were
aroused by the new experience. Through the honeysuckle trees she
could see fires, here and there little flickers of flame, which reminded
her of the vermilion-coloured azaleas in English gardens. There the

resemblance to England ended. There was a grandeur and a mystery about this strange land that was contained mostly in the smell of gum-trees. It was pervasive, and heightened by the crystal purity of the atmosphere. 'The air was clean as creation.'

George was delighted to be back in the Australian bush again. He told Angela how he had panned gold in the creeks. The boys bombarded George with questions. Why were the trees white? What sort of animals were in Australia? Could they go bathing? The trees, he explained, were gum-trees and the bark had been stripped off; hence their ghostly appearance. Out here in the bush the boys went to school on ponies. As for bathing, they would have to be careful. Sharks.

The party dined at an hotel. After the day's outing Angela was in good spirits and made everyone laugh. The boys were left with Mabel while she and the others went to a variety show at an open-air theatre. She enjoyed the broad humour and felt that she was making a good beginning in Australia.

When they finally disembarked at Port Melbourne after nine weeks at sea, the customs officials examined Angela's belongings. To her amazement they regarded the Dürer prints with great suspicion, considering them obscene.

Angela did not take them seriously at first, but it seemed clear after some discussion that her pictures really were in danger of being confiscated as undesirable objects. She quickly informed them that they were portraits of her ancestors and was allowed to keep them. This absurd incident at the customs-house was the culmination of an incredible voyage. While it was fresh in her mind she wrote it down: *What Happened on the Boat*.

The month was March. In England it would have been the beginning of spring. In Australia it was autumn. The Thirkell family took a taxi to Collins Street and the Oriental Hotel. Now it was George's turn to be Angela's guide on an exhaustive two days' sightseeing. Melbourne, Australia's second city and its cultural capital, seemed to Angela to be spacious and graceful with some fine parks and pleasant architecture.

They boarded another ship, the *Loongana* of 2,000 tons, and set forth to Tasmania, or 'Tassie' as George called the island. It was a long way from Melbourne and the waters around Tasmania were the most treacherous of the whole continent.

On the deck of the *Loongana*, George entertained Angela and the boys with blood-curdling tales of Tasmania's past. The island had a history of unparalleled brutality. In Port Phillips Bay, the powerful

current known as the Rip menaced all ships. The long estuary to
Launceston was lined with perpendicular cliffs shaped like organ pipes,
on which many a vessel had been wrecked. Above the cliffs was the
dreaded bush, which grew in horizontal layers and was impenetrably
thick. It sustained no animal life and convicts who escaped the slave
labour at Hobart and found themselves in the bush had either to
resort to cannibalism or to die a slow death from starvation.

The sea journey was followed by a long train journey. The exhausted
family arrived late at night to an emotional welcome from George's
family and a host of relations. Mrs Thirkell senior had not seen her son
for five years.

A cable from London awaited Angela. Lady Burne-Jones had died
ten days after she had left England.

405 Elizabeth Street was at the summit of a steep hill in the centre
of Hobart. Tramcars clattered up and down it. The large terrace house
lacked the splendid views of the mountains and the sea enjoyed by the
people on the other side of the street. The two boys were given a small
white-walled room at the back while George and Angela shared a
ground-floor room and Mabel slept upstairs.

There was a heroes' welcome for those Australians who had been at
the war, especially those who had fought at Anzac Cove. Their valour
assumed a legendary aspect, comparable to that of the ancient Greeks.
George was fêted; he had achieved glory for Australia and Tasmania.

George's father, Robert Anthony Claude Thirkell, was a fifth-
generation Tasmanian whose forebears had been Yorkshire landowners
in the early 1800s. The family were proud of their ancestry and traced
their descent from John of Gaunt, Duke of Lancaster. From one of
their forebears, Sir Lancelot Threlkeld, came the name of 'Lancelot'
which recurred in the family. The family of George's mother, too, had
owned land and property. But misfortune and mismanagement had
reduced the Thirkells' estate to this one house in Elizabeth Street,
Hobart, filled with cumbrous Victoriana.

Angela began her new life with zest and aplomb. Disdaining the
more homely words in which women address their in-laws, she called
George's mother 'Mama', soon changed to 'Meo', and George's father,
usually known as 'Dad', to 'Père'. It caused the family much amusement. At first they were a little bewildered, if not overawed, by this
tall, upright young woman with her Kensington vowel-sounds and
educated conversation.

Graham McInnes recalled that Meo 'radiated an aura of sweetness . . . She had a beautiful soft skin and a big round forehead, below
which were deep-set eyes with light mauve shadows . . . a retroussé nose
and a small sweet mouth.' George's father was 'gruffly genial' and
amused the boys with endless jokes. There were numerous relations.
One of them, Terence Crisp, was George's first cousin and a law
student at the University of Tasmania. He was fascinated by Angela's
range of literary references. In Tasmania and Australia at that time, a
well-read man, let alone a well-read woman, was a comparative rarity.
Sport was the preoccupation of young men in Tasmania. Terence
Crisp was dazzled by Angela and began to haunt his aunt's house.

A few weeks after their arrival, Angela found that she was pregnant
again, and their plans had to be reorganized. The boys were sent to
George's old school, Hutchin's, in Hobart. Angela explained to them
that at this school they would be known by their stepfather's name of
Thirkell. They had been 'adopted' by George Thirkell, although not
legally. George always referred to them as 'my boys', and they were
now going to be Australians. In a few months' time they would have
another brother or sister, though Angela did not tell them this.

For some years now she hadn't heard a word from James McInnes,
nor had the boys. She reasoned that it would be best if they all bore the
same name. She was discovering that a divorce was more of a disgrace
in Tasmania than in Kensington, and a stigma would be attached to her
sons if they bore a different name from herself and her husband. This
change of identity confused the boys and they, very naturally, resented
it, but made no protest. James Campbell McInnes, wrote Graham
McInnes, 'continued to lead a shadowy Plutonian existence'.

Angela and George left the boys in Mabel's charge and departed for
Melbourne.

June was the middle of winter in Melbourne. The water froze in
the ewers in the bedroom of the boarding-house where Angela and
George spent the next few months. George was working as an agent
for Brown, Firth, the Sheffield steel company. Their next address was
a small terracotta-roofed bungalow, 4 Grace Street, Malvern, in a
suburb of Melbourne. It was to be Angela's home for the next ten
years.

Angela's furniture arrived and was unpacked. They painted walls,
laid linoleum, hung pictures, put down carpets and rugs; Angela sewed
curtains. Then they worked in the garden. There was dark green paint

everywhere, so Angela painted the paling fence white. George planted English rose bushes, clipped the grass into a neat lawn, and put up a swing for the boys. There was a peach-tree and two small citrus trees. The outside lavatory was screened by a trellis, round which they trained a yellow jasmine. Everything about the kitchen was antiquated, even by Australian standards. There were two gas burners on which to cook, apart from the straw-filled wooden box, the 'fireless cooker', in which porridge and stews could be left to cook overnight. There was no hot water system, and of course, no refrigerator. A hole in the floor kept things cool. The bathroom heater was heated by a primitive wooden stove.

The baby was expected at the end of the year. By the early summer of Australia's November, Angela was ready to receive her sons again. The boys travelled to Melbourne with Mabel in charge, and they were soon attending Scotch College school daily, for which fees had to be paid.

Angela had now been in Australia long enough to realize that transplantation to a strange continent was more than a romantic adventure. Towards the end of her first year on the other side of the world, she began to develop symptoms which she could herself diagnose as 'home-sickness'. She constantly dreamed that she was at home with her parents. When she woke up and realized she was thousands of miles away, she burst into floods of tears. Every time she heard the church bells pealing, she closed her eyes and imagined herself in Oxford.

Melbourne, named after Queen Victoria's favourite Prime Minister, was utterly unlike the Victorian England she had known. English place-names abounded. Brighton, Sandringham, Malvern—all were dreary suburbs, and in the middle of one of them she had suddenly found herself. The people of Australia, although mainly of British stock, were vastly different from her Kensington neighbours. Beneath Australia's boasted egalitarianism was an enclosed and insular society that did not welcome newcomers. And the weather was upside down.

December 1920 was one of the hottest Australia had known since the 1890s. Day after day of torrid heat clamped the Melburnians into a lethargy. At 6 a.m. the temperature was in the 80s. The wind brought a suffocatingly thick red dust, a 'brickfielder', which permeated everywhere. In the eighth month of her pregnancy she made preparations for her first Christmas in Australia. She unpacked the delicate porcelain figures for the nativity crèche which Burne-Jones had brought from Italy for her when she was a little girl. With Mabel's help, she made puddings and mince-pies, and prepared a turkey. She knitted for the baby, and the wool, damp with sweat from her hands, made the stitches stick to the needles. The heat was disastrously prolonged and increased the danger of bush fires. When, for a few hours, the temperature dropped and rain fell, it was blood-coloured from the dust and soon afterwards the temperature rose again.

The preparations for Christmas heightened Angela's misery. Pink postal orders arrived for the boys and books for herself. She subscribed to the *Times Literary Supplement*, the *Cornhill Magazine*, and *Blackwoods*. George seemed unaware of Angela's homesickness. The boys, with their pocket money of threepence a week, went off on the tramcar with their friends to one of the beaches on the other side of Melbourne. The heat was so great that the tar melted on the roads, and on their return the boys trod black footprints on to Angela's fine rugs.

The baby was a boy, born in a private nursing-home in Armadale on 9 January 1921. George's christian names were reversed and he was baptized Lancelot George. Dr Gutteridge, her attendant at the birth, commented, 'He'll be having all the ladies of Shalott after him, won't he?' With his blue eyes he bore a remarkable resemblance to his grandfather, Dr Mackail. Almost every day of his babyhood was lyrically recorded in Angela's letters to Pembroke Gardens.

Under the Australian sun, Angela's complexion darkened and coarsened. She still wore her hair coiled round her head, sometimes with a cotton scarf to prevent it straggling into her eyes. When the day's housework and cooking were over, she went to the piano, played Beethoven, and sang her beloved Schubert songs. George would be at the Naval and Military Club.

Sometime during 1921, Angela wrote *Letters from a Shepherd in Arcady to a Little Girl* and sent it to the editor of the *Cornhill Magazine*. To her joy, it was accepted and its publication gave her much-needed encouragement. The title was suggested by *Arcady, for Better, for Worse*, a book written by her childhood friend, Canon Jessop, who was now dead. She had brought his letters with her to Australia. The essay was composed of extracts from Jessop's letters and reminiscences of a middle-class girl in Edwardian England.

The following June a second essay, entitled *An Evening with J. M. Barrie*, was published on the woman's page of the Australian weekly, *The Forum*. The women of Australia had hardly heard of Barrie and they found it entertaining. The editor sent Angela a modest cheque and asked her for more. In November, just before celebrating her second Christmas in Melbourne, she published another piece about her childhood: *Kipling and the Tourists*. The encouragement that the acceptance of these pieces gave her was more, much more, valuable than the fee. Slowly she built up a public in Australian newspapers and magazines, writing about different subjects—music, art, literature, theatre, the rearing of children, and even her great-uncle, the Methodist preacher, Fred Macdonald—always amusingly, and with verve. She began to be asked to literary parties in Melbourne. Her voice, described as a rich contralto, immediately attracted attention. Soon she was invited by the Australian Broadcasting Company to broadcast a weekly programme for children.

Angela joined the Melbourne Classical Association, and the Lyceum Club, and other cultural organizations. She gave more than one talk to the classicists, and in Latin too. The boys, with their Latin and Greek homework, found her useful. Every evening after tea, she read aloud to them from a variety of authors—Scott, Dickens, Thackeray, Captain Marryat, Jules Verne, Ballantyne, the Kingsleys—continuing the family tradition. To her youngest son, Lance, she repeatedly read her favourite children's story, *Mopsa and the Fairy* by Jean Ingelow. She acted most of the characters—Dickens was best for that—making the boys laugh and even cry.

Mindful of Ruddy's advice she read Australian authors. She particularly admired Charles Rischbieth Jury, known as the Adelaide poet, and published an essay on him.

Occasionally the family routine was enhanced by a dinner-party. The green-dragon plates were produced. The meal began with melon sprinkled with ginger, followed by steak cooked with herbs in a casserole. Next a mousse, French cheese, coffee. Wine was served, of course. Graham McInnes recalled that, after cooking the meal, Angela 'ripped off her apron, wiped her steaming visage and rushed to "put on her face" before greeting her guests'. Graham and Colin in their best blue suits and smart ties acted as waiters, and Mabel helped in the kitchen. George was coerced into a dinner-jacket.

A regular procession of distinguished people wended their way to Grace Street: Nellie Melba, the singer, then in her sixties; Sir John Monash, the Jewish general who led the Australians at Anzac; Ernest Scott, professor of history at Melbourne University; the dramatist Dion Boucicault, and others. Angela was becoming something of a lioness. There were times when 5 Grace Street took on the aspect of a 'salon'.

Angela's dinner-parties were considered extraordinary. For one thing, she did not leave the men to drink beer together, while the women gathered in another part of the room to talk about domestic affairs. Her marked enjoyment of men's company, and their appreciation of her company and conversation was a style of living which suburban society in Australia had not known before.

Angela's thoughts were increasingly directed towards the literary and artistic life in Melbourne. George acquired a motorbike. Angela refused to ride pillion, so he attached a cane-work side-car. And off they went to Melbourne.

He bought her a Baby Austin, but she never learned to drive it. It was replaced by a second-hand Chrysler, strictly speaking the property of the company of which George had become managing director.

In her first novel, *Ankle Deep*, she wrote of her heroine, 'One of a woman's worst misfortunes had happened to her, she had grown out of her husband.' It was also true in Angela's case. He may also have grown out of her. She had certainly not remained the kind of woman he had had in mind when he had married her. He spent more and more time drinking at the club. In *Ankle Deep*, the husband implores his wife to let him make love to her, whimpering to her to 'be kind' to him, but she refuses and in the end submits contemptuously. Years later, Angela described *Ankle Deep* as 'personal experience'.

In 1923 Angela's parents arrived in Australia. Dr Mackail's purpose in journeying to the other end of the world was twofold—to see his daughter and grandchildren, and to give a lecture at the University of Melbourne and at other Australian universities. He was the guest of a legal family in Melbourne, while Margaret Mackail stayed at Grace Street.

The subject of Dr Mackail's lecture was 'What is the Good of Greek?' The argument, in an increasingly technological world, still goes on. In an article, Colin MacInnes said that his grandfather believed that 'everything worth writing had been written long before 1910'. Dr Mackail's disparagement of contemporary poetry extended to W. H. Auden, of whose verses he pronounced, 'That is not poetry.'

Dr Mackail's strength as a scholar was not as a textual critic, but he could inspire in others a love for Greek poetry. His students had called him 'the great Mackail', and his enthusiasm for the classics made a strong impression on the Australians. It was said that Margaret Mackail's stay at Grace Street was not wholly successful. She was appalled by her grandsons, who had changed beyond recognition. In particular, she deplored their speech. Every morning, at Malvern, she drilled Colin and Graham in English diction, making them practise vowel-sounds and articulate consonants. Later, Colin McInnes described his grandmother as 'rather a demanding woman . . . The only work of art she had herself created was her own considerable personality.'

The Mackails brought news of home, Kensington, family, new books, new plays. Music was much discussed. And of course, painting.

Their departure from Melbourne plunged Angela into grief. She confided her feelings to Nellie Melba, herself a Melburnian, and something in the nature of a national heroine. The two women had known each other in London. Angela quoted Henry Kingsley:

> Only those who have done so, know how much effort it takes to say, 'I will go to a land where no one knows or cares for me', and few know the isolation, almost of terror, at having gone so far out of the bounds of ordinary life; the feeling of self-distrust and cowardice at being alone and friendless in the world, like a child in the dark.

Nellie Melba, who knew from personal experience what it was like to be far from home, wrote to Angela, 'My heart is with you'.

Angela was a keen theatre-goer and took the boys to the Little Playhouse, the only theatre in Melbourne where Shakespeare was regularly performed. When the famous Irish Players brought the plays of Synge and O'Casey to Melbourne, it was, for Melburnians, something rather different from the drawing-room comedies which they had been used to, and preferred. Angela saw every play in their repertoire and wrote a long letter in defence of the company to *The Home* magazine. It was headed 'The Irish Players and the Critics'. She also plunged into music criticism. For *The Forum* she wrote an article entitled 'British Music in Melbourne', satirizing the Melburnian attitude to serious music, which she thought over-solemn, even portentous. She was determined to see her views on any subject in print if she could. She aroused much hostility and one Australian journalist described her as 'insufferable'.

She thought the collection of pictures in the Melbourne Art Gallery rather meagre. In her view, there was little of interest there—a few Blake etchings, one doubtful Goya, which she thought a fake, and that was all. She offered the gallery the gift of a picture by her grandfather;

but Burne-Jones, by the mid-1920s was unfashionable, the directors declined the offer and she withdrew with hurt feelings. As for the only bookshop in Melbourne, it was small and poorly stocked. The new books she asked for were invariably unobtainable. 'It is a pity you are so literary, Mrs Thirkell,' the manager told her.

A disapproval of all that was meretricious had been part of Angela's upbringing. She found the Australian evening newspaper, the *Herald*, particularly meretricious. Every evening, George brought it home to Grace Street. It was a constant source of friction between them for Graham and Colin avidly read all the scandals in it. Angela tried to hide it from them, but the boys of course always managed to get hold of it. Above all, she thought it abominably written.

At this time, an Australian called Colin Ross committed rape and murder for which he was ultimately hanged. The *Herald* reported all the lurid details. It was not the type of news that Angela wanted her sons to read, and moreover the case reminded her of James McInnes who had also committed rape, although he had stopped short of murder. Angela implored George not to bring the *Herald* home. He flatly refused. At Scotch College, Colin, who had the same name as the accused, was jokingly identified with the crime.

Most of the boys in Malvern had 'trucks' which they rode in— Lance wanted one too. On his third birthday, he ran out into the little back garden and there, on the lawn, was a small glossy red truck. George had had it made in the TAMECO workshop. The perambulator-sized wheels had brass hub-caps which gleamed in the sunshine; the little wooden doors opened and shut perfectly. The pedals were arranged on the principle of a bicycle. Lance was ecstatically happy with it, and pedalled about in it incessantly. But Angela hated it and said that it ruined his shoes.

Angela's domestic standards were almost impossibly high; she drove herself and the boys hard. All the boys' recollections of their childhood were marred by the memory of the beatings which were regularly administered, on Angela's orders, by George. Lance Thirkell recalled that they were only superseded in severity by the bullying he encountered at his English prep-school.

In 1924, the Special Service Squadron of the Royal Navy, under the command of Sir Frederick Field, sailed round the world on a goodwill mission to Britain's overseas territories. The fleet of five cruisers and HMS *Hood* and HMS *Repulse* steamed into Melbourne in perfect autumn weather. The *Argus* reported:

It was a spectacle to stir the hearts of all true Australians, who felt a thrill of pride at the thought that they were of one blood with the great nation that has sent forth these emblems of her naval power . . .

Aboard one of the ships was Commander Roderick Tremayne Miles, whose family had been neighbours of the Mackails when they had lived in Young Street. Before leaving London, Mrs Mackail had given him Angela's address.

A hundred thousand exuberant Melburnians thronged the quayside, and when the ships docked they swarmed aboard; there was dancing on deck. The pressure was so great that soon visitors were banned for fear they would be swept overboard. Many had come for the Australian pastime of vandalism and the following day a number appeared in court charged with wilful damage.

There were 'At Homes' and children's parties. Commander Miles called on Angela, and Angela and George were guests of the Navy several times.

The Fleet continued to Hobart and Angela followed it. She left Lance to the care of her 'lady-help' for a few days' holiday—the first she had had since Lance's birth—to be the guests of a Colonel and Mrs Cass in their quarters, formerly the convicts' hospital, which was said to be haunted. She met Commander Miles again, taught him to dance, and walked alone with him up into the hills behind Hobart. When the Navy left Hobart, it was almost more than she could bear.

During 1923 two items of news from Britain were of especial interest to Angela and George. George's friend, Lady Elizabeth Bowes-Lyon, became engaged to the Duke of York, the second son of King George V; and Angela's cousin Stanley Baldwin became Prime Minister.

Lady Elizabeth's 2nd and 3rd names were nearly the same as Angela's -- Nagela Marguerite. The photograph that George Thirkell had taken of Lady Elizabeth was framed and placed on the upright piano in Grace Street. He repeatedly told the story of his convalescence at Glamis Castle and his friendship with 'the Dresden-china Cinderella', as Lady Elizabeth was now being called in the world's press. For the first time for centuries, a British royal Duke was not marrying into one of the European royal houses. The new Duchess would be British born and of British parentage.

In 1927 the Duke and Duchess of York embarked upon the long

sea-voyage to Australia. After visiting Tasmania, they went to Melbourne, which had prepared a great welcome for them. The earlier royal tours to Australia, notably the one by Edward, Prince of Wales, had been marred by scenes of violent enthusiasm; it had been a particularly arduous tour and the Prince's hand had been injured by the over-powerful Australian handshake.

The Royal couple were expected in Melbourne in late April. Angela helped George write a letter to the Duchess. He told her how happily he remembered his visits to Glamis and how he hoped to see her at some of the official functions. The *Herald* gave advice to Melburnians on what to wear. The city's emporia were stormed by ladies in search of the essential long white gloves. Gloves with twelve buttons cost 5s. 11d., with sixteen buttons, 9s. 11d., and with twenty buttons, 15s. 11d. The *Herald* also reported that the dancing teachers of Melbourne were busy instructing the ladies of the city how to curtsey. Short beaded dresses were *de rigueur* for evening. The ladies must curtsey without showing their knees to the royal couple, which was not so easily accomplished in view of the fashions of the day.

The competition for invitations to official functions was tremendous. Speeches were carefully prepared. Nellie Melba was to sing and Paderewski to play. Six thousand boy scouts were to greet the Duke. And there were to be no less than three grand balls, the most important of which was the State Ball given by the Governor-General at Government House, to which George and Angela received an invitation.

HMS *Renown* was obscured by early morning mist as it steamed past Brighton and Sandringham and into Port Melbourne on 22 April 1927—the first birthday of the Duke and Duchess's daughter Elizabeth, later Queen Elizabeth II. Melbourne was ablaze with decorations and all the important buildings were lavishly illuminated at night.

The visit coincided with Australia's Day of Remembrance—Anzac Day 25 April. Thirty thousand ex-service men, among whom were twenty-nine holders of the Victoria Cross, with Lieutenant-General Sir John Monash at their head, marched past the Duke and Duchess, George with them. The collective emotion was such that the barriers round the Cenotaph were broken. As George passed the Cenotaph he caught his first sight of Lady Elizabeth since he had said goodbye to her at Glamis in 1917.

Angela wrote a long letter to Lady Cynthia Asquith describing the effect the royal couple were having on Melbourne. The Duchess's delicate dresses were so fingered by the loyal people that one particular dress was unfit for further use. Her style of clothes excited enormous interest, and the whole of Australian womanhood blossomed into new hats. Angela wrote, 'Every girl with any pretence to looks, and many with none, wore a hat with a turned-up brim and was smiling more or less attractively.'

The day before the State Ball, a lady-in-waiting telephoned from Government House to Grace Street to inform George that Her Royal Highness invited him to tea the following afternoon. The Duchess greeted George in her sitting-room at Government House like an old friend. They had a long talk together. And afterwards George told Angela that it was like being at Glamis again.

For the Ball, Angela wore oyster-coloured brocade hung with lobelia-blue paillettes, a blue-beaded satin bandeau round her forehead, and long white kid gloves. George was in white tie and tails, white gloves, and his war medals. The Duchess danced first with the Prime Minister of Australia and secondly with the Governor-General, Lord Stonehaven. Her third choice was Captain George Thirkell. From the blue-carpeted dais on which the royal pair were seated on blue-velvet chairs under a canopy in the shape of a huge white rose, formed by hundreds of fresh white roses, an aide-de-camp was sent across to George and Angela. The music for this dance was the fox-trot, 'A'int She Sweet'.

Everyone was intrigued. Who was this good-looking young man? He wasn't in uniform and there were no noble orders emblazoned on his breast. 'The Smiling Duchess' as some called her, was a scintillating figure in a short dress of silver lamé interwoven with rose-coloured threads and trimmed with silver lace; she carried a rose-coloured feather fan. Round her forehead was a bandeau formed by five diamond clusters in the shape of roses—a wedding present from her father, the Earl of Strathmore. When the dance was concluded, the Duchess led George to the Duke. 'I want to introduce my husband to you,' she said.

The Empire Tour was a great success and on their return to London, the Duke said at the Guildhall, 'I return a thorough optimist. When one has seen how the grit and creative purpose of our kinsmen overseas have triumphed over the most tremendous difficulties, it is impossible to despair of the future of the British race.'

The Royal visit reactivated Angela's home-sickness. To Lady Cynthia Asquith she wrote, 'It is impossible to realize how cut-off one is in Australia.'

Every spring, like a torch-light through rain and mist, the yellow wattle in the Australian bush would explode into bloom, heralding the end of winter. The whole country woke up. Sheaves of the fluffy yellow flower, related to mimosa, were to be seen everywhere in the streets, and in most suburban windows.

Angela's Australian friends, Basil Yaldwin Hall and his wife Nell, lived at a house called Fairview at the village of Hurstbridge about twenty-five miles from Melbourne. The Halls and their neighbours at Hurstbridge supplied the Australian equivalent of England's county families, known as the 'squattocracy'. The English way of life, so familiar to Angela, was recreated there. The Halls' sitting-room was furnished with chintz-covered chairs and antique furniture. And here were copies of *Country Life*, *Punch* and *The Tatler*. The Australian dream George had told the boys about came true at Hurstbridge. They spent many holidays there. They rode bareback on ponies, hunted rabbits, shot pigeons, went crayfishing, and swam in natural pools in the hills. Angela was entranced by the wild beauty of the scenery. Beyond the pear and peach orchards, the purple alfalfa meadows and the vine-yards, were the romantic sights and sounds of the real Australia. The bush was alive with extraordinary animals and birds: kookaburras and wallabies, platypus, snakes and tarantulas. The distant mountains were capped with snow. Even an extinct volcano. The strange exotic land was scented with gum-trees, and in and out of these grey flat-leaved trees flew little brilliant parakeets. And all the while a hot sun shone.

There were also the country-house theatricals Angela had known in her youth. Plays were performed in a barn and she joined in happily.

Once, while staying with some friends in the country, Angela and Lance came upon a garden which had been abandoned by its owners because of a bush fire. A thick carpet of yellow daffodils and pink English roses caught her eye; then flowering cherry trees in full bloom. For a moment, it seemed to Angela that she was looking at a mirage of an English country garden.

George had sunk all his capital into T A M E C O—the Australian Metal Equipment Company—Metallurgical Engineers. 'The Works', as it was known, had premises at 124–126 York Street in South Melbourne and manufactured small engineering components. George's salary was a modest one, not really adequate for his family.

Angela worked in the house, economized as much as she could, wrote articles for local newspapers. Mabel Baden could not stay the course and was sent home. For a long time Angela had no domestic help at all. Her health began to suffer. To her horror, her face came out in carbuncles, which were extremely painful and had to be cut out. The doctor told her she was overworked and undernourished, and recommended a trip home.

5

'Ankle Deep'

At home in Pembroke Gardens, Angela quickly recovered her spirits and her physical health. To say that she was still a child beneath the skin is only partly true; if at the age of thirty-eight she was still emotionally a child, she was a remarkable child. Within the shelter of her childhood home her calm returned, and she was able to take stock of her life. The sad truth was that her marriage to George Thirkell was breaking up.

To the 8-year-old Lance, Kensington was a very strange place. Australia, with the freedom that a boy had there, was on the other side of the world. He accompanied the governess who had been engaged for him to play sedately in Kensington Gardens. His grandmother corrected his speech. The assistants in the shops called his mother 'Madam', and so did Annie, Mrs Mackail's maid.

After eight years absence, Angela saw England with new eyes. She was in a society she understood, in a milieu where she belonged. An appreciation of art, music and literature was taken for granted. Nobody was interested in Australia. There were hosts of old friends to see again.

Life in London had become gay once more. The war had been forgotten. Some of Angela's friends had transformed themselves; they painted their faces, wore their skirts above their knees, and cropped their hair. London was vibrant with fast popular tunes. In the houses of her friends, the flowing Morris designs had been replaced by the new geometrical patterns and subtle colours by startling ones. It was the jazz age.

Angela bought new clothes: a tweed coat with a shaggy fox collar, silk stockings, new-style shoes. But she did not wear her skirts very short, aware that her legs were not her best feature, and she firmly resisted the hairdresser's blandishments to cut her hair.

The gossip was all about clothes, *affaires*, and the Gargoyle Club in Soho, founded by Lady Glenconner's son Stephen Tennant, where 'everyone' went. Dr and Mrs Mackail strongly disapproved of the

Gargoyle Club in spite of its aristocratic associations. Neither had been there: it was said to be full of decadent young men and women, pansies and lesbians.

'I have to face a post-war world with a pre-war mind . . . It is so mortifying . . . to see other people one's own age doing cocktails and free love and self-expression, and to be quite incapable of it oneself,' wrote Angela at this time.

Life was less changed in the country. Lance went with his mother on a round of country-house visits and found it rather bewildering.

Lady Glenconner was now the second wife of Viscount Grey of Fallodon, Britain's Foreign Secretary in 1914, whose remark 'The lamps are going out all over Europe' is still remembered. Wilsford Manor had become a bird sanctuary, for ornithology was Lord Grey's passion. Wild birds flew about indoors, and Angela was entranced by the spectacle of her hostess reclining on a chaise-longue in her boudoir with birds flying about beneath the ceiling. It inspired her to write an effusive essay, 'The Charm of Birds', which was published in an Australian newspaper.

Several weeks were spent at Stanway which Sir James Barrie was annually renting from the Wemyss family; Lady Cynthia was his secretary and hostess. The Australian cricket team played there. Barrie was a beneficent tenant and even had a new pavilion built at his own expense, an elaborate structure designed like a log cabin on stilts. There were theatricals in the huge tithe barn, and endless luncheon and dinner parties.

Lord Balfour, Burne-Jones's old patron, was a guest while Angela was there; he inspired her to send an essay back to Australia on patronage. 'Art,' she declared, 'must always depend on the private patron . . . [It] produces the best work . . . Mr Balfour left the whole scheme in the painter's hands, knowing that he would receive the best that hand and brain could give him . . . The association between painter and politician over the pictures was one of deep sympathy.'

Stanley Baldwin invited her to stay at Chequers and at Astley Hall, his private country house high above the Severn River. 'Stan' blew kisses across the dinner table to his wife and called her his Queen. Barrie and Kipling were among the guests. The visit was the subject of yet another essay.

Angela wrote to Graham and Colin several times a week, told them she was longing to see them again, but as the months passed she realized that to return to Australia was the last thing she wanted to do.

been living away from home for a year. Colin was due to sit his School Certificate Examination.

Her parents were in their sixties. It seemed to Angela that they needed her more than her elder sons did. She was convinced that George would never leave Australia, so she made the momentous decision to leave herself, but told nobody. She wrote to her godfather, James Barrie. The famous dramatist had been a fairy godfather to many of his friends, principally Cynthia Asquith and the Llewellyn Davies family of five sons. It was said of him that he liked tall women who had strong characters; he certainly admired Angela. She told him that she was desperately home-sick and implored him for the fare for another trip home. Barrie sent her a cheque to cover one adult's return ticket. At the shipping-office, she bought instead a one-way ticket for herself and one for Lance. Freight was costly, and she had insufficient money for much baggage, but in any case to leave Australia with all the things that she would have liked to take with her would have aroused suspicion. A degree of subterfuge was necessary, because she needed George's written consent before she could leave the country.

Colin McInnes confided to his elder brother that he had overheard their mother speaking to her lawyer on the telephone, asking him about marine insurance on the Sargent portrait. Graham asked his mother if she was leaving Australia again. 'Yes, I am,' she replied. 'Dad's not earning any money . . . I shall take Lance with me, and Colin will follow.'

For George, Angela found a Mrs Biggs who brought her furniture and her husband, Colonel Biggs, to Grace Street. She would make George's bed and George's breakfast and whatever other meals he wanted. It was the best Angela could do. And in November 1929 she abandoned her home, cherished objets d'art—and her husband—and left Australia for good.

George, Graham and Colin were at the quayside to see her off on the *Themistocles*. It was the custom at Melbourne docks to throw coloured paper streamers to and from the decks of arriving and departing ships; they were bought by passengers and friends on the quayside. The ship was soon wrapped in a paper rainbow. A welcome or a farewell.

In the warmth of an Australian spring—autumn in England— Angela with Lance boarded the ship. She carried the Sargent portrait under her arm. Of all her possessions, it was to her the most precious. The pretence that she was going only for another trip home was maintained to the end but George knew otherwise. He never saw Angela again.

6

'High Rising'

Once again, sooner than they had expected, Angela and Lance found themselves in Pembroke Gardens. A few weeks later Colin joined them, having travelled as cheaply as it was possible on board the *Mooltan*. The worst gales of the century had buffeted the ship, and on disembarkation he was dazed and not in the best of health. It was the start of a chilly English winter, and the storms continued.

The welcome that Dr and Mrs Mackail extended to their daughter and her sons on this occasion was not as warm as it had been before. In fact, they were far from happy to have Angela and her troubles once more in their midst. And Mrs Mackail even made it clear that she did not wish her grandsons to be foisted indefinitely upon her.

Colin MacInnes at 16 was said to be extraordinarily beautiful, with an ethereal quality. He seemed to have stepped from one of his great-grandfather's works—Graham Robertson described him as 'a pure throw-back to Burne-Jones'. His temperament was not as angelic as his features. His roots were in Australia, and Kensington was completely alien to him, just as Melbourne had been to his mother. Unfortunately he did not get on with his grandmother—he rebelled at her attempts to change him—and there was constant friction between them.

Colin's education had been interrupted and his future was uncertain. He was passionately devoted to art, and was packed off to Switzerland —not to a finishing school but to an apprenticeship of a humble kind; what it was exactly, the present writer has been unable to find out, but it had nothing to do with art. Lance was luckier. After an uncomfortable Christmas at Pembroke Gardens, he was sent as a boarder to Colet Court, the prep school to St Paul's; but he was not very happy there and wrote miserable letters to his mother.

Angela's need to earn a living was urgent. The only occupation open to her was journalism. In the upstairs nursery, at an old-fashioned roll-top desk, she wrote article after article. The *Fortnightly Review* published a piece by her on the Finnish writer Frederika Bremer, whom she greatly admired, and in the *Cornhill* appeared her essay 'Shakespeare did not dine out', which brought an admiring letter from Falconer Maddan, one of the librarians at the Bodleian, Oxford, He told her that her theory that Shakespeare was ill-at-ease in polite society was confirmed by Aubrey. Maddan was not referring to anything in the celebrated *Brief Lives*, but to a remark in an unpublished manuscript of Aubrey's in the Bodleian. Angela's income from this occasional journalism was not very adequate for her needs, but it was fairly steady and, what was more, a constant encouragement.

She had made a few broadcasts in Australia. This encouraged her to approach the British Broadcasting Corporation, which asked her to submit something about her childhood, but the piece she wrote for them, 'A London Childhood in the 90s', was never used. She made a note on the typescript: 'Wrote this for the BBC but couldn't stand them and chucked it.' What exactly happened we are not told, but she decided there was no future for her at the BBC and that she must try her luck with fiction. In her luggage she had brought back a number of cheap exercise books, in which she had already written the account of two important episodes in her life—the journey on the troopship to Australia, and the romance with 'Valentine Ensor'. Throughout 1930, and during the greater part of 1931, she wrote stories, novels, plays; she was determined to become a professional writer. She also gathered together all her childhood reminiscences and divided them into three sections, on houses in which she had lived as a child: 27 Young Street, The Grange, and North End House, Rottingdean—the house in Pembroke Gardens was not included. Her childhood reminiscences ended at the age of 8. *Three Houses* was published by the Oxford University Press in December 1931. It was illustrated by photographs of all three houses and of Angela being adored by her famous grandfather.

The Observer gave it a two-column review by Enid Bagnold, who was living in one of the three houses—North End House, Rottingdean —at the time. She later wrote to Angela: 'The village hated me for doing it—and you for writing it ... But like all communities—when a little time had flowed—they were proud of their wounds and adored you for it.'

The book enjoyed a quiet success. *The Times* noted her 'minute, exact, and vivid memory,' and concluded, 'It is a very interesting little book, and it is very well and choicely written.'

Angela called her childhood a 'Golden Age'. To most, if not all, adults, childhood does seem the best age, to which they flee in times of

Angela Thirkell

difficulty. 'I always feel that with luck one may suddenly wake up and find oneself in it again,' she wrote. 'It is literally more real to me than today.'

Among the appreciative letters about her childhood reminiscences was one from Ernest Seymour Thomas, an Egyptologist and assistant curator of the Pitt-Rivers Museum at Oxford. Angela invited him to tea. The extensive Burne-Jones memorabilia in Pembroke Gardens immediately attracted his attention. Thomas adored Burne-Jones with quasi-religious fervour; he had come to admire Angela and he left worshipping her grandfather and his work. Another appreciative letter came from the artist Sir William Rothenstein, Principal of the Royal College of Art and a Trustee of the Tate Gallery. Thomas and Rothenstein were the moving force behind the Burne-Jones exhibition held in June 1933.

The success of *Three Houses* surprised Angela's friends. Graham Robertson gave a party for her, to which he invited, among others, the writer Clifford Bax and his brother Arnold, composer and Master of the King's Musick. The Bax brothers had met her twenty years before. 'Angela looking lovely with much of her old devil returned to her,' wrote Robertson. She was delighted and amazed at the interest her little autobiography had aroused.

Prominent among her literary friends was E. V. Lucas. Born in 1869, and brought up in Brighton, Lucas was a member of the cricket team founded by Barrie—the famous Allakhbarries—who played on the cricket ground at Stanway and elsewhere.

E. V. Lucas was a prolific writer of novels, an authority on Charles Lamb, and a frequent contributor to *Punch*. He occupied a cottage at Brittenden by Petworth in Sussex. A big man with a Johnsonian manner, he entertained his friends to gourmet meals, and gossipped about his neighbours, the Wyndhams, who owned Petworth Place, where Angela was a frequent guest.

E. V. Lucas, who was well-known for his help to budding authors, knew of Angela's ambition to become a professional writer and offered to help her by criticizing her work. She gave him a bundle of typescripts, which she had called *Three Sillies*; the title was from an English folk tale about two absurdly apprehensive parents and their childishly timorous daughter. This was her first attempt at a novel, and when E. V. Lucas read it he told her he believed that fiction was her métier and that if she would persist she had a future as a novelist. Then came the criticism: *Three Sillies* as it stood, was overlong, repetitive, poorly-shaped. Angela set to work, re-wrote it, and in due course submitted it to a number of publishers. The pile of rejection slips mounted. Lucas advised her to talk about her writing wherever she went. Word of mouth was a valuable form of self-advertisement. It was the right sort of advice for Angela Thirkell; she talked about herself boldly, in her characteristic rapid-fire speech. People found her droll. 'She was very very cheeky,' recalled Julian Ridsdale.

The second most important literary friend to Angela at this time was her long-standing admirer, W. Graham Robertson, who in 1932 was in his sixties. From an affluent boyhood, this talented and eclectic bachelor —a painter, writer, and a collector of William Blake—had become an important influence in the artistic life of London. In 1925, he edited a selection of the letters that Burne-Jones had written to a little girl called Katie Lewis, *Letters to Katie*. From an early age he had admired, and rather feared, Angela—'that limb of Satan', as he called her. Now, he wrote, she was a 'lovely, rather wistful woman, who has had a very bad time, and has been softened and sweetened by it'. He greatly admired *Three Houses*.

Graham Robertson and E. V. Lucas formed what Angela referred to as her 'advisory committee'. *Three Houses*, wrote Robertson, 'is going well, but I don't think the OUP has the enterprise and push of Jimmy'. This was a reference to James Hamilton, a young publisher who had recently set up on his own as Hamish Hamilton Ltd. Robertson arranged a dinner party for Hamilton and Angela to meet.

Hamilton was in his early thirties. He had been born in America of an American mother and a Scottish father, and it was said that his mission in life was 'to contribute something to the cause of Anglo-American understanding'.

During the autumn of 1932, Robertson wrote, 'My introduction of Jimmy to Angela has been a great success. She has just finished a novel which Jimmy induced her to let him read, and he writes that it is "perfectly delicious".' '*Three Sillies*. A. Thirkell' was entered in the book in which the firm of Hamish Hamilton recorded works submitted. It was read by L. T. Smith and Viscountess Lymington. The final entry was the single word, which carried so much for the author and the publisher too: 'Accepted'. The title, after careful thought, was altered to *Ankle Deep*.

The heroine of the novel was called Aurea—an unusual name, which begins and ends, like Angela's own name, with the letter 'a'. It was a name she had borrowed from a friend of her youth, Lady Aurea

Macleod. The surname of the heroine's parents was Howard—the family name of the Earls of Carlisle, the family of Lady Aurea Macleod.

The publication of *Ankle Deep* brought Angela apprehension as well as delight, for she had exposed herself and her feelings. More than that, she had written identifiable portraits of the hero, of various friends, and of her parents. 'She is in a slight panic,' wrote Graham Robertson, 'as she has never told her parents about the novel.' He advised her to 'follow Fanny Burney's example and dedicate it to "the authors of my being", and place the first published copy silently in their hands'. He told her that they would be proud of her. It was good advice, but it did not diminish Angela's anxiety.

1933 was to be a momentous year for Angela. The book was published in January, on her forty-third birthday. It was advertised as by 'Angela Thirkell (Mackail)'—in literary circles, Hamilton judged, the name Mackail would attract attention. Graham Robertson was jubilant. 'Do read her new novel,' he urged a friend. 'It's odd, almost plotless and very Angelesque, but is full of her strange humour, which might be bitter but isn't, and might not be engaging but is ... There is much real insight and an underlying pathos that is really rather poignant. The sketch of her own father is brilliant. She seems to know more about herself than most people.' The book was well-received and went well. There was a chorus of praise from the critics. 'Today is her birthday,' wrote Robertson to his friend. 'We will both wish her good luck. She needs it rather badly.'

Angela's apprehension about her parents was groundless. They recognized themselves of course, but they were not offended. On the contrary, 'they were kind enough to like it,' Angela commented. Hamilton was delighted. Graham Robertson wrote, 'Jimmy confidently expecting something really big from her someday.'

Angela did not rest on her laurels; she had already begun her second novel and made fair progress with it.

To help her financially, Hamilton engaged her as one of his readers. In December 1932, she read and declined twenty-six books. She also read French and German books for the firm.

On 9 May 1933 there was entered into Hamilton's submission book, 'No-title novel. A. Thirkell. Read by L. T. Smith. Accepted'. The no-title novel became *High Rising*, and it was published three months later, in September. Two novels in one year.

And as a diversion from writing, or 'divagation' as she would call it, she plunged into preparations for the Burne-Jones exhibition, which was scheduled for June, the month following the acceptance of *High Rising*. There was to be a private view on 14 June at the Tate Gallery. Angela was touched by E. S. Thomas's energy and love; he would brook no discouragement. She was even somewhat exhausted by his enthusiasm, but that did not stop her beginning another book.

Sydney Cockerell, the director of the Fitzwilliam Museum at Cambridge, where there were a number of works by Burne-Jones, had been especially dubious about the exhibition's success. The public had turned against Burne-Jones and Pre-Raphaelitism; 'modern Art' was distracting attention, especially among the young. 'I think, however,' Thomas wrote to Will Rothenstein, 'that the public would go if only to scoff, but I think many would remain to pray. There is something compelling in his work in the mass; the atmosphere of a cathedral.'

Angela was closely involved in all the arrangements. Baldwin was to be invited to speak on the opening day. 'Oh, and would anyone ask Kipling to write something about E B-J?' she asked Rothenstein at the end of May. 'His debt to and his affection for my grandparents was deep and real. He ought to—but perhaps knows nothing about it. He is so queer that his family can't well approach him.'

Excitement mounted as the opening day came nearer. 'I hear from Mr Thomas by nearly every post and fear that he may blow up,' said Angela.

'It was rather sad,' wrote Robertson, reporting on the exhibition. 'A little crowd of forlorn old survivals paying their last homage to the beauty and poetry now utterly scorned and rejected . . . the Critics— the few who have deigned even to look at the pictures—talk of E. B.-J.'s bad drawing and weak colour.'

Kipling declined to contribute anything, but 'Baldwin spoke quite beautifully and said just the right things in just the right way, which was very clever of him as he is up to his eyes in work and could only just manage to come at all,' wrote Robertson.

Among the distinguished visitors were Bernard Shaw, Forbes-Robertson the actor, with his daughter Jean, who three years earlier had married James Hamilton, William Morris's daughter May, Graham Robertson, Burne-Jones's last model, Mrs Gaskell. A painter in his nineties who had been an assistant of Burne-Jones was also present, T. M. Rooke. 'A glorious little show,' said Thomas. Margaret Mackail was conspicuous by her absence. She had been so overcome by nerves that she had stayed at home, and Angela was hostess in her place. 3,000 catalogues were sold.

The Times devoted a leader to the exhibition. In it the writer said that Burne-Jones 'was a lonely soul lingering in remote regions . . . thanking Heaven that had given him a passion for work . . . never quite so happy as when being bullied by some little girl'. This last remark was an allusion to his favourite granddaughter Angela Thirkell, whose own fame was growing.

The exhibition lasted until the end of August. On 21 September, Angela's second novel, *High Rising*, was published. The advertisement for it in *The Times* and the *Times Literary Supplement* was accompanied by a reproduction of the Sargent portrait. There was no mention of the Mackail name. Angela was now standing on her own feet. Potential readers were informed that the novel was 'intended for those who seek diversion in a disillusioned world'.

'Have you noticed Angela's wonderful reviews?' asked Graham Robertson. 'The reviewers seem to have thoroughly enjoyed themselves, which is rare. Jimmy will be jubilant and I myself feel jubilant in having rescued her from the OUP in which her first book was entombed. This one,' he concluded triumphantly, 'looks like a best-seller.' The rare enjoyment Graham Robertson detected in some of the reviewers' notices of *High Rising* may have been partly due to their recognition in the novel of two important figures in London's relatively small literary circles, James Hamilton and E. V. Lucas.

The reviews, in fact, were not so wonderful as Robertson wished to believe. And *High Rising* was not a best-seller. Neither *The Times* nor the *Times Literary Supplement* nor *John O'London's Weekly* were particularly enthusiastic. *The Times* remarked that 'the underlying impulse which holds it together comes of "feminism", but . . . Mrs Thirkell's women . . . have their *pudeur*, and would shrink from such a word . . . The men are only satellites and none the less that they may think themselves suns . . . It is to George to whom we owe the something it is about.' *John O'London's Weekly* dismissed it in a short paragraph and so did the *Times Literary Supplement*.

That week, in *John O'London's Weekly*, W. Somerset Maugham told an interviewer that, 'authorship is like any other profession—one has to mount by degrees . . .' He might have been commenting on Angela's position for she had not achieved, with *High Rising*, a 'breakthrough'. Some authors never achieve a dramatic break-through but mount the pinnacle of fame by slow steps as Maugham himself had done.

High Rising, like *Ankle Deep*, had a good deal of autobiography in it.

'Mrs Laura Morland', novelist, now appeared for the first time; she is Angela as Angela saw herself. 'Real life,' said Mrs Morland, 'is an untidy novel.' She was referring to the use she made of life for her own works of fiction. 'Somehow it all seeped through and was used with great effect in her next but one book.' This was just what Angela was doing, taking life as it occurred, and transmuting it into the stuff of fiction. In some ways Mrs Morland is Angela idealized; in other ways she is just as Angela appeared to the people who knew her.

The devoted Angela Thirkell reader could instantly recognize Mrs Morland when she reappeared in later novels, from her characteristics, as well as from her name; she had dishevelled hair, which spilled tortoiseshell hairpins, a somewhat brusque manner and a contralto voice. Angela admitted that Mrs Morland was herself. 'She is more or less myself,' she wrote to Susan, Lady Tweedsmuir, 'but much nicer than I am ... We each write the same book every year with unfailing regularity.' 'Mrs Morland' was in fact only one aspect of Angela Thirkell. If we compare her with Aurea, the heroine of *Ankle Deep*, who was no less Angela than Mrs Morland was, there is no resemblance. Angela was a versatile actress on paper.

Was the name Morland suggested by Jane Austen's *Northanger Abbey?* To create the character of a woman novelist earning her living in a country cottage, a name with rural associations was sought. Angela and Lucas were fond of the pastoral scenes painted by George Morland, to whom she occasionally referred in the novels. One of her favourite adjectives was 'Morlandesque'.

High Rising was written round the events which took place during Christmas 1932, which Angela and Lance had spent with their Australian friends Sunnie and Gerald Carr at the Old Vicarage, Tirley, in Gloucestershire. Mrs Morland is an impecunious novelist in her forties with a son, 'Tony', on holiday from prep school. She lives in a cottage at the village of High Rising. The two heroes of the novel are her darkly handsome publisher, 'Adrian Coates', ten years her junior, and 'George Knox', an older writer, a distinguished biographer, whose characteristics have much in common with those of E. V. Lucas.

Mrs Morland recalled her first meeting with her publisher, Adrian Coates. It was at a dinner-party, and she put herself over with these words: 'I could write some good bad books ... not very good books, you know, but good of a second-rate kind.' The publisher accepted her word for it, and when he received the typescript he found to his surprise that it was no less than Mrs Morland had claimed for it. He promptly published it, and publisher and author became good friends. 'She looked upon him as a contemporary of her eldest son—after all, she was only ten years older—while he found it difficult to remember that she was almost old enough to be his mother'.

The fourth main character in *High Rising* was 'Una Grey', George Knox's secretary, a young woman of uncertain background, disagreeably forward, neurotic, and harbouring a romantic attachment to her employer. Mrs Morland calls her 'the incubus'.

Angela's choice of this word to describe a character she heartily disliked is interesting: an incubus is a male demon who consorts with women in their sleep. It is not surprising that Mrs Morland, i.e. Angela, has nothing good to say of her. She is more than grey; she is black. Una is unquestionably an aspect of Angela, but it is not an obvious aspect. There was nothing of an incubus, or even of a succubus, about Angela Thirkell. Is Una perhaps the disagreeable, quarrelsome little girl that Angela had been? A door into Angela's heart is opened a fraction of an inch, and then closed; and Una, unlike the other chief characters in *High Rising* did not re-appear in any of the subsequent novels, nor is any one like her created in her place.

In 'Tony Morland', Mrs Morland's son, Angela created a lovable small boy whose particular passion was trains and who had a talent for non-stop conversation, which Angela also had. He was based on her own son, Lance, and his success as a character was reflected in the fan letters Angela received imploring her to write more about him.

In *High Rising*, she first became aware of her ability to write comic scenes which made people laugh out loud. One of her readers who laughed out loud was Monica Baldwin, a niece of Prime Minister Stanley Baldwin, and author herself of an autobiography, *I Leap Over The Wall*, an account of her departure from an enclosed convent after twenty-eight years. 'My métier is that of a female clown,' Angela wrote ruefully.

In *High Rising*, Mrs Morland is proposed to by her publisher, Adrian Coates. She rejects him. Coates was not the only man to be so inclined; there is a hint that George Knox is also romantically interested in her, but he held back because, 'much as he admired Laura, he was slightly in awe of her, which is not a good basis for matrimony'. In addition, George Knox finds that her large sons diminish her attractiveness as a prospective wife. At the end of the novel, Mrs Morland has found eminently suitable wives for both men, and she is left alone with her son, Tony. George Knox, himself a novelist, tells her that his next book will be about their romance: 'There is one form of very successful novel in which I am eminently qualified to succeed ... Awfully Dull Novels ... If you write dull novels, excessively dull ones, Laura, you obtain an immense reputation ... the plot is ... a mere vulgar intrigue between an unhappily married man and a woman of great charm, also unhappily mated.' George Knox continues his musings thus: 'What really interests readers? Seduction ... novel readers by thousands will read my book, each asking ... will seduction take place? ... It will. But so philosophically that hundreds and thousands of readers will feel that they are improving their minds by reading philosophy.'

This passage suggests that George Knox, or the man he was modelled upon—probably E. V. Lucas—was more important to Angela than a purely literary friendship would indicate. Once again, one asks—as if she were a character in a novel—did she or didn't she? It is doubtful if she overcame her romantic fastidiousness.

Whatever the truth of this relationship, Angela's comments in a letter to Hamilton reflect her views:

Women have much less time to make fools of themselves than you have ... Short of senile dementia or nymphomania, a woman of my age isn't ever going to care for anyone enough to make a glittering idiot of him and go mad. Whereas you have practically till the day of your death to think that a chorus girl or a sham intellectual is the goods, and the world wouldn't mock excessively, nor would you be left forlorn among irretrievable wreckage if you did.

In the name of Knox for her hero, she was using the surname of another famous 'E.V.', also a prolific contributor to *Punch*: E. V. Knox, brother of Monsignor Ronald Knox. It would appear from this thinnest of disguises, that Angela did not mind, at least where the London literary world was concerned, if her affection for E. V. Lucas was made known.

1934 was another productive and successful year for Angela and can be called her *annus mirabilis*. During that year she published three books: *Trooper to the Southern Cross*, *Wild Strawberries*, and *The Demon in the House*. The last, a collection of short stories, subtitled 'Stories of Tony Morland', was probably the first to be written.

The demon of the title was Mrs Morland's son Tony, and the title itself was a parody of the poem by Coventry Patmore, *The Angel in the*

House. In a prefatory note to the stories, she wrote, 'I came to love and hate him so much that I had to write down anything else that came into my mind about him.' The stories run through one academic year. The first story opens with the bald statement, 'He lived with his mother in the country. His father had died so long ago that he couldn't remember him, so he just thought that fathers were things other people had . . . His mother sometimes tried to be a little unkind to him, because she felt the responsibility of being a father and mother rolled into one, but she was not very successful.' This was far from being the real situation, for George Thirkell was still living in Melbourne.

Apart from this, the events and people in *The Demon in the House* once again reflected her own life at the time of writing. 'George Knox' was present in most of them.

E. V. Lucas was in his early sixties. From a promising start at the age of 16 as a journalist on a provincial newspaper, he went on to carve out a successful literary career. But unlike Barrie, whom Lucas loved, he did not achieve renown. For all his prodigious output, the touch of genius he was acknowledged to have did not manifest itself.

In *The Demon in the House*, 'Barchester' made its first appearance in Angela's work, and went quite unnoticed.

'Barsetshire,' she wrote, 'was a *pays de fantaisie*.' She herself forgot when she first used it. 'I don't know how it began,' she would say, with an assumption of vagueness that was not altogether genuine. 'It began to come in about my third or fourth novel and it got the upper hand of me.'

'Barsetshire,' was the county invented by Anthony Trollope. His *Framley Parsonage* was published in the *Cornhill*, even as Angela Thirkell's works appeared almost a century later. Angela found it very encouraging that she and Trollope shared the same initials. There were other 'links' between them: Both had written about Australia. And the illustrations to his novels Trollope most admired were those by John Everett Millais, one of the Pre-Raphaelite Brotherhood.

Cynthia Asquith wrote in her memoirs that during 1927 Barrie's reading 'turned violently towards Trollope'. He was not the only one. Trollope had died in 1882, and his modest prediction that his novels would remain in vogue for only twenty-five years after his death had not been fulfilled. A Trollope revival was imminent. Hence Angela's use of the name Barchester in *The Demon in the House*. Her projection of a series of novels set in the county of 'Barsetshire' came gradually, but in these novels she was not consciously imitating the great Victorian.

Angela had spent many holidays in the country near a cathedral city. Wilsford Manor and Clouds were both by Salisbury; Stanway was near Gloucester. Petworth Place was close to Chichester. In searching to cloak the identity of the cathedral city which Mrs Morland, Tony and George Knox visit in *The Demon in the House*, she thought it a justifiable literary conceit to borrow the name of a cathedral city already established in fiction and unidentifiable outside the pages of Trollope. In 1933, she was not yet aware that 'Barchester' would become a fixture in her imaginative life.

Trollope himself had begun to write of Barchester with similar unconcern. 'No one at their commencement could have had less reason than myself to presume himself able to write about clergymen,' he said. 'I never lived in any cathedral close, and at that time enjoyed no peculiar intimacy with any clergyman.'

In 1933 E. V. Lucas and Angela visited a small Elizabethan manor house, Mackerye End, and its adjacent farmhouse just outside the village of Wheathampstead in Hertfordshire, about five miles from St Albans. E.V. had a special interest in Mackerye End because Charles Lamb had written about it in his *Essays of Elia* (1823); Lamb's aunt had lived in the farmhouse and had been housekeeper to the manor. After admiring the rosy red-gabled façade—whether they were able to gain access to the house the present writer has been unable to find out—they went on to Hatfield to see in the Parish Church of St Etheldreda the rose-and-green Burne-Jones window, of especial loveliness, which commemorates the Drage family. They had lunch at the old coaching Inn, the White Hart, in St Albans, opposite the entrance to the cathedral on Holywell Hill. The White Hart in Trollope's Barchester, i.e. Salisbury, is several minutes' walk from the cathedral. Angela's Barchester was, initially, St Albans. But Hertfordshire was not a county she knew well. Her links with Salisbury, Gloucester and Chichester were stronger.

In *High Rising* and *The Demon in the House*, Angela was on the fringe of 'Barsetshire', but the real Kensington and Bloomsbury were still much in evidence. Barsetshire had not yet taken hold of her imagination.

The short stories were not so successful as the novels, but neither publisher nor author thought they would be. Still, she received many admiring letters, particularly from middle-aged women, who were enchanted with 'Tony'. Susan, Lady Tweedsmuir, then Mrs John Buchan, was one of them. She had recently published a children's book called *Arabella*, and sent Angela a copy of it. 'I nearly cried over the handkerchief the dead bird had been carried in,' Angela wrote in her letter of thanks to Mrs Buchan. 'There is one criticism no one should ever make about children's stories and that is that anything is impossible or improbable.' This was an echo of her favourite quotation from Charles Kingsley's *The Water Babies*: 'This is all a fairy-tale, and . . . you are not to believe a word of it, even if it is true.'

In one story in *The Demon in the House* she wrote, 'If you are born lonely, you die lonely . . . Loneliness gets to be a habit, like taking drugs. I'm not very good at making friends—I'm a bit stupid and stiff—so I shut myself up in my own dull self and am not too unhappy.' In spite of her great friendship with E. V. Lucas, she was still 'the solitary-hearted'.

In 1932, Mrs Mackail had received a volume of reminiscences, *A Family Memoir* by the Countess of Wemyss. The fly-leaf was decorated with one of the author's characteristic little water-colour drawings for which she was well known among her family and friends: birds, leaves and a vase. Lady Wemyss had inscribed the volume, 'For my sister-friend, Margaret, with the love that grows not cold. From Mary.'

With the book came this letter:

Darling, here is your book. I have great joy in giving it to you, giver to me of so much that is most precious in this world . . . People seem to love the book. Those that I love the most, like it most! I'm glad I did it, and hope that it will leave a more happy than sad taste for the young generation—but when I read the letters about it—I feel as if in a dream—and it leaves me confused, with a faint bewildered feeling but a sort of peace and gratitude. Surely life is a dream?

They are gone. I felt, while I was doing the book, that they were alive and laughing with or at me.

> So life is not all sadness!
> Life is not all madness.
> True love bringeth
>
> Peace
>
> Yr mad but loving
> Mary.

In another letter, Lady Wemyss commented on the drawing which she had spontaneously added to the fly-leaf: 'The common flower-pot with the green leaves of memory (I could not do a Greek vase!!) is really a Pot of Basil in which by Love's Enchantment sadness may turn into sweetness, sublimated therefore embalmed, and bittersweet.'

During the summer of 1933 Angela was invited by Lady Wemyss to Stanway for a few weeks. She was now something of celebrity, and it gave her enormous pleasure to be lionized by this aristocratic family and their distinguished friends as her famous grandfather had been.

Lady Wemyss, who so loved the company of artists and writers, welcomed her with enveloping warmth and sympathy. She offered Angela, in her new role of successful authoress, advice on how to dress in suitable style, and even gave her clothes. Angela still felt something of a Cinderella in the environment of Stanway.

To her, the Wemyss family was entrancing. They epitomized all the qualities that she associated with aristocracy—culture, beauty, wit, generosity. She had seen it all before, as a child and as a young woman, but after her return from her long sojourn in Australia she saw it anew. And now, as a novelist, she saw it with a creative eye, and what she saw, captivated her. When she emerged from her monastic life at Pembroke Gardens—she wrote alone in an upstairs room—and went into the country, her vision of England, and of the English upper classes was heightened. She felt as if she—like Alice—had stumbled into an old English water-colour painting.

The Wemyss family and its setting offered ideal material for the comic novelist. All the novelists Angela admired wrote about families. The temptation to write about them was something she could not possibly resist, and she wrote about them even with a sense of mission. They were the best of England. Her novelist's pencil transmuted the famous family from the realms of history, biography and gossip, into art. She plunged her readers into a delightful world in which it was always summer. The buildings were ancient, country activity was endless, and the persons inhabiting the landscape were adorably eccentric.

It was said of Angela that she worshipped the Wemyss family—and their way of life—with all the passion of the convert. She transferred her entranced state to her readers: they all fell in love with 'Lady Emily Leslie', who was a portrait of Lady Wemyss.

Kipling's sister 'Trix' had also been a guest of the family. And she left this loving sketch of Lady Wemyss:

A purple velvet hat wreathed with daffodils on an Easter morning— she wore it at church and looked lovely—but the sunny walk back wilted the flowers . . . She wore them triumphantly till tea time—

and they were then so limp and showed all the pins so much that Cynthia sat behind her and stealthily plucked them out one by one. That evening she was extra late for dinner . . . Another ten minutes and she wafted in, in a golden gown with cupped bare hands brimming over with rings and bracelets which she put in a gleaming heap before her while she refused soup and chose fish, and then thought she must have soup, and ate them both together while she threaded jewels on slender white arms and fingers, and collected all the threads of talk that were going on round her into a woven cable, as glittering as her bangles . . . 'I want plovers' eggs please.' She is a lovely lady, and everyone who knew her is the better for it.

When *Wild Strawberries* was published in 1934, Graham Robertson wrote, 'Jamie had an amusing party on Thursday to celebrate the appearance of Angela's new book *Wild Strawberries*. It is getting wonderful notices and is certainly quite funny.'

The distinguished novelist Compton Mackenzie was especially enthusiastic. 'A novel of laughter,' he wrote, 'with just enough sincere emotion, exquisitely conveyed . . . I have never been recommended a novel about which I felt so certain that everybody would enjoy every page of it.' And *Punch*'s reviewer acclaimed Angela to be 'the uncontested heiress of the English novel of pastoral England.' Norman Collins hailed her wit. 'A hundred and one times the reader is rewarded by the radiance of that inner grin which comes from sharing some entirely malicious piece of social observation that any man, and most women, would have missed completely.' She had arrived at last.

Wild Strawberries opened with the Vicar of St Mary's, Rushwater, waiting to begin mattins.

The Vicar of St Mary's, Rushwater, looked anxiously through the vestry window which commanded a view of the little gate in the churchyard wall. Through this gate the Leslie family had come to church with varying degrees of unpunctuality ever since the vicar had been at Rushwater, nor did it seem probable that they had been more punctual before his presentation to the living. It was a tribute to the personality of Lady Emily Leslie, the vicar reflected, that everyone who lived with her became a sharer in her unpunctuality, even to the week-end guests. When first the vicar had come to St Mary's, the four Leslie children were still in the nursery. Every Sunday had been a nervous exasperation for him as the whole family poured in, halfway through the General Confession, Lady Emily dropping prayer books and scarves and planning in loud loving whispers where everyone was to sit. During the War the eldest boy had been in France, John, the second boy, at sea, and Rushwater House was a convalescent home. But Lady Emily's vitality was unabated and her attendance at morning service more annoying than ever to the harassed vicar, as she shepherded her convalescent patients into her pew, giving unnecessary help with crutches, changing the position of hassocks, putting shawls round grateful embarassed men to protect them from imaginary draughts, talking in a penetrating whisper which distracted the vicar from his service, behaving altogether as if church was a friend's house . . . Rushwater adored her.

The identifiable portrait of Lady Wemyss did not amuse her family and friends. It has been said that they never forgave Angela Thirkell her audacity. It seemed to them that Angela had abused a privilege. Lady Wemyss, however, continued to invite Angela to stay with her, so she was not offended. When it was suggested to Angela that she should limit herself to writing on historical subjects where she would be less tempted to write portraits from life, her answer was, 'It is quite remarkable how much of history is not good fiction.' And later, she turned this judgement upside down and declared that fiction *was* history.

The question of libel had arisen in a discussion with her publisher the previous year and she had even promised him that there would in future be '*no* portraits'. Easier said than done. In later years, Angela's friends and acquaintances put up their guard when they met her unless they wanted to appear in her next book. They even warned one another not to ask her to their houses. She was, they said, like a butterfly collector, capturing, asphyxiating and pinning down specimens. It was a measure of her success and power.

Her creativity and success aroused envy among the less successful, as her grandfather's had. For the more intellectual members of London's literary society, her novels were 'too popular'. Angela knew this and their opinion gave her a sense of inferiority. She concluded, falsely, that writing that came so easily to her could be of little value. Nevertheless, James Hamilton and E. V. Lucas believed in her and assured her that she was an artist.

Early in December 1933 Angela wrote to James Hamilton, 'I am living inside the skin of an Australian officer—a type I know rather well—kind heart, insensitive, good in a crisis, maddening in private life, unconsciously sardonic, capable of almost brutal want of feeling, yet ready to make any kind of sacrifice for his men . . . I have invented nothing . . . If you think it all sounds impossible I shan't mind, for this is an objective piece of work and done for a lark.'

She was referring to *Trooper to the Southern Cross*, the story of her journey on a troopship to Australia. She had decided to write it as if she were a medical officer with the AIF, one 'Major Bowen'. Apart from the change in profession from engineer to doctor, the character of Bowen was George Thirkell. It was an affectionate, even loyal portrait. She wrote to James Hamilton, 'He is not at all literary . . . but he is a very good sort whom you would be glad to have at your side in a tight place . . . his temper is almost impossible to ruffle . . . Without him and a few like him I don't know how that hell-ship could ever have got to Australia.'

Hamilton declined it, and she submitted it elsewhere. She did not wish to publish it under her own name for a number of reasons, chief among which was her fear that the book, in which the Australian soldiery and the Australian military authorities were not portrayed in a flattering light, might produce an unpleasant furore, especially in official circles. She chose the pseudonym 'Leslie Parker', borrowing the name from a friend of Graham McInnes who was a fellow under-graduate at Melbourne University.

To her great satisfaction, *Trooper to the Southern Cross* was accepted by Faber and Faber. She was given £30 advance on royalties—a modest but not an insignificant sum in those days—and it was published in September during the following year.

The *Sunday Times* wrote, 'Major Bowen . . . must not be missed.' The *Morning Post* described the narrator as 'amazingly funny'. *The Times* wrote, 'Mr Parker has succeeded in a very clever study in character.' But the Australian reviewers were infuriated by it. *Trooper to the Southern Cross* was a virtuoso performance by a woman novelist who was also an accomplished actress, in a character role. Angela wrote that she 'was amused and flattered to find that all the reviewers took it for gospel truth (as indeed the facts were) and believed that the author was a real Australian soldier.' The most successful character-study in the novel was the portrait of the wife—a pliant, loyal little woman—as seen through the eyes of the officer/narrator. The Diggers were every-where—rumbustious, foul-mouthed, fighting. It was to be her only book about Australia.

7

'O, These Men, These Men!'

On a warm June day in 1934 a quite unexpected letter arrived for Angela at Pembroke Gardens—from her eldest son Graham. He was at sea, a passenger on the *President Roosevelt*; he asked her to meet him at Paddington station that afternoon. Angela had not seen Graham for four years. He had graduated from the University of Melbourne and gone to Canada in search of his father, a teacher of music in Toronto. Angela greeted him with composure. Graham recalled laconically that she 'was smoothly efficient'. In the taxi he blurted out that he had seen his father. 'Did you indeed, darling?' replied Angela coolly, and changed the subject.

Waiting for Angela at Pembroke Gardens was James Hamilton, with whom she had arranged to go to dinner. Graham McInnes described Hamilton at this time as 'a well-built young man with wavy black hair and a noble bashed-in nose'. Angela saw no reason to cancel her engagement with Hamilton, much to Graham's disappointment.

Graham had no career in mind, though he nursed vague aspirations to become, like his mother, a writer. He had inherited something of his father's talent for music and played the piano by ear brilliantly. Angela thought him handsome, and naturally wished to show him off to all her friends and family. She took him to a tailor and equipped him with, among other clothes, a dinner-jacket, a tail-coat and all the appropriate accoutrements. The London season was well under way. As Angela's personable son he was invited everywhere—dinner-parties, theatres, dances, country-house week-ends. Together they went to stay at Stanway.

Angela did what she could to help him. Through her efforts he was engaged to strum the piano, and even sing, at the Gargoyle Club. In his spare time he wrote songs, stories and sketches in the nursery upstairs at Pembroke Gardens. Hermione Gingold used some of his sketches in one of her revues.

At the height of the summer Angela was shocked by the news that James Campbell McInnes, now in his sixties, was back in London after an absence of nearly twenty years. Until Graham had dug him out in Toronto, neither of his sons had heard a word from him. He had a singing engagement at the Wigmore Hall and was staying at the Russell Hotel in Bloomsbury. She dreaded that he would seek her out and create a scene.

In one of his three autobiographical books, Graham McInnes wrote that when he met his father's secretary in Toronto, he came face to face with a young woman who bore a startling resemblance to his mother. James had lost Angela, but he had found a younger version.

The news of Angela's literary success had reached James in Canada. What he didn't know was that Angela's marriage to George Thirkell was at an end. Graham soon informed him.

Angela had thought she would never see James again. Her reaction to the news that he was again in London can only, for want of more definite evidence, be divined by her next novel, *O, These Men, These Men!* The title was a quotation from *Othello*.

So long as there was a chance of meeting James, so long would her fear live, beyond reasoning, beyond commonsense. Now it came back through every nerve, vague, overpowering . . . As she walked her eyes were nervously searching and yet avoiding the faces of the passers by. More than once she felt sick with fright when a man with a walk or a way of holding his head that reminded her of James crossed her path.

Angela did not flinch from calling her drunken villain 'James'. The heroine, 'Caroline', was another self-portrait. 'Caroline' was told that 'James' was as handsome as ever, and was being very charming to everyone. And it was reported that he was disarmingly contrite about the failure of their marriage. 'He has thought of you,' 'Caroline' was told, 'as a guiding star ever since.' He told everyone that 'Caroline' had been the perfect wife, that he had worshipped her and that he could never look at another woman. Finally, he passionately wished to see her and would not leave England until she had forgiven him. For her part, 'Caroline' declared that she had adored 'James' and that he had broken her heart.

It was suggested to 'Caroline' that she should nerve herself to see 'James', behave with compassion and tell him that all was forgiven. Her reply to this advice was terse. 'It isn't,' she said, and added, 'My baby isn't forgotten.' Angela was thinking of the child, Mary, who had died, and she was extremely annoyed when, at a party, the butler mistakenly announced her as 'Mrs Campbell McInnes'.

Angela immured herself in the upstairs nursery at Pembroke Gardens and refused to go out while James McInnes was prowling about. 'I live in a kind of mummy case,' she wrote of herself. 'And if I don't break out occasionally I shall become as dead as my case.' She reflected on the hardships and humiliations she had been through, and began to hate men altogether.

The weeks passed and she managed to avoid James. We are told by Graham McInnes that James telephoned Pembroke Gardens. Angela answered the telephone, but amazingly she did not recognize his voice. Graham adds that his father asked to speak to Angela as if he, for his part, had also failed to recognize her voice—or was he merely being formal? 'It's Jim,' he said. Angela instantly replaced the receiver. James McInnes returned to Canada, and Graham and Colin, out of sympathy for their father, changed their names back to McInnes.

In the autumn of 1934, Angela began to write another novel.

On New Year's Eve, 1934, Angela spent the day digging in a friend's garden at Shackleford in Surrey. She saw the new year in while drinking a mixture of port, whiskey and eggnog. Gardening and drinking were unusual activities for Angela.

The following day she wrote to James Hamilton, 'I can't write at all . . . I have a perfectly stiff back and trembling hands.' Her physical condition was due to her unwonted activities in the garden, but she was also in a state of anxiety about *O, These Men, These Men!*, the typescript of which she had given to Hamilton to read over Christmas. Would he or would he not like it? She herself had grave doubts over it. She had warned him that in this novel she had tried something new. It was, she said, 'rather sentimental'. She had wanted to get it out of the house so that when she saw it again she would be able to take a fresh view of it.

'Jamie', as James Hamilton was known to his friends, had given her his opinion of *O, These Men, These Men!*, and it was not a very encouraging one. 'Isn't it a fact,' she asked him, 'that your liking the book a lot *really* means that you don't like it very much?' This apparently contradictory remark conceals, or perhaps reveals, a subtle relationship between publisher and author. Hamilton handled Angela with tact and skill. He told her that in spite of one or two flaws he sincerely believed it was a better novel than *Wild Strawberries*. At the same time he doubted if it would be as popular as *Wild Strawberries*, which had sold extremely well, even better than *High Rising*. With this letter, he sent her several manuscripts on which he wanted her opinion—a crossword book, a travel book, and a children's book about an elephant.

'I *don't* find it much fun,' was her uncompromising verdict on the crossword book. About the children's book she wrote, shrewdly, 'The ground has been well-prepared by the *Babar* books . . . and it is often a good plan to bring out another book of the same kind—the public has become elephant-minded.'

Anxiety about the fate of her novel persisted. She felt as if her whole future was now in doubt, and she left it to Hamilton to publish or not.

Jamie's damning-faint-praise of liking it 'quite a lot' haunted her and plunged her into self-doubt and despondency. 'Are you going to ask me for another book, or has the quite-a-lotness put you off . . . I have never been so depressed in my (literary) life as over this book. Would you like to tear it up?' It was not so much Hamilton's disappointment as his travellers'. They were sorry that she had not written another 'strawberry soufflé'—her phrase. She knew that she 'had gone all gloomy and Russian', and her publisher's doubts, which she detected, started up her gloom all over again. She cheered herself up by going shopping. 'I have an enchanting new hat which makes me look like a dilapidated female cossack,' she told him. She was on her way to John and Susan Buchan in Oxfordshire; they planned to go that day for a long walk in the crisp January air.

While Angela did some re-writing and pruning, Hamilton did some calculating. *Wild Strawberries* was still 'moving', as they say in the book trade. At the end of the first year its sales totalled 3,017—'a very good showing'—and Hamilton felt that *O, These Men, These Men!* was well worth the financial risk. Angela's confidence in the novel slowly returned. She wrote to his secretary, James King, 'I thought of letting Mr Hamilton have the dedication of *O, These Men, These Men!* but it would be more amusing to make it a surprise. Can you see that "To J.H." goes on the dedication page without his knowing till the bound copies are received?'

Angela was once more assailed by apprehension. The portrait of her first husband in the novel was certainly recognizable, and as for Caroline, the heroine, Angela felt that she had done herself a disservice by making her as irritating and full of self-pity as she was herself. She begged Hamilton to print the novelists' disclaimer at the front of the book that 'all persons are imaginary', but he declined. 'It never cuts any ice either with the public or with lawyers in case of trouble, and so is a waste of space.'

Hamilton was unhappy about the design for the book's jacket, which he thought ineffective. Angela herself, with Lance's help, made some alternative sketches, but they did not meet with Hamilton's approval. 'I only pray to be in the Sahara or Tierra del Fuego next time you have a *"crise"*,' Angela told him. 'I am still sleepless and gibbering.' Had he exploded at her obduracy?

She was 'safely in the country' when the newspapers carrying reviews of the novel were published. She nerved herself to look at them.

'It's no good pretending that it hasn't been a disappointment to you,' she wrote to Hamilton after seeing Ralph Straus's review in the *Sunday Times*. 'I don't know what I think of it myself. First one is too close to one's offspring, and then when they have left the nest one loses all interest . . . Naturally one would like paeans of praise from a selling point of view, but otherwise it all is of so little value . . . I may have come to the end of myself. If I have, I hope you will find some other younger, cleverer more amusing woman who will do real best-sellers.'

Hamilton urged her not to be discouraged by Straus's review. And he tried to restore her confidence in herself by suggesting another project.

The idea of a book about the Regency courtesan, Harriette Wilson, had been simmering in her mind for some time; she had published in the *Cornhill* an essay on Harriette Wilson's novel *Clara Gazul*. She also wished to write a children's book. Hamilton did all he could to encourage these two projects, which he felt 'would make an admirably contrasted pair of winners for the autumn'.

Angela was still beset by doubts. She thought that Hamilton would probably lose money on *O, These Men, These Men!*; she didn't want that to happen with 'Harriette' as well. But Hamilton was enthusiastic, and he told her that her friend Gilbert Barker, whose opinion she valued, 'was impassioned' about her writing about Harriette.

'I would always rather do a heavy day's washing than have to make a decision,' she told him. 'I do *hate* it. You make it as easy as it can be made, but Lord! how I wish I were just a lady and nothing else.'

'Harriette' seemed to her to be an immense and daunting project. Illogically, she protested that she was no historian. 'You have far better qualifications than any dry-as-dust research student,' Hamilton replied, and he sent her the current issue of the *Cornhill*, in which Peter

Quennell had published an essay about Harriette. Angela commented 'How *ghastly* dull the poor *Cornhill* is'; and after reading Quennell's essay, her confidence began to reassert itself. 'I don't think Quennell knows any more about her than there is in the *Memoirs*,' she wrote. She was grateful to Hamilton for the support and tact. 'An occasional kind word will do wonders,' she told him.

But the book had still not seized her. She had heard that James Laver, the costume historian, was also contemplating a book about Harriette. She wrote to him, and received in reply a 'handsome letter' assuring her that he had no such project in mind, and, he added gallantly, if he had, he would abandon it. Angela also heard from Sir John Murray; he invited her to go to Albemarle Street to look at the Harriette Wilson letters in his rich archive of Byron material.

Meanwhile the Easter holiday was far from being the ideal opportunity in which to work. 'I am wondering how I am to get anything done at all in my "rustication",' she wrote, 'as, what with cooking and a certain number of friends in the neighbourhood, and walks, and then one fritters one's time away on housework, and feeling I mustn't neglect Lance, time flies like greased lightning.'

Hamilton added to her confidence by telling her of the interest which had been aroused by the publication of a historical novel called *The Bazalgettes*. It appeared anonymously, under the imprint of Hamish Hamilton, and all the critics were playing the game of 'guess the author'. Most people thought it was by Angela. In fact, the author was E. M. Delafield. 'What a marvellous press you are getting for *The Bazalgettes*,' Hamilton told Angela teasingly. He was delighted at the publicity he was reaping for *two* of his authors, and suggested that Angela write a letter to the *Times Literary Supplement* denying the authorship and thus giving a fillip to the press speculation.

After the holiday, Angela went up to the Midlands to stay with some friends near Buxton, and relaxed her brain and nerves by long walks, always a favourite form of exercise. She put the failure of *O, These Men, These Men!*—a novel which she was always to describe as 'crashingly bad'—behind her, and revelled in the countryside. She wrote to Hamilton:

We had a divine day yesterday . . . Down the bed of a marbled stream for about a mile—a romantic progress—then through a strange deserted Belle au Bois Dormant estate with rhododendrons and azaleas running riot, then into a valley where a dam is being made . . . Then for miles along a green track that used to be a mineral railway between two canals, then through a half-mile tunnel . . . frightened of the cold and the wetness . . . splashing darkness to the other end . . . then almost into Buxton, then back again by the old coach-road to the high moors . . . home in divine sleepy fatigue.

Back in London, she embarked on intensive research in the London Library, the British Museum, the Public Record Office and the newspaper library in Hendon, where she read the newspapers of the Regency period. She found the research fascinating and pursued it with energy and diligence, and not without a little relish. 'It *was* a gutter-press,' she remarked after a day's foray at Colindale.

'I have now fallen into the Record Office which is almost more fun than the B.M.,' she told Hamilton. 'Very empty and very exclusive and a faint F.O. atmosphere all about one. There I am reading the Granville Papers . . . so entranced by much of what I read that I want to edit it *all*. There are stacks of stuff waiting to be done by someone who really knows the period. I sit and laugh aloud over Poodle Byng's letters and Canning's despatches . . . The people who *could*, would naturally not think the subject worth treating. Indeed, I'm not sure about that point myself. Which all leads one to the interesting question, whether *anything* is worth while, except hot baths, good food, and a comfortable bed.'

But she had got the bit between her teeth now, and could not have stopped even if she had wanted to. 'You men of action have no idea of the joy, the excitement, the blood-lust, of tracking down one date, one allusion, at the cost of three days' work, most of which is wasted— I assure you it is as good as flying, or rowing, or squash, or making a night of it.'

Earlier, in March, Angela had written to Hamilton tentatively about the children's book she had in mind.

Do you know Ludwig Richter's drawings? If you don't there will be rather more explaining to be done. He did hundreds of exquisite drawings of German peasant and burgher life in the early part of the last century . . . I have been thinking that a few chosen tales, translated with a few picked drawings to go with them, might be something people might like. The drawings only need knowing to be loved and if one (I mean I) could do the translation in the

Grimm spirit, we might make something of it.

I have been doing one of the stories and I would like to show it to you together with the drawings that go with it. Unfortunately the drawings are all together in collected books, so I should have to bring the whole book to show you. Will you have any free time after lunch on Wednesday?

She had left her copies of the Richter books in Australia ('Alas!') and the only ones available to her in London belonged to her parents. She invited Jamie to dinner so he could see the pictures and discuss the project. 'You will have claustrophobia and agoraphobia and hydrophobia, but you know my parents . . .' she told him. 'Or, would you like me to come to your flat, complete with books? I am not cadging for a meal, nor do I require to be driven back, said she with morbid Scotch pride; but it is much more restful chez toi than chez moi. I love to think of your immediate reaction to both these suggestions, as that of a hunted animal scenting danger in the wind.'

The idea of the children's book met with a favourable response. While researching the Harriette book, she was also writing the children's stories. The book was to be called *The Grateful Sparrow*. 'We must get it all just right,' she said, 'and there must be no infelicities of taste. I warn you that I propose to be far more trouble about this child of other people's minds than about any child of my own. It has got to be perfect.'

On 30 May she handed in the typescript of five stories along with the books containing the illustrations. Some of the stories were happy, some unhappy. The title story was about a tired sparrow travelling with a bundle on its back, begging a little girl for some soup. Another was about a lawyer and his cross wife and their five quarrelsome children. A third was about an old grandfather's Christmas tree on a watchtower over the city gate; a fourth about some wicked gnomes who steal sausages at pig-killing time.

She wanted the illustrations to be in black and white, like the originals, and she was most upset to learn that they would have to be in colour. She wrote to her publisher: 'Now, will you and Clark seriously and *really pay attention*, reconsider the question of colour. You say one must have colour to sell a children's book, but the black and white of these is so excellent that it seems to me a great pity to try and improve them . . . And the question of type is very important. The sample you sent me was fine and clean, but by no means distinguished.'

Hamilton was adamant. The pictures must be coloured. Angela wrote early in June, 'If colour it must be, perhaps I had better try to do it myself. I know pretty well what I want.' Hamilton and Clark were impressed by her delicate work and the book went ahead. When the time came to lay out the title page Angela behaved in a very puzzling way. Hamilton asked, 'Do you really want the words "Taken from the German" on the cover and title page? Don't you think we might stretch a point and simply say "by Angela Thirkell?"' He was very reluctant to use the word 'taken'. His experience had taught him that there was undoubtedly a prejudice among booksellers if not among the reading public, against anything that was suggestive of translation. Apart from this minor difficulty, the firm was delighted with the book. With it, Hamilton hoped to make his entry into the children's book market. 'It should be one of the most attractive children's books in recent years,' he wrote to her.

Angela was worried by her publisher's insistence that the stories should be described as by Angela Thirkell. 'You and Clark both have some obscure feeling about it which I can't fathom . . . Is it that you think that the word "German" would be bad for the book?' Hamilton assured her that this was not the case. This forced Angela to tell the truth. They were not, as she had said, translations.

I wrote them all—they are very good pastiche (said she modestly) of the three writers to whom I have dedicated them: or rather, pastiche of the gifted translators whose names are unknown to fame. The snippets of poetry are a medley of various Volkslieder. *But* I thought I would feel safer and happier if I hid behind the decent obscurity of an imaginary German original. You can't think how pleasant anonymity is (talking of which Mr Leslie Parker has had a cheque for £2.1.2d from Faber). It would be nicer if people blamed or despised me . . . damn it all, how little it all matters compared with Time and Eternity and that being so do as you like. You see the whole trouble is my passionate wish to evade responsibility at almost any cost.

The trade were fairly optimistic about *The Grateful Sparrow*, and judged it most original and charming. But no American publisher made an offer for it, much to Hamilton's disappointment. The Viking Press and other American publishing houses turned it down.

The British press praised it, but it seems to have been far too delicate and original a book to have a wide appeal.

In the writing of it Angela had discovered a remarkable gift which she had not suspected in herself—that of automatic writing, a gift that another member of the family possessed. Kipling's sister Alice, 'Trix' Fleming, had become quite celebrated for her automatic writing and had been investigated by the Society for Psychical Research. The Society's *Proceedings* had devoted over a hundred pages to a report on 'Mrs Holland' as, owing to the disapproval of her family, she called herself. The immediate impulse for a Keatsian poem seven stanzas long that she wrote came from looking at a picture of St George painted by William de Morgan. Angela's new-found gift was of a similar order but less extreme. She had looked at the Richter pictures, the pencil in her hand moved upon the page, and the stories wrote themselves. She was herself curious about her gift of automatic writing and concluded that she was in some kind of trance.

During 1935, Angela continued to read foreign books and English typescripts for Hamish Hamilton. The fee, which she called 'the price of shame', was £1 a book. In the midst of all this activity, for she was writing her own books as well, she suddenly remembered that she had promised a Valentine's Day story about Tony Morland for an American magazine.

The telephone at Pembroke Gardens never stopped ringing: the calls were mostly for Angela, and her parents grew irritated by them. On several occasions they failed to pass on messages and they even refused to give her address to her publisher when she was away and he wanted urgently to get in touch with her. Angela felt the lack of privacy keenly. 'I shall have to invent a pseudonym for you if my family *will* listen in,' she told him. 'Not that I have any secrets, but it is a *bore* to be listened to and indirectly questioned. Could I call you Julia?' From now on when Angela telephoned her publisher, for the benefit of her family she was talking to 'Julia', the name of Harriette's confidante. Finally, Angela paid for a separate telephone to be installed upstairs in the nursery.

In August, Angela went to stay at a cottage in Ambleside, in Cumberland. The contract for the Harriette book was sent to her there. The terms were, she thought, too generous. 'Is it honest?' she asked. 'I am so worn out that I can't think straight and can only say that I'll try to do it anyway.' The thought of advance payment made her feel 'morbidly conscientious'.

She found the borrowed cottage somewhat primitive and country life frustrating. She had Lance with her, but she longed for adult company. 'The soot fell down the chimney,' she complained, 'and the pig has eaten one of my stockings.' But, she concluded thankfully, 'one can lift one's eyes to the hills'.

In Cumberland she once more indulged her passion for long walks. One day she calculated that she and Lance had walked twelve miles, 'but double that in climbing and rough going—and we saw all the kingdoms of the earth and were blown upon by twelve winds of heaven . . . Lance and I are enjoying the country so much . . . the fells . . . the grassy, rocky slopes, the flowers, the ferns, the mosses, the abundance of streams . . . and the perpetually changing light.'

The pig that had eaten her stocking was, she discovered, a sow. 'So like a woman,' she commented.

Her friend Gilbert Barker, 'the bat-eared Barker', as she called him, kept her supplied with data on Harriette.

About the middle of September, she learnt that Penguin Books wanted to publish *Wild Strawberries*. The new paperback trade was not very rewarding financially, but it spread her name far and wide. Australia had already enquired about serialising *O, These Men, These Men!* and there had been enquiries about foreign translations of *Wild Strawberries*, which had already appeared in America. The year 1935, after an unpromising start, was progressing well.

In the 1935 New Year's Honours List, it was announced that Dr Mackail had received the Order of Merit, the highest civil distinction. 'It was,' said Angela, 'about the only thing Papa wouldn't be too proud to take. He is really terribly pleased, though he would die sooner than mention it.' A shoal of congratulatory telegrams poured through the letter-box of Pembroke Gardens. Angela counted over two hundred. In due course, the white-haired scholar, clad in black silk knee-breeches and buckled shoes, went to Buckingham Palace to receive the Order from the hands of the monarch, George V.

Angela's success aroused envy, and even hostility, not only among other writers, but among her own family. It did not altogether please her younger brother, Denis Mackail, who was himself a far less successful novelist and writer. It was said of Denis that he looked like a ghost; his many published novels had something of his insubstantial quality about them. Angela's success diminished him even further. He went so far as to complain to Hamilton that publication of one of his sister's novels in the same week as the appearance of one of his own would ruin both their chances, and he asked for Angela's novel to be put forward.

As for Angela's sister Clare, her talent as an artist and musician had never developed. She was said to be intensely spiritual. Her nerves had never been strong, and in her teens she had suffered a severe nervous breakdown which recurred at regular intervals during the rest of her life. At 17 she fell into a condition of *anorexia nervosa* and ate so little that her life was despaired of. Angela's constant presence at Pembroke Gardens was abrasive to family concord. Denis and Clare kept their distance. Clare, who never married, shared a house with two women friends in Surrey.

Her mother, Margaret Mackail, had not found a role. She joined the Oxford Group; Angela commented, 'Alas, Buchmanism.' She attended house-parties at Hatfield House and elsewhere. She caused concern among her own family by retiring to her room for long hours, praying, and in subscribing handsome sums of money to the Group's funds. To her friends' surprise, she even lost her well-known reticence and openly discussed her new-found state of grace. 'As a rule,' commented Graham Robertson, 'she would die rather than tell you what she was going to have for dinner. Is this the effect of having "gone groupy"? . . . This expansive and voluble Margaret is new to me.' Dr Mackail and Angela were greatly perturbed but powerless. Margaret Mackail was a woman of independent temper and means.

Angela had always been a *fille de Papa*, and her literary success drew her and Dr Mackail closer together. In the evening, she read her latest novel aloud to her parents; she called it the 'dress-rehearsal'. Dr Mackail was her sternest critic and corrected occasional errors in style or grammar. 'Living with Papa one *must* be sure,' she wrote.

At the end of September 1935, Angela and her father boarded the train at St Pancras for Scotland, where they were to be the guests of Lady Wemyss at Harestanes, Longniddry, in East Lothian. Hamilton wanted her to exploit the opportunities for self-advertisement that this visit would provide. After all, she was one of his most successful and entertaining authors. He asked her to call on several booksellers in Glasgow and Edinburgh and vamp them. 'Your visits would be of the greatest help to the new book and to your future work,' he told her.

Their first stop was Ayr, where they spent the night and where, the following morning, a letter and a book from her publisher on which he wished for a report, awaited her. After spending part of the morning working, Angela walked round Ayr with her father. Later, they visited the Brig O'Doon which, she said, 'is all that Burns claimed for it', and watched men fishing and the salmon leaping under the autumn sun.

The following morning they went on to Glasgow. 'The only other occupant of our railway carriage (smoking, for Papa) was an aged shepherd, a glorious type of aged, ageless face, who spat without stopping . . . I had a stiff neck with looking out of my window, never daring to turn my head.'

In Glasgow, they left their luggage at the station and set off at Dr Mackail's insistence for the cathedral, 'along an interminable street half-way up a mountain, stinking to heaven of unwashed poor,' reported Angela. Dr Mackail read aloud the inscriptions on the memorials, and examined everything which was to be examined, with 'exhausting fervour'. For the next journey in the city, Angela suggested a taxi and even offered to pay for it, but her father wouldn't abide such extravagance; they took the tram. On their arrival at the Art Gallery, Angela noted with typical exaggeration that it was larger than the Louvre. To her relief, the greater part of it was closed for cleaning, but this did not deter the determined Dr Mackail, who called on the director, and introduced himself, but not his daughter, to whom he disconcertingly alluded as 'this lady', and asked to see the closed rooms. Angela commented, 'The director must have thought I was the family lunatic who had to be taken about and humoured.'

By three o'clock she 'was now beyond speech, thought, feeling, emotion, heaven or hell, and ready for anything, with a smiling though set, expression'. She still had to call upon the three Glasgow booksellers that her publisher had asked her to, but two were fortunately away for the day. Of W. H. Smith and Son, she reported, 'We caught your Mr Knox, a nice young man, to whom I gave real pleasure by introducing him to Papa, who was extremely amiable . . . So I have done my best for you, Mr Hamilton.'

On the last day of September they arrived at Harestanes, and were greeted by Lady Wemyss. The house was at the village of Longniddry, west of Gosford House, the magnificent eighteenth-century Adam mansion which this family also owned. At Longniddry, in the mid-seventeenth century, John Knox had been a tutor.

To Hamilton, Angela wrote:

Your letters are like the Hound of Heaven, following my footsteps— the Hound of Great Russell Street. I now have a sheaf of your communications to answer and two books to write about and here I am with a charming chatterer (female) chattering away to me and plans whirring about in my head and the Countess threatening to read aloud a pamphlet by Philip Kerr on How Never to Have another War and the Firth of Forth all grey and misty across the links, and trying to talk as I write, or write as I talk . . . Papa is being oracular: the door and window are open and a wild blast from the Forth is sweeping through the room because the butler has been sent to find a back number of *The Times* (nobody knows why), he moves back and forwards carrying mutilated copies rescued from coal-pit or dustbin: David Elcho [12th Earl of Wemyss] is darning his kilt and eating peppermints, while Clementina Mitford is trying to re-knit a bed-sock which Lady Wemyss's secretary has knitted all wrong—something to do with charity. If Lady Wemyss's chow barks all the time, that of course is merely its nature . . . I have a guilt complex, inferiority complex, old age complex, dullness complex, not-being-wanted-by-anyone-complex; but thank heaven one can laugh here.

Scotland and Harestanes refreshed her. Her recurring nightmares ceased—she did not say what the nightmares were—and for a change she had pleasant dreams. But she had no rest from the reading and reporting that she felt she had to do—the books arrived almost daily. Otherwise, it was a typical country holiday. They walked on the Pentland Hills, where Robert Louis Stevenson had walked. Angela went to Abbotsford and there was talk of Walter Scott. A trip to Edinburgh to see the cathedral followed, and in the evening they went to the theatre to see a comedy called *A Short Story*, in which Marie Tempest played the lead. Lady Wemyss asked Angela to extend her stay. Dr Mackail, O.M., returned to London and was seen off at the station. Angela was, of course, thinking about another novel. She asked herself, could she, or could she not, write another novel? 'Mrs T. She would like to in the abstract, but she has so little courage . . . What she would dearly love would be never to set pen to paper again . . . but write she must.'

During the autumn of 1934, Angela was under tremendous pressure. She had written and sent off to America the two Tony Morland stories for *Harper's Bazaar*, was now working at full stretch on the Harriette book, and on a 10,000 word serial for the *News Chronicle*. From time to time, she would take off a few days to spend with the editor of the *Observer*, J. L. Garvin, and his wife, who lived at Gregories, a house in Beaconsfield, Buckinghamshire. She avoided weekends with the Garvins. 'There are usually bores there and yet other bores come to tea,' she wrote.

During the work on the Harriette Wilson book, she often signed her letters 'Harriette', or with a monogram of Harriette's initials instead of her own. In the middle of November, Angela exuberantly addressed a letter to 'Darling Julia'—Harriette's close friend. The recipient was James Hamilton. She also saluted him, as 'Dear Stockdale', i.e. Harriette's publisher. And she sometimes prefaced he text of her letters with 'Angela Thirkell again! *Que diable m'écrit-elle?*' The French phrase was Harriette's.

Harriette Wilson was a gifted, high-spirited impudent letter-writer who never toadied to the nobility, with whom she was in frequent contact. In the opening pages of Angela's biography of Harriette there is this passage:

> She was a child of fearless and independent temper, extremely trying to her father ... When Harriette was about five years old she tore up one of his [mathematical] problems ... Her father swore to use the birch till she promised never to offend again, but the spirited little creature submitted to a thrashing that left her almost senseless sooner than apologise ... and in fact rather admired her father for this display of brutality.

The title was much discussed. *Angelick Harriette*, as some of the courtesan's admirers called her, was high on the list, especially since it linked with the author's Christian name, but this Angela rejected. The book went forward as *The Fortunes of Harriette: The Surprising Career of Harriette Wilson*. In America, where it had a simultaneous publication, it was called *Tribute to Harriette*. It was Angela's only work of biography.

Angela anxiously awaited the reaction of her father and mother to *The Grateful Sparrow*, and when it came, she was greatly relieved. 'My difficult parents are enchanted,' she wrote. Publication day of her children's book saw Angela at the offices of John Murray in Albemarle Street, where she had gone to supervise the photographing of Harriette's letters, one of which she used as an illustration. She could not resist taking a copy of *The Grateful Sparrow* with her to show Sir John Murray; John Grey Murray—the present head of the firm—was also there. They were both impressed, but Sir John rather more by

Hamilton's feat in putting the book on the market for the modest price of five shillings than with the book itself. John Grey Murray's summary description of Angela, when he recalled her at a much later date was: 'She was a *power*.'

A week later, the excitement of its publication was fading, and Angela was feeling thoroughly exhausted again and far from well. She put Harriette aside for a few days, 'because I can't drive myself beyond a certain point—but I hope and mean to get to grips with her again next week'.

She typed all her own work, and made a great many mistakes, not having mastered this difficult art. In addition, her spelling, which was usually excellent, underwent an extraordinary change between her mind and her fingers on the keys. It annoyed and puzzled her a great deal.

Early in December there were arguments about the jacket design. Dobell, the second-hand bookseller in the Charing Cross Road, had just acquired a miniature which was said to be of Harriette Wilson writing her memoirs. Angela hurried round to see it and made a sketch of it for the jacket. 'Something like this . . . she is sitting at her table with pen poised and the MSS in front of her, and inkpots all filled and ready.'

She delivered a first draft of the biography late in November. 'It has been a *hellish* job to sort out, correlate and bring together the best bits,' she wrote. Christmas 1935 found her ready, in spite of suffering again from insomnia, for a Christmas sherry party at Pembroke Gardens.

Angela began the new year by damning several French books she had been sent to report on. 'They are the lowest form of pseudo-scientific *ordure*,' was her uncompromising verdict. She had at last finished *The Fortunes of Harriette*. 'I hope to get Harriette really polished off over the week-end . . . I shall be very glad indeed, as I am rather *frappée en mort*, as Harriette so colloquially observed, and shall be thankful to take my mind off her for a couple of weeks.' She was planning a short post-Christmas break out of London. 'It will be very restful not to have to take a typewriter and have one's mind churning all night and waking one up with starts at three in the morning.' Two days later she wrote, 'I now want to re-write the *whole thing*, so it is time she left me.'

On 17 January Rudyard Kipling died, aged 70. He had been taken ill suddenly and operated on urgently. Three columns in *The Times* were devoted to his obituary: he was, the writer said, 'an ambassador of the Empire'. The adjoining column reported the news of the King's illness, which was causing some disquiet, and a few weeks later both King and poet were buried. Kipling's ashes were interred in Westminster Abbey, in Poet's Corner, next to Hardy and Dickens, but at his funeral, unlike Hardy's, not one literary personage acted as pallbearer; most were politicians or men prominent in society. One of them was Cousin Stanley Baldwin.

The columns of *The Times* were separated by thick black stripes of mourning for the dead sovereign. The new king was hailed: the handsome, boyish and much adored Edward VIII.

Early in April, Angela and Lance were once again installed in a borrowed country cottage—Cliff Cottage, Telscombe Cliffs, near Newhaven. 'There are an earwig and a spider here. At least the earwig is now dead, but the spider, who had at least nineteen legs, survives to plague me. Lance scours the downs on a pony, and I,' she added sourly, 'scour saucepans.'

Wild Strawberries had been a great success in America and Angela was now, in those relatively tax-free days, obliged to write out cheques for the Inland Revenue. 'It is an honour dearly bought,' she commented.

As a successful author, Angela aroused admiration and emulation, not to say envy, which occurred at all the stages of her career. In the beginning, there was Cynthia Asquith who, having learnt that Angela was making a success as a free-lance journalist, expressed her surprise and the view that she herself could do the same, for 'obviously [she is] no more a "born writer" than myself. If she could do such a thing, why not I?' Why not, indeed? Lady Cynthia began to publish articles on domestic subjects in *The Times* and elsewhere, and entered the field of royal biography.

Angela was vulnerable to some of her many friends and acquaintances who had ambitions to be professional writers and asked her for help. In particular, young men who wanted to get into publishing begged her for introductions and recommendations to Hamish Hamilton. To one aspirant she wrote: 'If it's love, I'll lunch any day next week. If it's business I'm still out of Town.'

Angela's gift for fantasy rose to the surface again, and she conjured up a vision of country life. Once more the pencil seemed to move of its own accord. In her new novel, which she began in the late spring of 1936, she sketched the topography of her *pays de fantaisie*. The names of all the places had associations with wool: Worsted, Fleece, Lamb's Piece, Winter Underclose, Winter Overcotes, Shearings, Skeynes, and Lambton. The Ram and Twins was the name of a public house near Dipping Ponds. There was no mention of Barchester or Barsetshire. She hoped that this novel would equal, if not excel, *Wild Strawberries*. The characters behaved with exquisite absurdity. None of the characters from either *Wild Strawberries* or *High Rising* were here; Mrs Morland and her Tony were forgotten in the sheer delight of creation.

'No one will ever know how a book comes into a writer's mind,' Angela wrote. 'Some novelists, one understands, have plotted the whole story before the writing begins. Others—as I in a small way can testify —sit down to write in a state of black despair, knowing that the Muse has fled and there is nothing but dust and ashes. Something must be written. Angrily the pen or pencil is forced to write one sentence. Then —with luck—something else takes over. The story begins, the people come to life of their own accord, and in lucky moments the pen is even busier than the mind. The thought is the master and the pen its servant, straining every nerve to keep up with it.' She quoted Thackeray: 'A pen is to an author like the wand of the necromancer, it compels the spell', and added, 'I have the honour to feel as Mr Thackeray felt . . . the characters, once created, *lead me* and I follow where they direct . . . Whenever a character gets into the round, so to speak, he or she takes control, and one can only run after them, pencil in hand . . . Some characters take the reins into their hands, and the bit between their teeth . . . and nothing will control them. They will go where they choose, marry whom they choose, break their hearts or anyone else's as they choose.'

Early in July it was finished, and the characters began to fade from her mind. 'I am quite *miserable* without all my friends at Worsted,' she wrote. 'I hadn't known them long, but you can't think how well we got on, and I am lonelier than usual.' When Hamilton read this novel, he was so delighted with it that he sent her an enormous sheaf of red carnations.

As usual, the title presented problems. 'Papa so far has no suggestions . . . I have been reading aloud to him. To his great pleasure I had looked up a reference to the Odyssey wrong . . . If I haven't an inspiration to-night, I'll have one tomorrow'. But no inspiration was forthcoming. 'I am all burnt-up and discouraged. What do you think of HOLI-DAY ROMANCE? The name is from a little story of Dickens'. Most people don't know it. I append the following from Shakespeare:

O brawling love!
Serious Vanity
Father of lead
Youth, whatsoever thou art
Unhardened youth
A youth, a kind of boy.
Shallow humorous youth
Flowering youth
In standing water (between a boy and a man)

I also thought of:

Youth in Idleness
August Folly
Chorus of Youth
Summer Interlude
Idle Hill of Summer
Not too serious

The novel was sent off to the printer and Angela went north to stay with friends at Tolson Hall, Kendal. She had hundreds of friends; who the friends at Tolson Hall were, the present writer has been unable to discover. The problem of the wrapper had not yet been broached; Angela sketched out her idea of what it would be like. 'I have every hope,' she wrote, 'that the matter of the jacket can be arranged in cool blood.' The artist Anna Zinkeisen, whose wrapper designs were far above the ordinary, solved the problem by making a delightful drawing which pleased both publisher and author and was reproduced in some of the reviews.

Angela was constantly meeting new people. In the London Library, during 1935, she made the acquaintance of a young man called Gilbert Welch Barker, whom she unflatteringly referred to as 'the bat-eared Barker'. Barker was the youngest son of Colonel F. G. Barker, CBE, Master of the Garth Hounds, and of his French wife Lucille. Before his birth, Mrs Barker had ardently wished for a daughter. There was something feminine and delicate about the boy, and his education was disrupted by poor health; he was said to be a 'sport' in the family on account of his artistic and intellectual interests. The Barkers lived at Stanlake Park, an Elizabethan house with Georgian additions, which was always full of dogs; the family was dedicated to country pursuits.

Angela encouraged Gilbert to write, and he, as well as she, would scribble away in exercise books, his interest being in art history. 'Those bloody exercise books!' exclaimed Colonel Barker as he retrieved one from the mouth of a dog.

In London, Gilbert and Angela were inseparable companions at dinner, concerts, galleries, the theatre; he followed her about everywhere. Did they or didn't they? It is unlikely. Later, he wrote of her: 'Her charm was so extraordinary, her wit as light as a butterfly, yet as sharp as a rapier. Above all, she had a wonderful capacity for friendship.' Barker's family did not share Gilbert's passion for French art, though his mother was French, and did not altogether care for Angela. They considered her insincere and affected, and overdressed in her habitual chiffons, with a cloud of pastel tulle round her head. And when Angela attempted to play the countrywoman in a tweed skirt, they thought she looked frumpish.

August Folly was a novel about a young man with bat-like ears, who was enamoured of an older woman.

At the end of August 1936, Angela and Lance went to Belgium for a holiday. They stayed at the Hotel Terlinck at Coxyde-sur-mer. Colin, who was working in Brussels, joined them at the weekend, and mother and sons swam, walked and played tennis together. 'The air and colours are clear and exquisitely lovely, and all the landscapes just like Flemish pictures,' she wrote to another new young friend, Ian Robertson, an assistant at the Ashmolean Museum at Oxford. 'Lance,' she wrote, 'is a *lovely* colour like a golden brown peach . . . I am quite ghastly like a weatherbeaten figurehead.'

While she was in Belgium she heard, to her delight, that *August Folly*, as the novel had been named, had been chosen as the 'Book of the Month' by the Book Society. 'I can only hope that the financial gain involved will counterbalance the moral degradation,' she wrote in her usual wry way to Hamilton's secretary, King. 'For the firm I am perfectly delighted, and hope it will be the beginning of a record season.' And to the publisher she sent 'millions of congratulations . . . and I hope we'll all roll in our Rollses . . . It would be interesting to know at what point in one's career the B[ook] S[ociety] does more harm than good.'

Angela had been invited again to Harestanes at the beginning of October, and she took copies of *August Folly* with her as presents for her friends. When she removed the wrapper she was agreeably surprised. 'The binding is *very nice*,' she commented to Hamilton, 'and has a kind of grown-up "arrived" appearance . . . *Do* come to Edinburgh next week while I'm there. You could come and dine at Harestanes—or we could make all the booksellers in Edinburgh drunk and get huge orders out of them.'

Books for her to report upon arrived at Harestanes. She was indefatigable:

Well, Mr Hamilton, you don't seem to have much feeling for us girls, sending us along jobs of work when we are supposed to be on holiday. As soon as I see the parcel I said to myself Well, men may be men, but they don't seem to have no consideration for us girls, and there's Mr Hamilton drinking champagne every night I daresay, in his new blue suit and brown boots and a carnation in his buttonhole, just thinking of himself and having no consideration for us girls at all. It's all very well, I said to myself, for him to sit there, telephoning to his lady friends and smoking cigarettes, but he doesn't seem to *consider*, I said to myself, that us girls are entitled to a little *consideration*, and we haven't got a lady secretary, I said sarcastically to myself, to write our letters for us, and he doesn't seem to consider that there mayn't be any ink in the house, and it's not fair to expect us girls to walk a mile to the village to get a penny bottle to write to him with, and very likely the rest just to be wasted, and the sea air taking all the wave out of a girl's perm, besides today being Sunday and all the shops shut, only just by luck the lady I am boarding with happened to have some ink in a drawer in the kitchen that she makes out the bills with. And as for him coming to Edinburgh, I said with a nasty laugh to myself, handsome is as handsome does, and it isn't likely he'll put himself out for *you*, my girl. Well, Mr Hamilton, I shall be at the above address till the end of the week, and then I am going to stay with my cousin in Edinburgh, the one that married a Colonel, and I shall be looking up those boy-friends of yours in the bookshops, but I don't suppose there'll be much to be got out of *them*. Now, if you had some boy-friends up here that would take a girl to the dogs, that would be *talking*, but us girls don't seem to have any luck . . .

Ivy [i.e. Angela]

She loved the Scottish countryside, and described it as 'too divine, with clear days of pale sunshine and an ever-changing view across the Firth of Forth to the Kingdom of Fife'.

It was to be her last year as guest of Lady Wemyss. The beautiful and sympathetic Countess was frail, and ageing rapidly. She had now to walk with a stick, and reclined on a chaise-longe enveloped in shawls and scarves fastened with innumerable valuable antique brooches, none of which were as bright as her dark 'hawk's eyes'. In *Love Among the Ruins* Angela described her hostess's room thus:

Lady Emily's room . . . was not unlike . . . the apothecary's shop in *Romeo and Juliet* in its crowd of miscellaneous and apparently un-related objects of all kinds. Watts's beautiful head of Lady Emily soon after her marriage; hundreds of photographs, from studio portraits signed by crowned heads and great statesmen and the Leslie children at every stage to snapshots of the 3rd housemaid's wedding; a set of asbestos mats on which her ladyship had painted red and gold birds, shawls, icons, Madonnas, a drawing of cats by Louis Wain, Sargent's head of her eldest son, books bristling with pieces of paper left in them by Lady Emily to mark a favourite passage, a large bureau covered with letters and bills with corners of papers sticking out of every drawer, and occasional tables covered with flowers, pencils, paints and stationery, a canary in a cage, an old-fashioned cheval glass which showed the room at an alarming tilt; and yet in spite of the muddle such a triumphant sense of the full-ness of life, such a bringing together of time past and present, that the rash beholder, felt the spirit of the room even more than she saw its untidyness.

True to her word, she called again on the Edinburgh booksellers. 'I am vamping the trade like anything,' she wrote gleefully. Before departing she gave a sherry party for them in an Edinburgh hotel. For-rester, one of the booksellers, presented her with a large sheaf of crim-son roses, which she took with her on the train to London.

Back in Pembroke Gardens, and not yet ready to write another novel, she began at the end of October to try her hand at writing a play. 'I have no hopes or illusions, because I can never think of any incidents and am too reticent to describe *passion*. But it keeps me from brooding.' She made little progress with the play, but an idea for a new novel finally came to her. She set off once again for the newspaper library at Hendon and immersed herself in *The Times*, the *Morning Post*, and *Bell's Sporting Life*, all for 1838—the year of Queen Victoria's corona-tion. Then she went home with all the pictures fresh in her mind, and conjured up a story, told in the first person by a young, provincial, well-do-do matron, in London to attend the coronation. The result was *Coronation Summer*. The text was embellished with reproductions of Victorian prints. Hamilton, to her chagrin, declined it, but it was accepted by the Oxford University Press, who found to their surprise that its announcement in their catalogue aroused a great deal of interest. They had to reprint before publication.

'The people are all my own invention', she told an admiring academic, Professor Gordon Haight, 'but every single fact is true ... I had great fun over it ... What was so enchanting was to meet Dickens's people—obviously seen by his quick eye and stored in his mind for future use. Especially Miss Flite in *Bleak House*, whom you will see in my book, word for word as a newspaper reporter described her, haunting the law courts.'

Throughout the year 1936 the world had been speculating about the future of the British monarchy, as well as about what Hitler's next move would be. A constitutional crisis loomed. Stanley Baldwin, his pipe in his mouth, was at the centre of the turmoil. Angela was living in another age—of almost a hundred years before—and she was concerned wholly with a happier coronation. As for the contemporary monarchy, she devoutly believed that someone, if not Edward VIII, would eventually be crowned. In December, Edward VIII made his abdication speech, and the Monarchy did an about-turn. George, Duke of York, became King, and Elizabeth, Duchess of York, Queen Consort.

The year ended with an ebullient Angela returning from the Cunard offices by Pall Mall where she had been addressed as 'Miss'. She had gone there to book her passage to America in the new year. In a letter to Hamilton she wrote, 'I feel generous and will spend 1½d on you.' She was referring to the cost of the stamp.

A great many people did not know that Angela had spent ten miserable years in Australia, for she neither wrote nor talked about her Australian past. Now she was off to America. Australia and America had something in common: they were egalitarian societies, which England was not. Graham Robertson was apprehensive that she would say some thoroughly disagreeable things about New York and other places. 'I hope she won't write a scarifying book about it on her return,' he said to a friend. He was thinking of Anthony Trollope's redoubtable mother, Frances, who, during the previous century, had published *Domestic Manners of the Americans*, which had caused a furore of indignation.

On 29 January 1937, the Court Circular in *The Times* carried the following announcement: 'Mrs G. L. Thirkell has left London for the United States and will be away until Easter. Letters will not be forwarded.' Angela always insisted on this form of address. On her writing paper and printed postcards she was always 'Mrs G. L. Thirkell'. To her extreme indignation, she was often addressed as 'Miss Angela Thirkell', or even just 'Angela Thirkell'. Although she was obviously alone, she was still married. Punctiliousness over details was not her only reason for insisting on this form of address. It has been said that, as a result of her two failed marriages, she suffered from a sense of inferiority. Whether this was so or not, she was certainly proud of her married status.

Before she sailed for America, she fought off an attack of flu with rum and quinine. On the boat she read Ford Madox Ford's *Great Trade Route*, which she described as 'queer and rambling'. Ford's description of Grand Central Station she found excellent and exact. She was to spend one night in New York, before going on to Boston, where she was to stay for several weeks. Then on to Canada to see Graham.

Her American publishers, Alfred and Blanche Knopf, met her with an enormous box of long gladioli, which she regretfully left behind the following day. New York did not please her. She wrote: 'I so *hated &* *loathed* N.Y.... It is a *nasty, paltry* ... *negligeable* place'.

On arrival at Boston she was in a state of physical and mental exhaustion and took to her bed. Her pleasant room faced south and was warm with central heating; in addition, a wood fire blazed in the hearth. Her Boston hostess was Miss Elizabeth Gaskell Norton, whose forbears had been friends of the Burne-Jones's. Miss Norton's house at 19 Chestnut Street, was 'a spacious red-brick early 19th century house, full of perfect furniture, pictures and what-not'. Of Miss Norton herself, Angela wrote, 'She is a wonderful remnant of the Flowering of New England, still managing to have servants, to "entertain" and wearing the most dashing pink and apricot negligées in the evening ... Boston is charming and as for Harvard and Cambridge, they are quite exquisite ... I shall be very happy here if the strength lasts out.'

The warmth and enthusiasm that she had fallen into thawed her and she began to enjoy herself. 'My first sight of Harvard, driving up the Charles River, with its beautiful new buildings and their white spire and lanterns in the winter sun, was unforgettable.' Boston suited her 'dull and frumpish' tastes, as she put it. 'An atmosphere of dignified red brick houses, old linen, silver, glass, furniture, pictures. My hostess has never bought a cup and saucer in her life . . . such being the family possessions.'

She was subjected to the inevitable ladies' luncheon parties, and found herself unequal to them. 'I haven't much to say anyway, and a weak voice, and often I sit through a meal almost in silence, amused by it all, but physically unable to make headway against the shrieking chatter of my fellow guests . . . My hostess says she sees me sometimes open and shut my mouth, but nothing comes out of it.'

Americans, for their part, looked upon Angela as a typical English lady, rejoicing in her very English qualities—her reserve, her accent (which they thought quaint), her air of distinction and her evident good breeding. A good deal of her father's stately academic manner had rubbed off on her. Americans listened to her with respect, admiration and even delight, fascinated by her knowledge of England, English families and their intricate ways of life. She told one astounded American, that in order to understand the British caste system, 'one should read, and *memorise*, a page of Debrett every day'. Privately, however, she admitted that she could make neither head nor tail of Debrett's *Complete Peerage*.

On leaving Boston, she went to Washington, where she spent 'a blissful couple of hours' in the Library of Congress, and then on to Mount Vernon, which enraptured her. As a result of the Abdication, Mrs Wallis Simpson's house at Baltimore had become a place of pilgrimage, and, rather uncharacteristically, Angela paid it a visit. Next stop, Ottawa.

The novelist John Buchan, Lord Tweedsmuir, was now Governor-General of Canada. He was fifteen years older than Angela, a tall, handsome, frosty-eyed Scot, whose background was similar to Dr Mackail's. Both were the sons of Scottish clergymen of modest means and both, while at Oxford, had won the Newdigate Prize for Poetry. Angela simply idolized him.

Buchan's wife, Susan, was also a writer, and Angela spent a happy weekend with them,' gossiping with Her Ex[cellency] and talking about Scott, Augustus, the *Noctes Ambrosianae*, Mrs Simpson and Osbert Sitwell'. Buchan spent the weekend in bed, 'there holding audiences'. Had he been exhausted by Angela?

Harold Macmillan was at this time a fellow guest. Angela found him dull. She also thought Canada dull. Lady Tweedsmuir, who loved Canada, tried to convert her to a different view: Canada was a land of contrasts, she told Angela.

On 16 March, Graham McInnes met her and took her to Montreal and Quebec for a few days. The weather was very bad, 'a real Canadian blizzard'. Graham was well settled in Canada and had taken out Canadian citizenship. 'He has lots of artist and communist friends,' Angela wrote, 'all very nice and entirely self-centred.'

Back in Boston, she summed up her views of America thus: 'I have *loved* USA, and rather disloyally find it much nicer than Canada . . . *very* glad to be back among the rebels . . . I'll have to come back again if writing pays.'

August Folly had been well-received by the American press. '*Very* praising', she wrote, 'but that doesn't mean much. The *New Yorker* approves in six lines, the *Herald Tribune* in a column.' The time in Boston went by very quickly, and early in April she prepared for the return journey on the *Brittanic*, which was due to leave on the 15th. Her last social engagement was at the Food and Wine Society. 'To-night I dine with two middle-aged pansies (one with an anti-mother complex) . . . So you see, Boston is not unlike London.'

The cold English spring to which she returned and Pembroke Gardens depressed her. 'It is *awfully* flat after USA and I feel more unappreciated than ever.' She and Lance went to the Lake District for the Whitsun holiday, but even the Lakeland scenery, which she loved, did not charm her this time, or compensate for the warmth and hospitality and cheerfulness of America. In retrospect, the New York she had disliked assumed an unexpected glamour, and she longed to return.

The following month she was more cheerful. *Coronation Summer* appeared, was widely reviewed, and sold over two thousand copies—which was not very many, compared with her novels, but she liked the look and feel of the book. It was described by one reviewer as an amusing pastiche in the manner of Jane Austen. Its publication coincided with the coronation in Westminster Abbey, the third in her lifetime. Amid all the pomp and pageantry, the King and Queen were crowned on the day that had been arranged for the coronation of Edward VIII: 12 May. And during this exciting season, Gilbert Barker took her out night after night, to dinners, concerts, theatres, the opera. It was calf-love on his part. From her point of view, she was pleased, even at times elated, to have a handsome, cultured young man of good family as her escort.

She was now in the thick of another novel. 'I am trying to produce, but genius doesn't burn—I lick my pencil twenty times for a word and then don't like it! However, it's dogged as does it, and I shall plod on.'

Now, for the first time, she committed herself wholeheartedly to Barsetshire. Her decision to do this—at the risk of incurring the displeasure of all Trollopians—may have been strengthened by the fact that Monsignor Ronald Knox had, the previous year, published a novel called *Barchester Pilgrimage*. There is no record that Ronald Knox and Angela Thirkell ever met, though they had many friends in common. In a prefatory note to Knox's novel, Maurice Baring wrote that the author did not believe anyone would read it, 'because practically nobody has ever heard of Barchester'. And Knox himself wrote:

> My readers may be few enough; but it will be something to have told your non-readers—the people who will put down the book in disgust at this point—that you think as poorly of them as I do, for taking so little interest in Trollope . . . To me Barset has been a real county, and its city a real city: and the spires and towers have been before my eyes, and the voices of the people are known to my ears, and the pavements of the city ways are familiar to my footsteps. Barchester was a welcome escape from real life . . . And then I suppose I must have looked once too often—that image of a cathedral town began to flicker before my eyes; what had become a motionless piece of sculpture turned all at once into a newsreel . . . the world was moving, and Barchester had to move with it.

Angela set her new novel in a boys' public school near a cathedral city. In it, Tony Morland, now seventeen, reappeared. And she invented a delightful companion for him, an embryonic classical scholar called Hacker, whose pet chameleon provided fine comedy. And for the first time she borrowed, not only the imaginary 'Barchester' but a whole family from Trollope, that of Dean Crawley. She wrote steadily, and by the middle of July the novel was finished. 'I have thought of these titles,' she wrote to Hamilton. '"Waistcoat Buttons", "A Spray of Honeysuckle", "Summer Half."'

Once again Hamilton was pleased with the novel, which he felt sure would be another winner and responded with flowers. 'Thank you so much, Jamie dear,' Angela wrote, 'for the battalion of red roses which today are all opening and embalming the air.'

In May 1937, Lady Wemyss died. She was buried at Stanway in a primrose-lined grave to the sound of the cuckoo. 'So vital was her living personality that her spirit seemed to be flitting around enhancing the sense of poignant sadness but divesting the scene of any "tragic element",'

Angela Thirkell

wrote Violet Lady Leconfield in *The Times* obituary. She was mourned as 'the perfect friend'. 'Trix' Kipling wrote: 'It is right merry in Heaven . . . I couldn't sleep for imagining her welcome.'

Barrie, too, died that month, and was buried in Westminster Abbey. To the rage and despair of his family, he left his huge fortune to Cynthia Asquith.

At the end of July, Angela and Lance were at the Francis Hotel, Bath, 'not to take the waters, but to repose ourselves and see the sights'. There she sketched designs for the book's wrapper. 'A bright coloured cover—perhaps bright blue, with contrasting lettering . . . to be GOOD, like Cape's, which we haven't achieved yet.' She was so tired, she said, untruthfully, that she wouldn't care if it was bright yellow, like Gollancz wrappers.

She began to suffer from eye-strain. Hamilton proposed that she should not read the proofs of her new novel and that he would have them read for her at the office. Angela demurred, and insisted that only she could do the job properly. She was also afflicted with rheumatic headaches, and felt 'entirely disintegrated'. Her doctor suggested a holiday, which to Angela meant staying with friends. Fortunately, the Garvins invited her to Montreux. She took Lance with her.

'Perfectly lovely place for walks and view. I have a room with a huge balcony and view of the lake . . . millions of lights at night all round . . . Snow is falling on the mountains.' Tramping round the snow-covered Swiss hills restored her. 'I am much better', she announced on her return to Pembroke Gardens, but 'today a miserable nostalgic wretch.'

Towards the end of the year she was at Newell Grange, Redditch. 'There is a girl here who is so *exactly* like my Rose in my last book that it does my heart good. It must be genius when the brain conceives what the eye has not seen!' Rose was one of her more amusing young women, lovely but inane and given to repeating a particular phrase—'foully dispiriting'. It was said later that Angela's catch-phrases ranked with Dickens's.

The Times critic wrote of *Summer Half*, 'Here is Mrs Thirkell at her liveliest and best, laughing gently at her people . . . for our delectation. I enjoyed every page'; and she was hailed in *Punch* as 'one of the great humorous writers of our time'.

Hamilton noted that E. V. Lucas was not among the guests at the party Angela gave at the end of November 1937, and he mentioned the fact. Angela affected surprise. E.V. had been a great friend of hers.

But apparently he wasn't any longer. One can speculate endlessly on the subject. It was common gossip in literary circles that E.V. had many affairs with women. Was Angela among his conquests? It must have been in his mind as a possibility, if not in hers. But he was now sixty-nine and ailing. A. A. Milne said of him, 'To be a writer and to have him for a friend was to feel that whatever he wrote was written, in a special sense, for him; so that the thought "E.V. will like that", gave one a new conceit.' Certainly, his faith in her talent had sustained her during the first years as a professional writer.

In December, she was trying to get on with another novel but was unwell again. 'I have been having words with the Muse,' she wrote crossly. 'She is willing, but what is going to make it all very difficult is that even two days' "work" have put me back into blinding stupefying headaches. And no one seems to know what they are or why, it is not amusing. To have one's tools and means of livelihood (exaggeration—means of holidays, treats for Lance, taxis and other unnecessary outlay on oneself)—broken in one's hands is beyond fair play. There it is. We shall do what we can.'

Early in January 1938, Angela finished *Pomfret Towers*, and wrote the blurb: 'The whole is written in Mrs T's inimitable vein of sardonic kindliness.' In the usual thorny discussions over the wrapper, she wrote the description of the house in which most of the action takes place:

> It was built by the sixth Earl of Pomfret under the influence of Ruskin and the Gothic revival and was, as I take pains to point out, exactly like St Pancras Station, from the ramp leading up to it and the medley of Gothic windows, turrets, steep roofs and chimney stacks, to the Victorian clock from which Lord Pomfret's flag as Lord Lieutenant flies when he is in residence.

'If you know anyone who could make it imposing, funny, hideous enough, go ahead.'

She was fettered to the typewriter for several weeks preparing a final typescript. 'I think you'll find the book no worse than the others.'

There was some anxiety about the name of Pomfret and Angela was asked to make sure that there was no risk of libel.

'(a) There is no *title*. The only Pomfret existing is in Burke's Landed Gentry. His name is Virgil Pomfret. I wouldn't have thought of that. (b) Pontefract, or Pomfret Castle, well known to you as a student of Shakespeare is, according to Murray's 1904 Guide, only a few ruins . . . I have thought of it so much as Pomfret Castle, that I can't think, *pro.tem.* of any other name. If I don't call the *book* Pomfret Castle, I don't see why I shouldn't go on using the name *inside*, as I make it clear that Pomfret Castle was founded by a Pomfret, and there was no such family as Pontefract, which was founded by the de Lacys and probably called after a place in Normandy.'

The novel was renamed *Pomfret Towers*.

In the middle of March she was a guest of Percy Matheson, a retired classics don, at Headington near Oxford and there she met Ian Robertson again. Both 'collected' what might be called aesthetic experiences.

Go into the Botanical Gardens, straight through to the Alpine plants, then turn to the left, there is a Cydonia Japonica, espaliered against the stone wall, facing south, which is *well* worth your attention for its qualities of shape and colour. I have *never* seen such a perfect piece of decoration.

The correspondence led to her spending a weekend at Robertson's house at Coombe, a small village near Oxford. Robertson who shared the house with Archie Balfour, was an art historian who collected the work of the nineteenth-century surrealist Richard Dadd. The charming house and the witty company brought out the best in Angela. She was reluctant to return to 'horrible London'. Ian Robertson recalls her scintillating company, in particular her gift for verbal duelling of a very high order. 'I have the greatest pleasure in the world in differing from you: we can do it so amiably', she told him. 'So much laughing, I really felt infinite happiness and refreshment . . . I have never been in a house where one could do as one liked with such complete confidence in not displeasing anyone. There was also often a *surréaliste* tone in the conversation that amused me excessively—I felt we talked only in asterisks and brackets sometimes, but so brilliantly.' Robertson, above all, admired her looks at that time. She was always at her best in the evening, coming downstairs for dinner and making a grand entrance with her lovely head and neck swathed in clouds of tulle.

That was only an interlude in her life of hard work. Rheumatic headaches still plagued her and her doctor suggested that she should take the waters at Rheinfelden in Switzerland, near the German border.

Angela stayed at the Hotel Krone-am-Rhein. 'I am in full blast of drinking waters, having baths, extensive and boring amounts of rest, massage etc . . . and much ashamed of being so reduced to thinking of my own horrible self . . . it is the remains of an enchanting little walled town with towers and storks' nests. Over the bridge is Germany, who have much the best bits of it as they get a lovely view of us, whereas our view of them is mostly factories. The country inland from here is *very* lovely—mostly hilly orchards and vineyards among beech woods.'

She went to Zurich, 'and very pretty it was and we drank beer under the flowering chestnuts on an island in the lake. And such enchanting medieval towns in the Rhein all steep cobbled streets and gabled houses falling over each other and astoundingly clean.'

Ian Robertson had suggested to her that black lace would suit her porcelain complexion. She had remembered this, and while in Switzerland she bought a black lace mantilla, the type of triangular head-covering Catholic women commonly wore to Mass. It softened the long line of her now not-so-young neck and shoulders, and had the effect of making her feel alluringly feminine. The weather was hot and the flowering chestnut cast romantic shadows. She was not alone. She flirted, but it was all very innocent.

On her return to London, Hamilton took her out to lunch, and he told her he needed some photographs of her for publicity purposes. At the end of May she went with her mantilla to the studios of Howard Coster and was photographed wearing it.

She was unusually docile before the camera. The photographer was 'a rum bird: addressed me as "my dear" and (I *think*) "darling"; interlarded his talk with "dear God!" and "dear crucified Christ!" and told me what he thought about things—so I agreed amiably with everything.'

The results pleased her. She said that the black lace mantilla made her look like 'a distinguished woman who has been Through Much'. That description was the way she now saw herself; she enjoyed the role, and played it for all it was worth.

Towards the end of June, she was being pressed for another book, but she was once more suffering from fatigue. 'I haven't got near thinking of a book—finding living from day to day (what a lot of present participles . . . I use them too freely) as much as I can compass. I haven't forgotten, but the minute I try to do a little more it is too much.'

She enjoyed a day at Henley with Lance, who was a keen rower. July passed and she was still without a compelling idea for a novel. 'I have been so *souffrante* this summer with perpetual headaches which knock the stuffing out of me.' She took herself, without much hope of improvement, to a new doctor. Her headaches and general fatigue seemed to her to be more like an 'Act of God', than an illness which would arouse the interest of the medical profession.

August 1938 brought her a German translation of *The Grateful Sparrow* which she found so charming it moved her to tears, 'So it *must* be good'.

She went to Varengeville in the South of France, and there, in the Hotel de la Terrasse, inspiration seized her and she began to scribble. In the somnolent and sensuous heat, she imagined herself wearing a black lace mantilla while reclining on a chaise-longue under a large Spanish chestnut. The fantasy grew.

Early in September she was back in London with her three sons. 'Graham is here, full of plans, very busy. He, Colin and Lance all at once are overpowering—I feel a little like Gulliver in Brobdingnag. I am taking them all to *Nine Sharp* on Monday, and oh, how my head does ache.'

After a long courtship by correspondence, Graham McInnes proposed marriage to a Melburnian girl called Joan whom he had known while an undergraduate at Melbourne University. Graham came to London to meet her and the wedding was arranged. Joan, of course, knew few people in London, and Angela arranged for her to stay with a Kensington friend of hers, Mrs Cissie Craies, née Ionides, a descendant of the well-known Greek family who had been patrons and friends of Burne-Jones. Angela put her work aside, braved her headaches, and took her future daughter-in-law shopping for her trousseau.

In spite of all this, her new novel made progress. 'I see an end of a new book in sight, but not too soon as I have to side-track into a stupid short story for Harper's Bazaar, and I *can't* write short stories as no one knows better than myself.' She was aiming to finish the novel by Christmas. Somewhere in the middle of it, she realized with surprise that it was pleasing her enormously. The heroine, a flirtatious middle-aged woman who wears a black lace mantilla, is entertained, or bored, by one man after another. The atmosphere throughout, at least in the scenes concerning the heroine, is somnolent and sensuous. There is a lot of fruit-picking, and the heroine is always in a condition of languor. Towards the end of it, Angela was drawn into the frantic search for a title. 'You Shouldn't Say Such Things' and 'You Shouldn't Talk Like That' occurred to her and were rejected. 'Lavinia Brandon,' the name of the languid heroine, was a third possible title. In a letter of Christmas greetings to Hamilton, she signed herself, 'your affectionate female Author'.

Angela could still talk pictures very happily with Robertson, and to him she sent a card from Prunier's seafood restaurant in St James's, where Gilbert Barker had taken her for dinner. The card was of an unrealistic yellow-and-white fish floating over a black lobster, which was resting on a white table. 'This delightful picture is for your collection,' she wrote. And in a letter composed shortly afterwards, she reported on the exhibition of pictures at the Royal Academy, to which she had gone with Barker. 'A dismal show except for the *perfect* Alan Ramsay room and about half the Raeburns, but it was a morbid pleasure to see the two Noel Patons of Midsummer Night's Dream, which I always adore in Edinburgh. But I saw in them what had never struck me before, a horrible resemblance between his fairies and Dadd's people. Had this ever struck you? There is a *surréalisme* in both, a glittering terror of the eyes, an entire absence of scale or proportion as between the different figures: only Paton, being a respectable mid-Victorian who had a large family and chiefly painted religious figures, has a lewdness from which Dadd is free. The two little Dadds at the Burlington Fine Arts are exquisitely drawn.'

Christmas and the turn of the year invariably and inexplicably depressed her. It was a season she could never summon up any enthusiasm for. 'I have never felt so low physically, spiritually, mentally,' she wrote.

The Brandons was the title finally chosen for the new novel. She roundly condemned all the wrapper designs which were submitted. 'It is very sad, but there it is, I think you'll have to decline them,' she told her publisher. Damn all jackets I say. Cape has the best type in the trade—I wonder where he gets his.'

But the jacket, like all book jackets, was finally agreed upon.

When *The Brandons* was published in late March 1939, it gathered the chorus of praise which Angela, by now, was accustomed to and fully expected. In 1939 she was at the peak of her creativity and career. Sir Hugh Walpole—'Lord Walpole' as Angela called him—himself a prolific and successful novelist, praised it highly but deplored the lack of a plot. 'Not even for him . . . can Miss Thirkell invent a plot—she must go on being a "clever lady" . . . in her own way', she wrote.

She was compared with Jane Austen by the reviewer in *Punch*. 'No more than the late Miss Austen does she pay heed to wars and rumours of wars.' There is not a hint in the novel of Hitler and the gathering storm clouds. The farcical Munich agreement had come and gone, and the world was bowing its head to the inevitable catastrophe, but the characters in *The Brandons* were wholly preoccupied with other interests. The *Daily Telegraph* hailed her in these words: 'Such a writer is a blessing in a work-a-day world.'

She put on her black lace mantilla to go to a literary party which Duckworth were giving at the Book Wine Shop in Bloomsbury, and as she turned into Great Russell Street by the British Museum, she naturally stopped to look in the window of her own publisher. It was filled with his latest publications including of course *The Brandons*. The position of her novel in the window annoyed her; it had been relegated, as she thought, to one corner, elbowed aside by more important works. But a few days later she recovered her good humour when she read the advertisement for *The Brandons* in the Sunday papers. She wrote the following note to Hamilton:

> ### The Blurb Society
> The Directors of the above Society have much pleasure in informing
> #### Mr Hamish Hamilton
> that his advertisement in today's *Observer* and *Sunday Times* has been chosen as Blurb of the Month.

What she had especially liked about the advertisement was the reproduction of a curled-up cat, smiling happily while holding in its paws a copy of her novel. The cat's face was that of the critic James Agate, whose remark about *The Brandons* was quoted: 'All the time I was reading it I purred like my kitten.' Indeed it was the novel 'that made Walpole chuckle-headed and Agate purr'.

In America *The Brandons* sold 8,000 copies before publication. In addition, it was chosen by the Book of the Month Club and jumped into the best-seller list. Almost dazed by this success, she wrote, 'I'm very much surprised to find myself above Dos Passos and Maugham.' Soon to head the list of best-sellers was John Steinbeck's *The Grapes of Wrath*. For one delirious week, *The Brandons* was in second place.

Her friend Gilbert Barker was also enjoying, in a smaller way, a success with his biography of Watteau, of which Angela had scrutinized and criticized every chapter. In the copy Barker gave to her, he quoted the following extract from the Goncourt *Journals*:

Ne rien faire qu'écouter son coeur, et laisser parler son esprit, et laisser venir les rafraîchissements, et laisser marcher le soleil, et laisser le monde aller, et laisser les petites filles tourmenter les chiens qui n'obéient pas.

(Do naught but listen to your heart, and let your soul speak; be refreshed, and watch the sun set; let the world go by, and let the maidens tease their disobedient dogs.)

It is a curious quotation, and suggests a clue to their relationship. Did Angela tease Barker? It is said that Angela led him on like a little poodle, and indeed he literally followed her about everywhere. Barker added, 'Love, blessings and gratitude.' Barker was a dilettante and without her help he probably wouldn't have brought *Watteau* to a successful conclusion.

E. V. Lucas had died the previous year. At the funeral, Edward Knoblock, the dramatist, read Kipling's poem about Sussex, the county which Lucas had loved and made his own. Lucas had bequeathed his cottage at Brittenden in Sussex to a woman friend, who shortly afterwards sold it to Hamilton. Angela told Hamilton: 'A friend of Mother's has had psychic communication with E.V.L. He sent a message to his secretary but none to you.' Nevertheless, Hamilton commissioned a potter to make a plaque in memory of Lucas, which was put up on the wall of the cottage.

During July, when Alfred Knopf was in London, Hamilton invited him, Angela and Barker to dinner at his newly-acquired Sussex cottage. 'I am having my hair washed and set in Alfred's honour,' Angela wrote. 'Do you think we shall talk business a little, or is it to be all gaiety and joie de vivre? Is it a *party*? . . . Gilbert is on a strict diet . . . a plain grilled cutlet or a grilled sole that is *all*—no vegetables or sauces—and he may only drink gin or brandy, poor thing. But I will eat lark's brains with you and drink Tokay.'

Barker drove Angela down. She wore, of course, the black lace mantilla and a frock of floating pastel chiffon. It was said that she looked, and was, at this time, 'sinuously feminine'. It was a day of rejoicing—the last they were all to have for a long time, for war was about to break out.

Angela had already done 'half, a small half', of another novel and, with an unexpected burst of energy, it was finished by the beginning of August. She described it as just like the others, and not so funny as *The Brandons*.

But in fact it was not like any of her previous novels. Although some of the minor characters reappeared, and some of the places recurred, the Barsetshire flavour was absent. *Before Lunch*, as it was called, was a romantic comedy concerning two middle-aged women, a middle-aged man and a young brother and sister. It was her most delicate and atmospheric novel. The three women characters were different aspects of Angela herself; the cumulative effect of this triple self-portrait was elegiac. In the main, she was Catherine Middleton, the middle-aged woman with whom the delicate young man falls in love:

> She would have given a year's life to be the receiver and not the giver. Her longing to step aside for a moment, to lean on a shoulder, to give gratitude as freely as she gave help was very great . . . Good friends she had, but none to whom she spoke much of herself, except in a gentle sardonic way that made them find her good if baffling company.

Angela was still the 'solitary-hearted'.

By the end of the summer she felt completely exhausted. Her doctor advised a long holiday. 'He wanted me to have some vices because they help one to relax. Poor female Trollope—*elle n'est pas capable*—not even of smoking.' She handed in the new novel and went off with Lance to St Jean de Luz in the South of France for three weeks.

Her stay at the Hotel Erléac at St Jean de Luz was peaceful. She returned to London in time to hear Neville Chamberlain's radio announcement that Britain was at war with Germany.

A mass evacuation of children had begun—adults too—which was described as 'The Greatest Organized Movement of Human Population Ever.' Nine of the principal routes out of London were declared one-way streets and banned from ordinary traffic. Children, with labels tied to their coats and gas-masks hanging from their shoulders, boarded trains and coaches for the country, which some of them had never seen before.

Newspapers advised their readers what to do in the event of an air raid, and after twenty years of uneasy peace the streets were once more full of uniforms. The *Daily Mail* reprinted the poem by Kipling which it had published on the outbreak of war twenty five years earlier.

For all we have and are,
For all our children's fate,
Stand up and take the war.
The Hun is at the gate!

Our world has passed away
In wantonness o'erthrown.
There is nothing left today
But fire and steel and stone!

Though all we know depart,
The old Commandments stand:—
'In courage keep your heart.
In strength lift up your hand.'

The German Chargé d'Affaires was photographed smiling and shaking hands with his chauffeur before departing for Germany. Shortly afterwards there was perpetrated an outrage that sent crowds of young men rushing to enlist in the Armed Forces: the liner *Athenia*, full of holidaymakers, was torpedoed by a German submarine in the Atlantic ocean.

Angela helped her parents to dust-sheet the furniture at Pembroke Gardens. Then they departed for the Noel Arms at Chipping Camden in Gloucestershire. 'Nature, banal though it sounds,' wrote Angela, 'is the one comfort, and this country is *heavenly*, and the little town, which I hadn't seen for years, is absolutely unspoiled . . . I expect to be here for some time.'

Gilbert Barker's family house, Stanlake Park, at Twyford in Berkshire, had been invaded by a dozen children from the poorer parts of London, with two teachers who were supposed to be in charge of them. Angela was horrified when she heard about it, because the house was full of valuable old furniture, paintings, and other treasures, not to mention Barker's elderly and infirm parents. Barker had thrown himself into the changed times with zest, and while waiting to be called up had become a warden with the ARP—Air Raid Precautions—and spent every night at a rectory in Wokingham. Petrol, of course, was rationed. He therefore acquired a motorbike, put on a mackintosh and a tweed cap, mounted his motorbike and roared away.

The outbreak of the war was followed by a lull, and people began to take a more realistic view of the situation. Angela made day trips to London, went shopping for warm winter clothing, looked in at Pembroke Gardens. Half London's population had gone. 'I was so frightened that I forgot my latch-key and my gas-mask and dropped everything and was thoroughly ashamed of myself . . . I am a lily-livered coward with a yellow streak.'

She did not stay long at the hotel in Chipping Camden. Apart from the expense it was too far from London, and she moved to Beaconsfield, to be near her friends the Garvins.

'I shall be a P.G. for an indefinite period with a Miss Collins,' Angela wrote. Dorothy Collins had been secretary to G. K. Chesterton, a prominent Roman Catholic. Angela was unsure whether such a milieu would suit her: 'I daresay the spirit of John Knox will sustain me,' she wrote.

The house was Top Meadow, in Beaconsfield, near the local hospital and opposite some film studios. Dorothy had only recently moved there and the house was not yet in order when Angela joined her. It was mainly a 'half-way house' for unmarried mothers, who stayed there until they were in labour, when they moved over to the hospital. Dorothy Collins ran the household with one daily woman and was engaged in war work in the village as well.

Angela neither helped with the washing-up nor made her own bed, and she even left her flat-heeled black leather shoes outside her bedroom door at night and was surprised to find that no one had cleaned them by the morning. Dorothy was soon thinking that her guest was a most inconsiderate woman. It was true that she paid two pounds ten shillings a week, but there *was* a war on. Finally, confusion arose when a vanload of furniture arrived from Dorothy's old home. Hard-pressed, she asked her guest to leave for a few days while order was restored. Angela did leave, but to Dorothy's annoyance and surprise returned the following day. Dorothy could not understand why Angela, who was after all fairly well off, did not spend a week in a nearby hotel, and summed her up as a very selfish woman. Angela merely said, 'Beaconsfield always suits me.'

Angela's earnings from her writings were now substantial. Earlier in the year she had received a cheque from Knopf for nearly $5,000, 'A frightening amount of money,' she commented. And indeed in those days it was quite a sum.

Angela was in the middle of her next novel, and the material she was using was mainly compounded of all the wartime activities of Dorothy Collins and the other women in Beaconsfield. Angela was a fascinated spectator and took in all that she heard and saw.

She was a frequent guest of the Garvins. 'Garve is marvellous—so is the riotous waste in the kitchen, unsubdued by war. They eat more than ever and we are heavily rationed. If all England is a smoking ruin, the kitchen at Gregories will be having eggs-and-bacon and cocoa five times a day. We had a hilarious budget night—Garve always cheers up under certainty—he drank Cointreau and I made poetry and he quoted largely from Wordsworth and Friedrich Habal and sang songs from the Beggar's Opera.'

She suggested to P. P. Howe, Hamilton's partner, that *Before Lunch* should be subtitled *But Read It After Dinner*. He asked her to luncheon. She replied, 'If A. Hitler has offered his peace terms and we have said what we think of him and he begins to bomb us I shan't come. Otherwise, complete with gas-mask (or more likely having forgotten it, as I usually do) and rushing from one ARP shelter to another, you may see America's alas only sixth best-seller . . . appear, a nervous wreck.'

Before Lunch was reviewed in December 1939. It was a quieter novel than its immediate predecessor. *The Times* described it as 'a suite instead of a symphony'. They also compared her to Jane Austen. 'No one would suppose from her novels that the French Revolution and the Napoleonic Wars were contemporary with them . . . She has taken from Miss Austen as well as from Trollope. Longbourn is now much nearer than Barchester . . . Miss Austen was probably right when she dwelt on the Bennets and ignored the Buonapartes.'

Most of the time she now wore black, and her tall dark figure striding through the village was an object of curiosity. Her talent for outspokenness or, one could say, lack of inhibition, increased with the years. She began to lose weight, either through anxiety or through eating less, and she remarked, 'My clothes hang on me like a scarecrow.' She was always happy to go to Oxford, where Lance, at Magdalen, was now an undergraduate.

Hamish Hamilton's spring list in 1940 announced no new Angela Thirkell novel, and she never again achieved her two-novels-a-year output. She contemplated taking up some sort of war work, but her friends implored her to 'go on amusing us, for God's sake, with your books'. She was still surprised and modest about her success. 'I never expect people—I mean real people—to read my books.' Everywhere she went she was asked about her methods of work. 'As a matter of fact,' she would explain, 'I seem to spin things out of my inside like a spider.'

Hamilton was now in the army and expected to be sent abroad. 'I don't intend to indulge in heroics, but I shall think of you with much affection, as always,' Angela wrote. 'And with a gratitude that doesn't forget your kind but firm handling of me ever since we met at Graham's house. I have been very lucky in having a publisher who has been such a good friend. Bless you and much love from A.'

During that Christmas week 1939 Angela paid another visit to a deserted London, and learnt that the bookshops in Oxford had no copies of the Penguin *Wild Strawberries*. She sent a card to her publishers. 'Could you . . . ginger up the book trade in Oxford?'

She left Top Meadow to live in what she called, distastefully, 'rooms', in Beaconsfield. 'I have never lived quite alone before and of course I may go mad or take to the bottle.'

8

'Cheerfulness Breaks In'

By the spring of 1940, Angela's new novel, which she called ironically 'My Great War Novel', was more than half finished. It was a view of the war from the village of Beaconsfield.

She sent Hamilton and his new wife, the former Countess Pallavicini, a copy of her childhood reminiscences, the slender *Three Houses*. It was a strange wedding present, especially from someone so conventional as Angela. 'Here is a book for you. A dull present I admit, but it is the one Real Book I shall ever write, and you liked it years ago, and it led to our very happy (for me) literary partnership, during which, in spite of occasional provocation from both sides, there has *never* been a word or a blow exchanged in anger . . . *Three Houses* comes with all love and blessings to you both, Loving A.' The gift of *Three Houses* from Angela was something special, an intimate and most precious part of herself. Was it the little girl in Angela asking for love?

When she had sent her completed typescript of 'My Great War Novel' to her publisher, she wrote, 'I think this is perhaps as good as I have done . . . As for jackets, I hope that particular form of trouble has been removed by the War . . . Can we make Hitler an excuse for not having jackets?'

At the end of May, in beautiful weather, the Germans drove down the Somme Valley to the Channel, isolating the Allied armies, who withdrew to Dunkirk. A mass rescue by big and little ships was organized and 225,000 men were saved from death or capture. 'The Dunkirk spirit' was the phrase which summarized the heroism and the sacrifice of those involved in this mass exodus of Allied soldiers from the encircling German armies. Angela mentioned this great feat at the end of her novel. 'If we are all dead it won't matter. If we aren't, Dunkirk will not be forgotten . . . I couldn't feel a funny scene at the end.'

Her publisher preferred the title *Cheerfulness Breaks In*. 'I have tried too in my time to be a philosopher,' said Mr Edwards to Samuel Johnson, 'but I don't know how, cheerfulness was always breaking in.'

A typescript had gone to her American publisher, but Howe warned her that they might not like it. In August his fears were confirmed when Angela received the following letter from Knopf:

I have just read carefully *Cheerfulness Breaks In*, and have had another reader, Mr Smith, report on it too. I hope you will not misunderstand me if I write you with great frankness about it, for I think it my duty as a publisher to tell you what we think.

The first half of the book I found, if anything, more readable than your other novels, and that is saying a good deal. But then there creeps into the book increasingly, until you come to the last fifty or seventy-five pages, a note that I am afraid your American readers are going to find a bit startling—an acid quality far bitterer than has ever turned up in your work before . . . Now it happens that only yesterday I was hearing at great length about the behaviour of these evacuated slum children, and I realize that so far as the facts go, you haven't been in the least misrepresented. But for reasons which are fairly obvious, Americans have become pretty sentimental about English children these days—one reason I guess is that you haven't sent over many from the slums, and the papers are full of photographs of the most gorgeous looking young ones. So Americans are going to gather from this book, I'm afraid, that you are a rather upstage and nasty sort of person who checks with the Left Wingers' idea of a member of the British upper classes—which simply isn't true. This is perfectly all right if you want it that way, but it will, I think, adversely affect the sale of this book and your immediate market here. I hope you will sense what I mean and realize that I am not asking you to change the book, or expressing an unfavourable personal opinion of it. I am simply telling you what I think a lot of people who have liked your books are going to feel when they read, or read about, this one.

Another matter is a little more difficult for me to speak about. As a Jew I am not particularly sensitive about how we are pictured in novels. I have met and expressed myself all too frankly about too many unpleasant Jews in my time. But the Warburgs are really laid on too thick—they aren't real people but caricatures, particularly as you put them in the film business with which we over here are pretty familiar. Certain Jews will, of course, object and I'd no doubt hear about it, but I'm not concerned about them and I don't think they'll do you any damage. I think that many Christian readers will.

It would be almost impossible, I think, to eliminate these three characters, or at least, tone down some of their most incredible remarks. Or, if you want to take advantage of present sentiments over here, no less I imagine than on your side, make them naturalized German Aryans, or naturalized any other kind of central European. In any case, believe that this paragraph is written to you purely on professional and not personal grounds.

Now, however, I come to one smaller matter which is largely personal. I would hate to print a book with such objectionable people *geboren* Warburg in it. Because Warburg over here is the name of probably our finest and most universally respected Jewish family. They are mere acquaintances of mine and not in any sense friends, but I would certainly not want, even indirectly, to hurt their feelings, and I think I should come in for much justified reproach if the name stood. You can surely devise one that is more common.

Forgive this long letter and take it as from a friend who wants to sell all the books possible for you and make all he can for you in the process...

Yours ever,
Alfred

After receiving this letter, Angela changed the name of Warburg to Warbury and unburdened her feelings to Howe. 'His [Alfred Knopf's] point of view is so Jewish. My Warburys are alas! only too true and the things they say not overstated in the least . . . if it were really necessary I could make them Christians . . . the Warburys are no more representative of Jews than say Fagin . . . If one is to alter one's characters because one's publisher is a Jew, R.C., Plymouth Brother, or Four Square Evangelist, life will be even more difficult.'

She saw, however, that there was nothing to be gained by upsetting her American publisher. 'I have altered three cracks about Jews, and written Alfred a CHARMING *letter* (though why Alfred, I don't know, he should be Habbakuk) if he knew with what good-natured contempt I have done it he would *frizzle*. But the evacuees must take their luck with the great sloppy-hearted USA public . . . they are far worse than anything I have said and the whole scheme has been a gigantic blunder.'

There was general approval of Angela's adjustments to her text. 'My letter [to Knopf] was really a model,' she assured Howe, 'dignified, apologetic, full of nobility and readiness to oblige.'

She was pleased with the book's wrapper. 'Cheerfulness has broken in charmingly with the dado and the frieze—I am so grateful . . . for jackets break my spirit.' The novel was well-received by the press. When Angela read Straus's review she wrote sardonically, 'Dear Old Ralph is always *so* kind to us girls, and so un-understanding.' The *New Statesman* however, detested her novels. One of their critics wrote, 'Perhaps the next epoch will call for Stakhanovite heroines, then we shall witness an *auto da fé* . . . and the tweeded dummies of this pygmy Barsetshire will be the first to burn.'

In the early summer of 1940, it seemed as if Britain, like France, would fall to the Germans. Squadrons of fighter pilots downed the Luftwaffe in the Battle of Britain. The crucial day was 15 September. Churchill compared it to the Battle of Waterloo. The Fuhrer's planned invasion was 'postponed'.

As the Germans switched to night bombing, the wail of the siren warning of the enemy's approach became a familiar sound. The underground stations were lined with sleeping, swaddled forms. The city woke in the mornings to the sound of the 'all clear' and the work of removing the debris began.

Angela described London as a sad shambles. Houses around Green Park, in Jermyn Street and King Street were still smouldering wrecks, the Red Cross headquarters in St James's Palace were covered in soot. But everyone was 'so good and cheerful'. Clare Mackail was hurt in a raid. Pembroke Gardens was slightly damaged. 'I made a vow never to be nice to *any* foreigner again,' wrote Angela.

Alfred Knopf was not the only person to be offended by some of the characters in *Cheerfulness Breaks In*. The portraits of a state school headmaster and his wife, evacuated with their pupils to a public school in the country, also met with criticism. It was said that she was unkind and inexact. 'You should know,' wrote a critical correspondent from Maida Vale, 'that most London secondary school headmasters are Oxford or Cambridge men and that all are conversant with dinner jackets and sherry. I am speaking from knowledge as I have relations in those professions and a brother who is a senior army officer.' Angela was unrepentant.

She was now, for the first time in her life, a member of a small country community at Beaconsfield, instead of merely a visitor to the 'big house'. The whole village community was united against the enemy, and this broke down or weakened the traditional class barriers.

In *Cheerfulness Breaks In*, the Dean's wife, Mrs Crawley spoke her thoughts:

> Mrs Crawley did her best to be broad-minded about social changes and managed to have faith that the next generation would make the world a little better, but all her broadmindedness could not make her think that it would not be so happy for the people of her own age who had seen the golden Edwardian prime. Whatever happened it would mean eating other people's mental bread and treading strange stairs, and Mrs Crawley sometimes felt that she would like to shut herself up in the Deanery, stop her ears, and there gently decay in a corner, living in a dream of the past.

By February 1941 Angela had written more than half of her next novel, which she confidently expected to finish by the end of March. She wrote the blurb with ease:

> In her latest book Mrs Thirkell is, if we may so express ourselves, more Thirkellish than ever. As escape from the War appears to be impossible, she continues her 'Barsetshire War Survey' ... Cheerfulness goes on breaking in.

Its title was *Northbridge Rectory*, which her friend Sir Humphrey Milford, publisher to the University of Oxford and a distinguished literary figure, thought commonplace. Angela disagreed. For her, it was a good Trollopian title.

Printers' staffs were all under 18 or over 41 or unfit for military service. The proofs of *Northbridge Rectory* were full of printers' errors, which nearly drove Angela demented. 'They have behaved shockingly ... and have made several maddening corrections on their own ... I could kill them. As for my beautiful rendering of the siren ... they have given it up in despair.' Angela's attempt to put the sound of the air raid warning into print was a series of graduated 'ees' and 'ows' around a central explosion of printers' marks. 'Could the printers compose a kind of bouquet +*!? all jumbled together? I admit it is unusual but so is the siren.' The novel opened with one of her most accomplished pieces of descriptive writing, of the High Street of Chipping Camden:

> The High Street with its lovely curve is the whole town. At the

upper end are the gentry houses, still in many cases inhabited by descendants of the wool-staplers, or prosperous graziers who had built them three or four hundred years ago of honey-coloured stone that has weathered to soft greys and browns lightly stained with lichen here and there, the roofs made of thin stone slabs. Just where the street swings round the curve that is known to every tourist, stands the little Town Hall on its twelve stone legs, the little open market place below it. Beyond the Town Hall the houses are newer, late eighteenth and early nineteenth century, flat-fronted, with great sash windows on the ground and first floors . . . A good many of them have fine plaster ceilings and there are one or two circular staircases whose curve is like a reflection of the High Street and the despair of every architect that tries to copy them, though their designer left no name . . . And beyond them the street tails off into the picturesque and insanitary cottages of wood and clay, lath and plaster, white-washed with thatched roofs, descendants of the original mud huts . . . At the end of the High Street is the river. There was a ford hereabouts as long as history can tell . . . the church stands on a little eminence and behind it is the rectory, an ugly but commodious house whose long garden slopes to the river.

As for the jacket, which aimed to sketch 'Northbridge', 'I am no judge,' she said, 'because curiously I cannot visualize *any* of the places I describe . . . it all looks very pleasant.'

Northbridge Rectory was published at the end of August 1941. She liked the look of the book. She also liked several earlier novels which her publisher had reissued in compact grey linen volumes with blue lettering. 'Five shillings is a good selling price . . . the novels of A.T. look extremely impressive,' she wrote.

Reviews of *Cheerfulness Breaks In* were arriving from America. In its toned-down form the book apparently offended no one, but it was only doing moderately well. 'I don't call 10,000 to date—even fair,' complained Angela, 'not their fault—it must seem a bit queer to outsiders.'

Ian Robertson was now Ordinary Seaman O/S P/ JX 263310 Ian Robertson, serving on *HMS Ark Royal*. He had bought, read and enjoyed *Cheerfulness Breaks In*, and wrote to tell Angela so. 'It was very sweet of you to give my foolish scribble a testimonial,' she told him on 7 April 1941. 'I have just finished a new one—totally indistinguishable from the others, which should be out this summer.' She was suffering from writer's cramp and could not use her hand, so Veronica Turleigh, the actress, wrote the letter at her dictation.

Robertson had a friend, Lady Helen Smith, at whose family house, Bere Court, in Hampshire, he spent some of his leaves. Lady Helen admired Angela's novels, expressed a wish to meet her, and invited her to Bere for a weekend. Angela was put in what she called sarcastically, 'that little slip of a room next to the bathroom'; she was accustomed to more royal treatment. Archie Balfour was a fellow-guest. Another member of the household was a Miss Bennet, known as Benny, a retired governess who had formerly taught the family.

Angela and Archie Balfour walked about the park in the fine autumn weather, talked about music, played word games with their hostess after dinner, and made friends with the four children. Angela's pleasure was marred by a consciousness that her clothes did not match the romantic surroundings. 'I feel intensely the need for the proper clothes for certain décors, and this called for something much more silken and flowing than a tweed tailor-made and a camel-hair coat.' She enjoyed the company of the children. She described babies always as 'highly agreeable'.

'Thanks in the first place to you,' she wrote to Robertson, 'I had the most delightful week-end at Bere. I don't know when I've had such a nice time. Lady Helen is such a delicious mixture of kindness, bonhomie, and pretty manners that I was enchanted.' Angela told Robertson that she hoped Lady Helen would invite her again, 'for it is a very happy house. I am more grateful to you than I can say for suggesting the visit originally.'

In the blurb for her next novel, *Marling Hall*, Angela wrote: 'A slight but deeply observed portrait . . . touches a deeper chord than any the author has yet struck.' The model for this portrait was the governess at Bere, Miss Bennet. In *Marling Hall* she was introduced as Miss Bunting, or Bunny. 'A short, spare, grey-haired, elderly woman in a nondescript dark knitted suit, with a piece of black ribbon tied around her faded neck.'

In the character of Miss Bunting, Angela also put a good deal of herself. It was said of Angela that, as she aged, she developed the severity of a strict old-fashioned governess and that she was even spinsterish. She now used a lorgnette—a word she disdained, insisting that it be called a *face à main*—and her manner was didactic.

Marling Hall was finished by February 1942. Howe was almost more enthusiastic about it than any of its predecessors, and Angela was of course immensely relieved and pleased. There was some discussion about the title, but she now felt, without conceit, that it didn't matter very much. 'It is only a label for another bottle from the same cellar.'

To her surprise and pleasure, *Northbridge Rectory* had done far better in America than anybody had expected, and Hamilton was reissuing *The Grateful Sparrow*—which delighted her, for after *Three Houses* it was the favourite of all her books. In addition to her overseas earnings her income from UK sales amounted at this time to the fairly comfortable sum of about £1,500 a year.

' Towards the end of June she was once more put in a rage by the printers' errors. 'Not only have they punctuated to their own taste . . . I counted forty-odd commas *added* by them in 80 pages, but they have made the most ignorant and pretentious emendations and suggestions.' It has been said that Angela Thirkell's sentences were far too long and rambling. Evidently the printers thought so too. 'My apparent eccentricities are deliberate,' she wrote angrily. She did not wish the reader to be unnecessarily interrupted by a lot of commas and short sentences, but to be carried along by her flow of words.

Marling Hall appeared in August. Agate was especially kind again. Mrs Thirkell, he said, 'puts our more portentous novelists to bed'. Angela was exultant, and she gave a 'Marling Lunch' to her friends at Beaconsfield—plovers, prawns, and *spam*, the new wartime food.

When her Hampshire hostess, Lady Helen Smith, read the novel, she was distressed and furious to find in it a portrait of her beloved governess lightly disguised under a very similar name. She was afraid that Benny would discover it, since she was plainly described down to the smallest detail—such as the black velvet bow which she wore in the evening to dress up her scanty grey hair, and the way she would sit on a chair just outside the family circle in the drawing-room.

Miss Bunting had spent forty years of her life in instructing the gilded early youth of England before it went to its preparatory school, sometimes residing in the country mansions of its parents.

[She] had that sense of her own worth that only the old governess and the old nannie possess . . . Sustained by her intimate acquaintance with so many of England's gilded youth and fortified by Debrett, [she] pounced upon every relationship . . . and rejoiced that she knew her Peerage and her Landed Gentry so well.

Lady Helen bought up and destroyed all the copies she could find in the district. And she didn't invite Angela to spend another weekend at Bere. Ian Robertson was equally upset. Miss Bennet, he declared, had been ruthlessly and cruelly pilloried by Angela, and what she had done was unforgivable. The friendship between him and Angela foundered.

Angela's fame continued to spread, and brought, inevitably, requests for the stage, radio and screen rights in her novels—mostly from amateurs. She had no agent and she replied sympathetically and hopefully herself to all these letters. But what at that time touched her most were the letters of appreciation from serving soldiers and prisoners-of-war. In her novels, they said, was depicted the England they were fighting for. Sir John Martin-Harvey, the actor, wrote to tell her that her books had given great pleasure to his blind wife, to whom he read them aloud. Most of them had been turned into braille. A letter from a French admirer addressed her as 'Lady Thirkell'.

Angela was, she said, indifferent to hostile reviews, but that was only her defence against them. Her name, anyway was by now a household word. She was particularly scornful of the *New Statesman*, which invariably wrote hostile reviews of her novels. Angela was unconcerned: her public did not read the *New Statesman*. As long ago as 1941, Philip Toynbee had dismissed her in its pages as 'the safest bet for oblivion,' but she had proved him wrong. The one critic whose views she especially valued was Elizabeth Bowen. 'What a cool mind she has, *very* refreshing. The people who like me attribute to me virtues of which I am unconscious—I hope they are right. As for the people who hate me, I would feel dishonoured by their Red-Left approval.' Angela stoutly maintained that she told the truth.

In the novel she published in 1943, *Growing Up*, Hamilton objected to some of the views she had put into the mouth of the local station-master:

> Changes grieved Mr Beedle, a staunch upholder of the old order, but even more was he grieved that first-class carriages, except on a few long-distance trains, had been abolished . . . the abolition . . . struck to his heart, and Mrs Beedle was able to state with truth that he hadn't never seemed to fancy his supper since. Mr Beedle was loyal to the core . . . his personal sense of shame at having nothing better than third-class to offer to his own local magnates did not lessen with time.

Angela protested that she had merely taken his views from the local

station-masters known to her at Beaconsfield whose views were far
from egalitarian. '*My characters* are Direct Inspiration—and what they
say I report,' was her answer.

'Herewith *Thirkell* 1944,' she announced in January of that year to
Hamilton when she sent him the typescript of *The Headmistress*. She
added: 'I shall be 54 on Sunday. What a very dull age. But I like all
my ages because they are *mine*.'

The new novel extended her war chronicles. New characters were
introduced. 'It is *so* like the rest,' she told Howe, 'except for Heather
Adams of whom I ackcherley found myself getting quite fond.'
Heather Adams was the unattractive and socially gauche daughter of a
self-made industrialist—a character quite unlike the charming well-
bred girls of most of the novels. As time went on, and the chronicles
progressed, Heather Adams and her father, Sam Adams, became more
prominent. It was beginning to be said of Angela that she was more
than a writer of light novels—she was a social historian.

She anticipated the usual wrangle about titles for the next book. 'I do
hate titles. I don't mean Dukes or Marquesses for whom I have an
affection amounting to idolatry.'

A review of *Northbridge Rectory* in a Canadian newspaper, the
Peterborough Examiner pleased her immensely. She sent it to her
publisher.

> If England is to be completely changed, as we are assured it will
> be, why do so many people want to read books about an aspect of
> English life which would not survive a revolution? Second, if county
> society and Old Families are objects of mockery to the young
> Britons of today, why do they lap up these books which glorify these
> things? . . . Mrs Thirkell knows what she is doing better than the
> post-war planners.

The Headmistress was published in December, and was declared by
Ralph Straus 'another brilliant Thirkell'. The social scene in Barsetshire had been developed further. The Belton family, driven into
genteel poverty by an increasing overdraft, let their Palladian mansion,
in which they have lived for five hundred years, to an evacuated
London girls' school. The family discuss the changes in their lives.
Elsa Belton reflects:

'As a matter of fact, it must be much nicer not to be a lady now, because then one would have a lot more friends. Being a lady makes one a bit particular even if one tries not to be . . . I suppose I'm a perfectly beastly snob, but I can't help it.'

Mrs Belton thought of her own youth, so sheltered, among girls of her own sort who might look funny now with their heavy knobs or puffs of hair, their long skirts, their unadorned lips and fingernails, their mother's eye always more or less over them, but were all what she roughly called one's own sort . . . All this mixing might be a good thing, but she felt too old for it and frankly hated it . . .

'It's a queer mixed lot on the Bench now,' said Mr Belton. 'There are men on the Bench that don't know a gamekeeper from a poacher and think kindness pays with young hooligans that steal, and destroy other people's property. There's a man sitting with me now that employs two thousand men at Hogglestock and heaven knows how many more over the other side of Barchester, and dresses like something on the stage. He may be all right, I don't say he isn't, but he throws his weight about and gets petrol when nobody else does, and frankly the less of him I see the better pleased I am.'

'Bad luck, Father,' said Commander Belton sympathetically. 'Of course we do get a few queer fish at the Admiralty, but taking it by and large the Navy isn't too bad. When you're all doing things together everything shakes down.'

'As a matter of fact,' said Charles . . . 'If you get awfully mucky and sweaty with a lot of fellows over your tank, you find they're all right.'

'If only life were one long crisis, everyone would be perfect,' said Mrs Belton.

Mrs Belton's attitude offended a great many readers, particularly the clergy, the bereaved, and those who were putting heroic efforts into winning the war. The incredible atrocities of Belsen and Buchenwald were still to be revealed. Some readers asked, did people like Mrs Belton really want this state of affairs to continue? Angela herself had two sons in the forces.

When Angela's royalty statement arrived in time for Christmas she was astonished. 'Pleased is not the word; I am overcome by the *fantasticness* of the whole thing, that I can't express it. I feel like Marguerite in Faust, "*Est-ce moi? réponds, réponds vite*". Whatever bricks are thrown at publishers I always stand up for them; for where would *us authors* be without their unwinking vigilance?' And when she heard that there was to be an Indian edition of one of her novels, she asked mockingly, 'Do I sign anything or is Our Gracious Permission enough?' She sent her publisher love, 'from Successful and Sardonic Female Trollope'.

'I am giving myself a treat on Tuesday by going to old Rothenstein's Memorial Service,' wrote Angela in February 1945. 'I adore Memorial Services and look upon them as a social function.' But new difficulties cropped up in her life. Dr Mackail suffered a slight stroke early in the year and Margaret Mackail was taken to hospital at Oxford with an inoperable kidney complaint. Angela was distracted with anxiety. Both her elderly parents were dependent upon her and she was far more competent at dealing with these difficulties than either her brother or sister. She made all the arrangements for the care of her parents. For a time, Dr Mackail was in a nursing-home. He was bewildered and unhappy, surrounded by strangers. In desperation, Angela decided that she must re-open the house in Pembroke Gardens and take care of her father herself, with the help of a nurse.

A year earlier, in 1944, her distant cousin Monica Baldwin had written to her. The two women had not met since before the First World War, when both of them had been guests of Monica's uncle Stanley, at Astley Hall. Monica remembered Angela as 'a lovely and attractive girl who had dazzled and rather alarmed me across the dinner-table'. Meanwhile Monica had been a nun in an enclosed convent; but now, after twenty-eight years, she had emerged and was writing a book about her experiences.

Angela described Monica as 'very intelligent and charming . . . utterly unlike a nun'. She suggested that Monica should help her to re-open Pembroke Gardens. Monica agreed and moved in with a Siamese cat, 'the one great love of my post-conventual life'. Angela named the cat Me Wang, a river in Siam. The two women together removed the dust-sheets over the furniture and pictures.

Dr Mackail was brought home. His mind, as far as conversation was concerned, was unimpaired. 'The intellectual standard of Angela's circle was so much above my head that I soon gave up any attempt to be more than an admiring listener and looker-on.' Monica began to find the house rather alarming and did not stay much longer. When she had finished writing the story of her life as a nun, Angela introduced her to Hamilton, who promptly accepted the book.

The next 'Thirkell' was *Miss Bunting*, in which the governess who had played a minor role in *Marling Hall* was promoted to a leading part. In it Angela contrasted the traditional values with post-war attitudes. On the one hand is the delicate daughter of Sir Robert and Lady Fielding—she adores poetry and is not strong enough to go to school, so she has a tutor, Miss Bunting. On the other hand, Heather Adams, a brilliant mathematician is taught by Miss Holly; they represent the contemporary materialistic elements in life and society. The story was set in a village which was rapidly becoming a town.

As may be imagined, the town on the hill did not mix with the town beyond the railway, and society fell tacitly into two groups: the Old Town, consisting of the original inhabitants of the stone houses and aboriginal cottages and work-people, and the New Town, the status of whose citizens was almost indefinable, but may be expressed in the words of Engineer-Admiral Palliser at Hallbury House who . . . remarked that those houses . . . were always changing hands, and so dismissed the whole affair.

This state of affairs was a reflection of what was happening throughout England. In *Miss Bunting* the opposing forces were well and evenly matched. Towards the end of the novel Miss Bunting dies, and Anne Fielding and Heather Adams become friends, while the rich industrialist leaves his non-conformist chapel to worship at the Parish Church of England. One of Angela's characters remarked, 'Read Disraeli's *Two Nations*. Nothing has changed.'

When *Miss Bunting* was published, Elizabeth Bowen wrote, 'If the social historian of the future does not refer to this writer's novels, he will not know his business.' But another critic with wider sympathies remarked, 'Barsetshire is closing in on Mrs Thirkell.' Knopf in America had not liked *Miss Bunting*. Nevertheless, the novel about two middle-aged spinsters and two innocent young girls of different social backgrounds, won many admirers in the States, where sales passed the 16,000 mark. 'Not bad for my "too English" novels!' remarked the author.

Hamilton had now returned from the war. He surprised Angela by a beautiful Christmas present, which was to become an annual event: a specially bound copy of her latest novel. 'I can't thank you enough for the thought and for the trouble that must have gone to the planning of it. It would be an ornament to the library of any nobleman or any gentleman and is now sitting in a bookshelf despising all its clothbound neighbours. It was really *very.*dear of you.'

To add to her pleasure, an old friend of hers, Eric Mitt, a Keeper of Manuscripts at the British Museum, asked for the manuscript; he wanted the Museum to have it. 'O.K. boy!' replied Angela. 'There's fame for you!' she remarked to her friends.

Life was grim at Pembroke Gardens. 'Papa slowly declines and if *he* doesn't die soon, *I* shall,' said Angela.

9

'Peace Breaks Out'

Just before Christmas 1945, Dr Mackail suddenly died. Tributes to the great scholar and humanist, whose last work had been *The Sayings of Christ*, poured into Pembroke Gardens. 'I am submerged in Papa's papers—he destroyed *nothing*,' Angela wrote. 'I destroy everything—almost everything.' Dr Mackail's death deprived Angela of a cherished companion, and her work became ever more important to her. She had plunged into yet another novel, 'which will have cost me my remaining eyesight,' she wrote. She gave it a topical title: *Peace Breaks Out*.

It was a peace which brought Labour to power.

In Barsetshire, Angela recorded what was happening all over the country. Sam Adams, socialist, defeated Sir Robert Fielding M.P., who commented, 'There's nothing so conservative as a good labour man.' Mrs Morland held a contrary view: 'It is really goodbye to everything nice for ever,' she said.

Colin MacInnes and Lance Thirkell returned from the war, and in the summer of 1946 Lance became engaged to Kate Lowinsky. Angela knew Kate's parents, for Katherine, oddly enough, had been born in the same house and even in the same room in which Margaret Mackail had been born; and Kate's parents had rented Stanway during several summers after Barrie's tenancy ceased. As a wedding present, Clare gave Kate the string of coral beads which can be seen in some of Rossetti's and Burne-Jones's paintings.

The wedding took place at the village of Aldbourne near Salisbury in glorious summer weather. After the ceremony the bridal party walked through the village. Angela wore a black tailor-made suit, black shoes, and a black hat trimmed with a black-and-white feather. She was in mourning for the married state but in any case clothes could only be bought with coupons. She was exhausted; she had had too much excitement and felt like a holiday, so she accompanied Lance and Kate to Crans-sur-Sierre in Switzerland to spend part of the honeymoon with them. This seemed to her a perfectly natural thing to do.

Margaret Mackail was now more or less an invalid. 'Mother has a fine nuisance-value,' wrote Angela, 'and criticizes everything and everybody.' For long periods Mrs Mackail just sat about in Pembroke Gardens and refused to speak to Angela at all. 'Time we were all dead,' wrote Angela, 'though I daresay Heaven would be just as bad'.

The autumn, however, was enlivened by a visit to the theatre to see a new revue at the Piccadilly Theatre, *Sigh No More*. Most of the material was by Noel Coward but there was one song written by Joyce Grenfell with music by Richard Addinsell, *Oh! Mr du Maurier*, in which the Pre-Raphaelites were satirized:

I have stood for Mr Millais, and I've sat for Madox Brown;
I've been graceful for D. G. Rossetti, in a florrissy Morrissy gown.
I seem to delight each Pre-Raphaelite, Mister Holman Hunt takes
 me to lunch;
I've been done in half-tones by Sir Edward Burne-Jones, but I've
 never appeared in *Punch*.

Angela was greatly amused by it, and wrote a fan postcard to Joyce Grenfell. She began the communication with the words, 'Talented creature!' Joyce Grenfell recalled that she said 'kind and generous things that I can remember enjoying and being warmed by'. Afterwards the two women used to meet while shopping in the King's Road and they occasionally had tea together. Angela wrote: 'The stream may still be running underground . . . the PRB may yet be known by its fruits.'

Another novel: *Private Enterprise*. The title reflected her political opinions which she put into the mouths of most of her characters. Barsetshire had now become for her more than a literary terrain; it was also a means of escape from post-war England and the author's personal problems. She went thankfully to Barsetshire now. In the blurb she wrote: 'The first post-war summer, with its strong resemblance to a winter of discontent, is providing a full helping of the horrors of peace. Barsetshire complains with the rest of us, but cheerfulness keeps breaking in, as ever, and kindliness, and wit.'

A great many loyal readers could not agree. They had not found much kindliness in *Private Enterprise*. With each book, the acid note in her work had become more marked. It was also reflected in her face. People who knew her, said she looked like 'a junior witch', with 'a smile that cut like a knife'. And in her conversation. 'The once-lovely mouth could be seen twisting rapidly, forming poisonous words.' When they issued forth, they stung her hearers. Somewhere, on the road to success, Angela had parted company with most of her kindliness. Her son Colin put it bluntly: 'The whole of her writing years were those when she had ceased to love the world'. This is not quite true. It was the Conservatives' defeat at the general election that marked a turning point in her work. The character Lord Stoke says in *Peace Breaks Out*, 'World's got to go on somehow.' And another character, Lady Graham, says: 'But you will write another book, Mrs Morland, won't you?' 'Mrs Morland', i.e. Angela, did write another novel—in fact, several. But by now the loss of kindliness was manifest. And in her fan mail there were an increasing number of what she called 'hate letters'.

To her great surprise, she received just before Christmas 1946 a letter of appreciation accompanying a parcel from Margaret Mitchell, the author of *Gone With The Wind*, from America. Angela said that it made her very conceited. Of *Gone With The Wind*, she said that 'once taken up, you cannot put it down, and once laid down, nothing would ever induce you to take it up again'. Margaret Mitchell had long admired the novels of Angela Thirkell. For more than a year her husband, John Marsh, had been seriously ill. 'For many months I read him a chapter from one of Miss Thirkell's books every night,' wrote Margaret Mitchell. 'He says they saved his life . . . I hope he is out of danger, so I take this occasion to try and send something to Miss Thirkell as a token of both genuine and serious appreciation of her books and what they have meant to me and my husband during a very worrying year.' There were still food shortages in Britain at that time, and the parcel that Margaret Mitchell sent to Angela consisted of 'a big fruit cake and a big can of anchovies, a box of candy, guava jelly in cans, liver pâté in cans, mushrooms in butter—also in cans, canned tomato sauce with onions'. It was so large and heavy that Margaret Mitchell could not carry it alone to the post office.

Angela was greatly touched by the gesture and much enjoyed the contents of the parcel. A lively correspondence sprang up between the two women. Margaret Mitchell 'seems to be a nice ordinary woman just like me,' Angela wrote. She tried to discuss *Gone With The Wind* with her, asking in particular whether Rhett Butler ever returned to Scarlett O'Hara; but the author of that celebrated southern novel was not to be drawn.

To Margaret Mitchell's pleasure, a prominent American literary critic, Isabel Paterson, wrote an appreciation of the Thirkell novels for the *New York Herald Tribune*. This sparked off a correspondence in its columns on the subject of the 'Bishop of Barchester' and Angela's novels in general. The feud between the bishop's palace and the deanery had been set by Trollope, although most of Angela's readers were unfamiliar with Trollope's novels and this tradition.

By February, *T 1947* was ready and typed. Angela was pleased with it, although conscious of what she called too many mannerisms in the text. She was planning to go to USA and Canada in April. A few weeks before she left for the States she received a letter from Professor Gordon Haight, who was researching on George Eliot. Haight had been working on George Eliot since 1933, and had already published one book on her.

'Do any of your young people read her?' Angela asked him. 'What a power she was in her day.' Were there any George Eliot letters or references among her mother's papers? Angela told him that it was not at all easy for her to trouble her aged mother. 'If I hear of anything I will let you know—but fear it is a useless quest.'

Margaret Mackail recalled that George Eliot used to wear a black lace mantilla, sometimes fastened with a cameo brooch. She believed it was somewhere among her treasures. The brooch was found, with a note in Lady Burne-Jones's handwriting authenticating it. Angela sailed for America in the Queen Elizabeth, taking the brooch with her.

In New York she had dinner with Alfred and Blanche Knopf and met their son. New York was shrouded in snow and a blizzard raged. Angela remarked, 'Here there are no lions and I find myself a small lioness.' From New York, she went to Boston to stay with her old friend Miss Gaskell Norton; then on to Canada to meet for the first time her two grandchildren, Susan and Michael McInnes. From Canada she wrote to Haight, offering him the 'rather depressing cameo brooch', which had belonged to George Eliot. 'If it would be of any interest to you, I would gladly let you have it, as I would never wear it.' Haight wrote an enthusiastic acceptance, and what had begun as a polite academic enquiry ripened into friendship.

On her return to the States Angela met Gordon Haight and his wife Mary and gave them the cameo brooch. She learnt that it was mentioned in George Eliot's correspondence, which Haight was editing. Angela, for her part, was able to supply Haight with a recollection of John Cross, whom George Eliot had married after George Lewes's death. 'I have him most distinctly in my memory's eye in his neat blacks as befits a London banker, with his curly white beard, and such charming manners to the stout growing up girl I was then.'

She heard of more Eliot letters through a woman who worked for an estate agent; they belonged to the woman's mother, but before Angela could get to them, she incomprehensibly destroyed them. 'One doesn't know what to say, nor what to do about the question of letters. I sometimes feel that they A L L should be destroyed . . . But where is one to draw the line between the personal and what will interest or help posterity?'

The day of her return to London, her new granddaughter, Georgiana Thirkell was born. 'I have come back to a welter of life-duties,' she wrote. 'Lance is alone as the "daily" walked out on them just before the baby was born, and my devil of a cook goes off to-morrow for a month and Mother and her nurse are at loggerheads and Old Mrs Thirkell has to be and do sixty people and things at once.' Victor Hugo, she declared, would have written '*quite* differently if he had to look after the little darlings . . . George Eliot didn't know what *life* was.'

In September, she was trying to begin *Thirkell 1948*, but was showing such symptoms of strain and exhaustion that Colin and Lance insisted that she leave Pembroke Gardens. She spent a few weeks in Bath, and on her return to London, she stayed at 10 Bywater Street, Lance's house, while her son and daughter-in-law Kate were in Budapest. She began to look for a house or a flat of her own. 'It is high time, for I am en train for a really spectacular breakdown after 2½ years of dotty and dying parents,' she wrote.

After so many years under her parents' roof, the little house in Bywater Street seemed strange and a little bare—the Thirkells had taken some of their furniture to Hungary with them. Angela commented wryly, 'All my things are still in Australia!' But she was able to get on with her next novel. 'We are in great trouble, as we don't know who is going to marry whom', she wrote absorbed.

It gave her a feeling of immense pride to receive an invitation to the wedding of Princess Elizabeth to Lieutenant Philip Mountbatten. The royal family, it was said, were among her greatest fans. Among the silk and lace, and jewellery-laden women, Angela wore her customary black tailor-made suit, flat-heeled black shoes, and the small black hat with the black-and-white feathers.

Angela spent Christmas 1947 at Stanlake Park with Gilbert Barker and his father—they promised to have the central heating full on—and Angela returned to Bywater Street to criticize a number of foreign translations of her novels. 'The German woman is a pretentious bore,' she wrote of the translator of *Cheerfulness Breaks In*. 'I am really serious about seeing translations before they are passed, if in French, German or Italian—I never saw her *Cheerfulness* and I feel sure from her letter that there will be more than one complete misunderstanding of ME and the English.' To her surprise, the name of her French translator, Marguerite Scialtiel, was familiar to her. She remembered from her youth a Mlle Scialtiel who used to recite French poetry in Edwardian drawing-rooms. Was it the same person? It was. They corresponded but did not meet.

She attended a lecture on Tennyson given by John Betjeman to the English Association. 'He was gibbering with nerves and it was not good, but he read aloud delightfully. I had him back for a drink afterwards with one or two people and he got so excited that he took us all to dinner at the Café Royal—so you see going to lectures at learned societies is sometimes rewarded.'

In April 1948 she wrote that she was '*very old* and racked with *lumbago*'. But in spite of all her aches and pains her work was proceeding. She was now succumbing fairly regularly to winter attacks of bronchitis, and wrote in bed, or sitting in a chair, wearing a fur coat, wrapped in rugs, a hot-water bottle on her lap, with the electric fire on.

Her sales were falling slightly. 'This I quite expected,' she wrote, 'owing to the general stagnation of everything . . . I expect there will be more slump before we die.' But she was cheered by a visit from Monica Baldwin, who had become, through her *I Leap Over the Wall*, an overnight celebrity. Miss Baldwin was now settled in a cottage in Cornwall and reported that the black magician Aleister Crowley had performed a black mass nearby. 'She says it is Mortal Sin,' reported Angela, 'and I say it is just *damn silly*.'

In late September, in her fifty-ninth year, she finally found the flat she wanted. 'I am in negotiation for a delightful flat in Cheyne Walk on the nursery floor of one of the loveliest houses.' It faced the Thames and the whole area was steeped in literary and art history. The neighbouring houses all had most precious associations with the past. Rossetti, Morris, Sargent, Wilde and many other famous figures from the near and distant past had lived in the vicinity. To crown her pleasure, she discovered that George Eliot, her grandmother's great friend, had lived in the house, though not for more than a few weeks before her death. It was the house which George Eliot, at the age of sixty-two, and her young husband, John Cross, had bought. 'A very pleasant and airy perspective,' Angela wrote.

Angela moved in without delay. The staircase, walls, and ceiling had been decorated, so it was believed, by Thornhill, 'with gods and goddesses on clouds'.

She received invitations from Princeton, Columbia, Yale and Harvard to lecture on any subject she chose. 'Fee only $200, but I would get hospitality and combine it with Canada ... It sounds a Good Thing to me,' she wrote.

Angela's 1948 novel, *Love Among The Ruins*, named from a picture by Burne-Jones—but the title also fitted post-war England—was not a great success. There were too many endless and aimless conversations and the novel was far too long. A critic pointed out that one sentence contained no less than 250 words. The *New Statesman* slighted it as usual; the *Times Literary Supplement* too.

Angela had included in the text part of a letter of criticism she had received from a Miss Vera Telfer. Angela called the writer 'Miss V. Lefter'. Miss Telfer's solicitors wrote to Hamilton and threatened a libel action. The case was settled out of court, but Angela was obliged to apologize and pay a share of the legal costs. Hamilton agreed to excise the offending passage in subsequent editions. In a later novel, she wrote some lampoons on Sir Stafford Cripps, the Minister of Food, calling him 'Kripps'. 'Even as I write his loathsome name a ladder, nay a double ladder, has just rushed down my stocking,' she wrote. She was persuaded to delete the 'Kripps' lampoons.

She was invited to attend the opening of the Morris Gallery at Walthamstow. She went there in a mood of conflict, for she had remembered that Morris, her grandfather's friend and colleague was a socialist, and none other than Clement Attlee, the Prime Minister, whom she heartily disliked, was to perform the opening ceremony. In his speech, to her great satisfaction, he misquoted Kipling, a fact which she reported as 'Mrs Morland' in her next novel.

In April 1949, Angela again visited America, travelling on the *Queen Mary*. She spent six days in New York, staying at the Cosmopolitan Club. 'I saw several million magazine people, all women and *most* agreeable,' she wrote. Then to Boston and Miss Gaskell Norton.

'Like millions of Americans, we have never left England,' one American woman told her. 'When I was a little girl "stone" was pronounced "stun" in our local patois ... we brought the language and pronunciation of the county from which we came. Is the sound "stun" familiar to you?' Everywhere she went in America, her English accent gave pleasure. One of the journalists interviewing her asked her about this. Angela explained: 'When I was young, I was always surrounded by people who spoke correctly.'

Bennet Cerf's column in the *Saturday Review* carried an anecdote about an indignant woman being turned away from a library which had no Thirkell novels available. 'I thought this was a genuine Thirkellating library,' she was reported as saying. This witticism led some of Angela's American fans to form groups calling themselves 'Thirkell Circles'.

At Yale, Princeton, Harvard and Columbia she was in her element. One would have expected her to speak on an English writer but she chose to speak about Dumas père. It was a talk which she had given earlier in London to the English Association, to a markedly appreciative audience. Not only had they cheered, but, Angela noted happily, even Dame Edith Sitwell had laughed. She believed that no one living knew Dumas' works as intimately as she did, and in her talk she traced the influence on Dumas of Walter Scott. 'It was really all clowning,' she said, but it was 'great fun and a very sympathetic audience'. The Haights were her hosts at Yale. They surrounded her with comfort and attention and made her thoroughly happy. Angela wrote, 'U.S.A. is the only place that I feel at all at home in, out of England.'

With her she took the manuscript of *Private Enterprise*. Haight had requested one of her manuscripts for the university library. Once again, she was amazed. 'It never occurred to me before that anyone would want the illegible pencillings when they could read a nice printed book,' she wrote. 'Nobody will ever look at it again . . . nor do I much care, for I write my books to earn my living, and it is only when they are in print and selling that they are real.' Her income from her writing was now considerable and she no longer needed to write in order to live. She wrote because she had to and she loved the appreciation of her many readers; it was the most important thing in her life, but she maintained the myth of her poverty.

An American academic, Bradford Booth, at the University of Los Angeles was editing the *Journal of Victorian Fiction*, formerly *The Trollopian*. Angela accepted an invitation to be on the editorial board and was asked to contribute. She chose to write on the neglected novels of Henry Kingsley, the brother of Charles. 'I wanted to draw people's attention to him.' She loved in particular *The Hillyars and the Burtons* with its evocation of the Chelsea she had known as a child. Her strong attachment to the flawed and little known novels of Henry Kingsley was partly due to the fact that he too had lived in Australia where his house was now a place of pilgrimage. One incident in his novel *Ravenshoe* concerned a boy playing a game in the street and was so vivid to her that whenever she passed the actual spot by the church in Eaton Square, she looked for the mark on the wall the boy had made. She borrowed several incidents from Henry Kingsley's novels, and also some of the folklore, for example the case of the witch who appears in the form of a black hare.

From America she went to Canada. It saddened her to see her son Graham so Americanized. She now had three Canadian grandchildren, who were, she said, 'darlings . . . plenty of good looks'; but she did not approve entirely of the way they were being brought up, 'in the school of self-expression'. The baby, Michael, won her heart, as babies always did. 'A good, fat, placid angel, ready to laugh at anything and entertaining himself by the hour.' Canada was too provincial for her tastes. 'No arts of any kind—no theatre—social life is small . . . the shops can hardly be called shops.'

In July, she returned to London on the Empress of France, vowing that she would never visit Canada again. 'Next time I want a change I shall go to Clacton—it could hardly be duller and would be less expensive.'

In the autumn *The Old Bank House*, all of 136,000 words long, was published. 'The prevailing note is still kindliness spiced with wit. Though it must be admitted that the note tends to tremble at the mention of Them,' she wrote in the blurb. By 'Them' she meant the Labour government.

David Gurney took photographs of her. 'It is high time I looked my age in my photographs,' she wrote, but she certainly did not look her age. Again, she wore the black lace mantilla, and the photograph was used to illustrate the review of her novel by Richard Church in *John O'London's Weekly*. Church declared: 'The book is a social document of contemporary account.'

'Sam Adams, M.P.' goes from strength to strength. He buys a period house, is accepted by the gentry, and becomes engaged to the spinster daughter of the squire of Marling Hall. His own daughter, Heather, has different aspirations; she does not particularly want to belong to the gentry. She marries Ted Pilward, the son of a prosperous brewer. Their children, declared Angela, would never be accepted by the gentry.

In *The Old Bank House* she introduced the rare and repellent plant *Palafox Borealis*, which flowers only once every seven years and arouses the envy of other gardeners in the county:

a clump of rather ugly serrated leaves, fleshy and covered with a kind of whitish bristles as if they had forgotten to shave, from which rose a short grey-green stalk crowned by a sticky knob from which depended, apparently, three strips of housemaid's flannel.

The character of Sam Adams was admired by many, including Professor Haight. 'I became *very* fond of Mr Adams too,' Angela told him. 'And the rum thing is that *I* didn't do it, he literally raised *himself* by his own exertions and his general probity and I only chronicled—I can't explain this—but characters do get out of hand. I wonder if G[eorge] E[liot]'s did?'

She wrote to the London County Council, proposing that they put up one of their blue plaques on the wall of the house in Cheyne Walk, telling the world that George Eliot had lived and died there. In due course the plaque was erected and unveiled, to Angela's great pride.

In January 1950, Angela was taken to see *A King's Rhapsody* by Ivor Novello, whose music she loved. She was astounded to see that among the cast was 'Madame Koska, a dressmaker'. Madame Koska was the name Angela had given to the character of a dressmaker in 'Mrs Morland's' novels. After the performance, Angela went backstage to see Novello, who confessed to being a great admirer of hers. Yes, he used the name she had invented. 'Did I mind his having used the name?' she echoed. She was absolutely thrilled. 'It was the Night of my Life . . . I have never been so complimented,' she wrote.

In spite of fatigue and the annual bout of bronchitis, she was hard at work. 'What I need is a Protector,' she wrote; 'but Heaven evidently thinks that having looked after myself and boys for the last thirty years I can jolly well go on.' She was resigned to her falling sales. The competition of television had had a disastrous effect on the sales of all books.

'I shall go on turning the handle and hope for the best while undoubtedly expecting the worst. It is my only way of earning money . . . we must go on.'

In the autumn she spent a few weeks in Bath. The Bath musical festival had been inaugurated and she was enraptured by the singing of Flagstad who 'unleashed her *magnificent* organ in the Passion and in the Schlagdoch cantata . . . It fascinated me to watch that magnificent voice with apparently no effort . . . with the added and immense charm of a so handsome head and throat.' Angela was a guest at the mayoral reception in the Guildhall, 'the finest city room I have ever seen with lustres unequalled anywhere for shape and for rainbow lights in every piece of glass'. And in this superb setting, she was approached by the admiring Bishop of Bath and Wells. He told her how much he liked her novels and how true her pictures of the clergy were, and invited her to be his guest at the Palace in Wells when she was next in the West Country.

The book critic of the *Church Times* had detected an error in *County Chronicle*, the novel Angela published in 1951:

> I have a bone to pick with Miss Thirkell. In this otherwise excellent entertainment, I came across the sentence, 'The Church of England does not hold with confession (except for the amiable eccentrics who *she* in her wisdom keeps within her fold)'. Normally Miss Thirkell is well-informed on matters ecclesiastical; such an error in a matter of fact is inexcusable. Miss Thirkell can hardly maintain that the Prayer Book shows any discountenance to the practice of confession, and if she speaks mainly of authority in the Church of England (other than a few admitted eccentrics) who hold recourse to the Sacrament of penance unlawful or universally undesirable? Can it be that the only authority for this statement is Miss Thirkell herself? She seems to have been caught tripping—my typewriter almost refused to write the second P.

Angela apologized for her error. At the same time she informed the reviewer that she was a grandmother and *Mrs* Thirkell. Many of her most loyal fans were clergymen, and most of them praised her for drawing portraits of real and sympathetic parsons. In addition they and their families enjoyed identifying the innumerable literary quotations and allusions in her novels. In her post-war books she introduced a new-style Church of England parson. 'Mr Parkinson' had not been educated at a public school; he had no private means and his children attended a state school. Gradually, in the chronicles, Parkinson and his family became accepted into the middle-class county families; they were 'shiningly and unself-consciously good'. The *Church Times* devoted a long article to the clergymen created by English women novelists: Charlotte Yonge, George Eliot, Charlotte Brontë, and the supreme creator of the famous 'Mr Collins', Jane Austen. Angela was not among this illustrious company, although her 'Tubby Fewling', 'Mr Moxon', 'Dr Thomas', 'Mr Parkinson', and the 'Colonial Bishop of

Mngangaland'—all clergymen—were in the same great tradition. 'How very good and sane English books about the life and surroundings of the clergy are, and so humane,' she wrote.

After the criticism in the *Church Times*, she decided to seek the advice of the Reverend Peter Dennis of Gateshead-on-Tyne. She had never met Mr Dennis, but he was one of her clerical fans. And she sent him, to his surprise, the entire typescript of her latest novel for him to check. For the love of her, he readily complied. When the novel was published, one of the first copies was posted to him, inscribed 'to my clerical adviser'. The partnership continued.

In her novels—and indeed in her conversation—she regularly quoted from the Bible, which she frequently read. During her country-house visits, she usually went to church, and upbraided her hosts if they did not accompany her. She grew to love the liturgy with a passionate sincerity, and deplored the changes that were taking place in the church services. 'The way they "muck" it up and have the wrong tunes is literally driving me away from the fold.' She wrote furiously to the newspapers on the subject. The quality of spoken English as broadcast by the BBC also incurred her wrath and she spent hours making lists of mispronounced words. More angry letters were dispatched. 'Always the governess,' she confessed.

A Mrs Margaret Bird in *County Chronicle* detected a number of errors, and wrote to Angela. They were in the nature of anomalies in the complicated family relationships in the Barsetshire novels. For example, one couple were expecting a child before they were married, an unthinkable situation in a novel by Mrs Thirkell. 'I've never had a secretary—it is all done by hand,' Angela replied in her letter of thanks and apology. 'I always miss my old father. He had your quick ear and eye for discrepancies and it was the greatest help to me. People in books are as muddling as one's own friends.'

Margaret Bird was a trained secretary. She was soon typing Angela's manuscripts as well as performing the valuable service of reading the work for errors and omissions. Angela explained her method:

I register Book I (I write in excercise books) to you and you acknowledge it as quickly as possible. I have one top copy on *good* paper and two carbons on thinner paper (but not 'flimsies'). Then if you will return the MS together with 2 typescripts, I shall register Book 2 to you. When you have done Book 2 you send me your two top copies and also the second copy of Book 1.

She acknowledged that the method was fussy, 'but it means that there is only *one* point at which a book could be lost—while in the registered post from me to you'. She worried a good deal when the manuscript was on its way to Mrs Bird, for she had no copy of it.

Angela wrote her novels in ordinary red exercise books, which became less and less available. One day she walked determinedly all round Chelsea in search of them. When she did find a new stock of them, to her annoyance they did not contain the same number of pages and the price had gone up to half-a-crown.

Margaret Bird was a frequent visitor to Cheyne Walk, when she and Angela would 'go to Barsetshire'. 'I should like to think that it waits for me somewhere, with all the old friends alive and as they were,' she wrote. 'And perhaps Mr Trollope among them, fresh from his desk, or the hunting field, so that I may thank him as best I can for what he has given us.'

In 1950, Angela was asked to write an introduction to a new edition of Mrs Gaskell's *Cranford*. The editor described her essay as admirable but rambling all over the place. And to her pleasure and satisfaction, she heard from the Oxford University Press that *Three Houses*, her first book, was still in print and regularly in demand. Geoffrey Cumberlege of OUP wrote: 'I think I can say that there are very few publishers who would have kept the book on all these years.' Angela commented tartly, 'I think I can say that there are very few books which would have sold for 19 years on their merits alone.'

She spent August Bank Holiday with Lady Milner at her house in Hawkhurst in Sussex. Angela always enjoyed seeing nearby the ancient and lovely castle of Bodiam. The two women talked about old times. The biography of Rudyard Kipling by Hilton Brown and the 'peculiarities' of the Kipling family were much discussed. Lady Milner was one of the few people that Kipling's daughter Elsie admitted to the family circle. 'All that family, including of course, Lady Milner, are *characters*,' Angela said. Among Angela's speaking engagements that year was a talk to Lady Milner's Women's Institute, the Horatian Society's annual dinner and the London Library's Annual General Meeting. 'I have a strong suspicion that I am looked upon as a useful buffoon,' she wrote. 'If this is so, I shall use to the full the buffoon's privilege of saying exactly what comes into his or her head.'

The lease of the flat in Cheyne Walk was unhappily a short one. Obliged to look for another home, she contemplated leaving London for a cottage in the country as her mythical 'Mrs Morland' had done.

London had changed and was full of foreigners, she said. But she could not leave it. 'It is hellish but one's own old home and all one's friends are there.'

She worked busily at her next novel, and also at a long short-story to be serialized in *Homes and Gardens*. She was enraged to find that it was mistakenly advertised as 'A New Novel by Angela Thirkell' and she blamed the editor, who, she declared, 'was really impossible to deal with as she is full of ideas and very careless and inaccurate.'

She spoke to Townswomen's Guilds and to Working Men's Clubs, and at the book exhibition in Grosvenor House, Park Lane. 'It is a dreadful sight to see so many books in one place and to know how few of them are worth writing,' she commented afterwards. She went to the West Country again, where she had been asked to give a number of talks. 'It will include a weekend with friends who still have a *mansion* and what is more, letter-paper with a steel engraving of the house,' she wrote loftily. She addressed the Bristol University Arts Faculty Club on the art of fiction, and also spoke at Girton College, Cambridge. 'What a nice lot of girls there, and what *are* they going to do? Every one of them wants a job.' She stayed in the college and was enraptured by the glass and newly-cleaned stone of King's College Chapel. As for Girton, 'it is a *perfect* women's idea of life. Bitterly cold, endless tiled corridors, one bathroom to every 600 residents, tepid coffee, tepid boiled eggs. But they all love it, bless them.'

Angela especially enjoyed speaking to university groups, conscious that she herself had not had an academic career. She believed that a university training would have turned her into a pedant and inhibited her creativity. 'Thank God I was never educated!' she would say.

10

'Old Mrs T'

The year 1951 saw the Festival of Britain, a hundred years after the Great Exhibition of 1851. At the first concert in the Royal Festival Hall, the King, the Queen, Princess Elizabeth, Prince Philip and Princess Margaret were present. Angela treated the events with the greatest scorn, but she agreed nevertheless to be interviewed on the 'telecinema', which was part of the celebrations.

It was a marvellous experience . . . exactly what I had expected. One conceited mass of expensive idiocy, plastics, transparencies, cigarette ends, waste paper, well-advertised W.C.s, folly, extravagance and boredom . . . Outside the telecinema was a long queue which I am told is there all day and all night. Once over the sacred threshold we were wafted up by a manly young pansy to the first floor where I found Bruce Belfrage, the compère for the show. We had both been refugees at Beaconsfield during the war . . . He had a sports coat, the lapels bound with leather, and it was all very perfect. The heat intense, with million watt lights everywhere, and [he] said the electric people work in anything from 95 to 105 degrees all the time; sweated labour I call it. Then BB sat himself on what is known in refined circles as a couch, at right angles to a kind of television set in which he could see himself, and talked in a bland and reassuring way to his audience . . . and then to his surprise there was Old Mrs T. So I sat by him and we 'chatted' just like royalty. I got in a few cracks.

The audience laughed as soon as she said one of her catch-words, 'Ackcherley'. She was voted a great success.

In May she signed a lease for a three-storey terrace house in Shawfield Street, just off the King's Road. It was to be, she declared, 'my *last* home'. While moving in, she fell down the front steps and hurt her back and her leg, but not seriously.

During the autumn she broadcast for Columbia radio to America, and sent loving messages to all her fans who might be listening. A review of her last book by 'someone called Lasky' brought a rush to her defence. She had never heard of this critic, and she was moved by her readers' love for her. 'I had to write and tell you how cross it made me,' wrote one admirer. 'Tiresome creature; I think she must be a socialist.' Marghanita Laski had written of the novel's 'high-class grumbling . . . [a] sense of grievance that is rapidly overwhelming her sense of fun'. Angela wrote, 'I remain calm.' The novel was *The Duke's Daughter*, an echo of Trollope's *The Duke's Children*. She chose the following epigraph:

> *Les gens du monde se representent volontiers les livres comme une espèce de cube dont une face est enlevée, si bien que l'auteur se depêche de 'faire entrer' dedans les personnes qu'il rencontre.*
>
> Proust.

(Society people think that books are a sort of cube, one side of which is opened so that the author can hurry to let into the box the people he meets.)

Towards the end of *The Duke's Daughter*, she wrote a sort of reprise in which many of the earlier characters were re-introduced briefly, as if the novel were, indeed, a box of conjuring tricks.

In 1952, *Happy Returns* was published. The Conservative Party was re-elected to power; hence the title. By now she was aware how important Barsetshire was to her personally. She explained, in the guise of Mrs Morland, that she was 'in the company of people who . . . were almost as real to her as her old friends; people to whose conversation she listened intently . . . often sorely thwarted by her own roving ungovernable mind which would stray.' The characters who were real friends to her were also real friends to her readers. A lonely schoolmistress wrote to say that when she scanned the obituaries and her eye caught the name of one of the Barsetshire families she feared for a moment that it was a real friend who had died.

Jutland Cottage, 1953, is a very simple Cinderella story. The heroine is an impoverished spinster daughter of a retired admiral—plain, shapeless, and over forty. In it, one of Angela's most glamorous young women, Rose Fairweather, takes poor Margot in hand. They shop for a new corset and a twin-set, and visit a good tailor and a hairdresser. Rose gives Margot a string of artificial pearls. The end finds Margot engaged to a rich market gardener. There is much truth in the character of Margot, for all over England there were, and are, women like Margot Phelps.

In 1953, after long years as a permanent invalid, Margaret Mackail died. Angela wrote to Gordon Haight, 'Oh to go out with a *bang*!' She spent weeks sorting out papers and belongings. 'I hope to leave no papers when I die, and to spend the rest of eternity reading new Scotts and Dickenses.' The accumulation of letters and papers oppressed her. 'Whenever I opened a drawer or a chest I found more—many of them were letters between my parents, carefully docketed and marked *destroy*. Oh why the *hell* did they *not* destroy. I have had to tear and tear till my fingers ached . . . I worked among them till nearly demented . . . Now all is cleared, but I am on the edge of a bad breakdown.' She found some letters from John Ruskin to her mother, 'the kind of letter that Mr Ruskin ought not to have written to a young girl,' she wrote, and quickly burned them.

One result highly gratifying to Haight was the discovery of some George Eliot letters, which she sent off to him. 'I am glad to think of them being in good hands . . . One dated March 20th 1873 is to my grandfather; all the rest are to my grandmother. The last is from John Cross to tell her of G.E.'s death'. And after that, Angela collapsed with mental strain and physical fatigue. She was ordered to a nursing-home. The clearing of her parents' house, she maintained, was a task from which she never really recovered.

In 1954, *What Did It Mean?* was published. The enigmatic title cloaked the mixture as before. In it she summed up her feelings about the country society she wrote about: 'Some families gently came up while others as gently declined . . . These are things that no Gotha Almanach can fathom and go partly by centuries of unwritten custom and partly, we believe, by what English cottages feel.' Gradually, more and more of her childhood memories crept into her novels and remarks were put into the mouths of quite unsuitable characters. Incidents from the earlier novels were recalled and repeated *ad nauseam*. 'Everything gets queerer and queerer,' she told Margaret Bird, 'and perhaps my writing has too . . . It gets worse and worse, largely through *fatigue*.' What bewildered her most were the restrictions on length that the post-war economy dictated. She found it almost impossible to write to limits; the computation of words was beyond her. Margaret Bird helped her as much as she could. 'When one is young,' Angela told her, 'one can do so much more than when one is older. When I think what I did in Australia between 1920 and 1930 . . . I often wonder why I am alive. I might have been aliver had not all this happened, but anyway it did . . . One gets through it with courage and goodwill—but one leaves some of one's fleece in the hedge.'

To her aches and pains, and annual bronchitis, was added failing memory.

She wrote an introduction to Thackeray's *The Newcomes*, but was extremely indignant about Edward Ardizzone's illustrations. He was not, in her view, an artist, and she declared that he could not draw at all. 'All fuss and fuzz and no line.'

She received from Gordon Haight the first volumes of his edition of the letters of George Eliot. In her letter to him, she described the book as 'a repaying for the brooch a hundredfold'.

She was enormously pleased to see the Haights again during the summer of 1954. They all went down to the Sussex coast on the Brighton Belle, 'lunched in style,' had tea with some of her Kipling cousins, and then went on to Rottingdean. There they called on Enid Bagnold who let them wander round North End House where she had spent so many childhood years with her grandparents. Gordon Haight took colour photographs of Angela in front of the church. She did not think the results flattering. 'I am obviously Being English, with my coat drooping at the back all muffled round the throat. However, I *am* English, so what?'

In her correspondence with Haight she discussed her loves and hates in literature. 'I go entirely on my passions,' she wrote. She reflected on German literature which, she thought, had deteriorated during her lifetime. As a girl, she had loved the poems of Heine. 'But could you read *any* of Schiller? Not I. And of Goethe very little beyond the poems that Schubert and Schumann have immortalized. I wish some real scholar would think about this and tell me . . . It is to me as if German literature had never been, except in so far as music has kept it alive.'

Her friendship with Haight took her back to George Eliot's novels. She read *Middlemarch*, for, she said, 'the Dunnamanieth time'. She wrote to Haight, 'I feel that the Lord has laid it on me to write to you and tell you *what* a good book it is . . . *what* a book . . . Middlemarch itself is the hero and heroine and *what* a one! All that small town life is so piercingly acute and so compassionate and so un-funny and un-priggish. And the clergy are the best scenes from clerical life that she ever did.'

On Christmas Day 1954, while sitting in the drawing-room in Shawfield Street, she reflected that she had had a year of 'terrible unwellness'; she had worked harder than ever, not just at her novels, but at public speaking, which involved much tiring travel and expenditure of nervous energy. She now had so much correspondence that, in addition to Margaret Bird's typing and 'vetting' of her novels, she had to engage a typist several days a week.

Hamilton had asked her to consider another children's book. The idea appealed to her. She thought nostalgically of her much-loved *The Grateful Sparrow*, and concluded that it was, in botanical terms, a 'sport' which she could not repeat. 'Most of child literature has been so "Blyted" that one wonders any.child has any brains left . . . No little Noddy rubbish for us,' she wrote. As for producing more than one novel a year, she felt that her public could scarcely bear it. She had just finished another, *Enter Sir Robert*, the title of which was an allusion to her youngest grandson Robert Thirkell, and she was free to go again across the Atlantic. 'This book is possibly the last "life-blood of a master-spirit",' she said to Hamilton. 'I am bloody and considerably bowed.' And she signed herself, 'Very Old Mrs Thirkell.'

On Sunday 2 January 1955 she was at home listening to the radio. Paul Dehn was broadcasting a programme of children's poetry. To Angela's astonishment, among the poems read was one which she herself had written, and which had been printed in *High Rising*, her second novel. She wrote at once to her publisher. 'Would you be kind enough to take it up with the BBC? I have not the faintest objection to their quoting from my immortal works till I am black in the face, *but* they must ask your or my permission and *pay* for same.'

She sailed for America on the Queen Elizabeth early in January 1955. After a week in New York, spent mostly at the Cosmopolitan Club, she found herself alone for the weekend with Alfred Knopf in his apartment on Madison Avenue. Angela was touched by his efforts to entertain her, and in particular she was much amused by a gramophone record called *The Interrogators*, a skit on the McCarthy anti-Communist activities. 'One of the funniest and wittiest things the gramophone has produced . . . We both laughed till we ached.' When the time came for her to go, she was further touched by his pressing into her hand a wad of dollars with which to tip the servants. 'Extremely nice of him.'

She went again to New England. 'I feel I may have seen some of my Boston friends for the last time,' she wrote. In Boston she gave two talks, and at the Chiltern Club she read from her own works. Miss Gaskell Norton was now over eighty and this time she stayed with a Mr and Mrs W. G. Constable. She also stayed with Margaret Mitchell's sister-in-law and her husband, Mr and Mrs Rollin Zane. (Margaret Mitchell had died tragically in a car crash before Angela and she could meet.) Next stop, Chicago. Then on through the middle west where she had been booked to speak to the English-Speaking Union for the fee of $75, which she thought niggardly. There were other speaking engagements too. 'I feel more confused by this strange land (which I love) and the pace at which they live and the richness of everyone. I have only met *one* person who is anything near being not quite well-off—yet my friends are very ordinary.' For the first time, she was nerving herself to fly—to Minneapolis, to an ardent and wealthy fan who would not take no for an answer, and who was paying the fare. Unexpectedly, it was so warm that she had to carry her shabby old fur coat everywhere.

On her return to London, she considered again the question of a higher output. Hamilton had suggested that she deliver another book before Christmas. She had been reading a biography of Elinor Glyn. '*What* a woman—and what a lesson to us all in Hard Work. But she also, it seems, had *faith* in herself, lucky creature.' She pointed out that Knopf preferred longer spaces between each book. 'It does make one feel rather nervous and also is more work for the Old Lady who is now 65. But anything to oblige the gentlemen.'

At the end of September 1955 she was writing, 'I still feel *highly* confused as to *T 1956*. I am trying to write a bit, but I can't tell you *how* worrying and maddening this business of so many 1000 words is— during the *free* and *happy* war years I could write as much as I wanted or didn't want. It *quite honestly* takes some of the heart out of one and makes it a Task rather than a pleasure, and a. Perpetual Worry and Nightmare.'

Roger Machell, Hamilton's new editor, asked her to luncheon, which she greatly enjoyed. 'Albany is so dashing to my Victorian mind and it makes me feel like the bit of Proust where he finds his bachelor uncle entertaining Odette de Crécy—but alas! I have neither her charm nor her peculiar gifts.'

Nothing seemed to please her. She described the Royal Society of Literature as 'an honourable and quite useless Society now'. She was a Council member and was a regular attendant at meetings. There she sat with her back to the window and surveyed her colleagues. One of her *bêtes noires* in the literary world was Charles Morgan, also a Council member. To her intense indignation, it was reported that she had been seen dining with him at the Garrick Club. 'I have every opportunity of seeing, in the full light of day, the peevish, suspicious, irritable, self-satisfied Welsh face of one whose great appeal to the Reading Public (so-called) is the theme of Delayed Seduction; which was far better dealt with by the late and quite-honest-about-it Miss Ethel M. Dell.'

In fact, her host at the Garrick Club had been an old friend, Orlo Williams, an authority on Leopardi and Clerk of Committees to the House of Commons.

The mistaken identity rankled. She fumed, and at the next Council meeting she found herself sitting next to the 'Arch-Impostor' Charles Morgan. She studied him with interest, '*seamed* with the wrinkles of discontent and peevishness'. It was all a projection of her own discontent. Her formidable personality earned her the title of the *grande dame sans merci* of the London literary world.

She was not a member of the English-Speaking Union, but in November, perhaps because she was a cousin of Rudyard Kipling, she was asked to take the chair at a meeting at which the speaker was to be Charles Carrington, who had replaced Lord Birkenhead as Kipling's biographer. 'Of course, Elsie was ill-advised to turn Birkenhead down,' she wrote. 'There are the makings of an agreeable storm in an ink-well.' She prepared herself to display tact on this occasion. Carrington she thought dull and uninspired, but, Angela wrote, 'one has to remember that between F.B's book and his [Carrington's] so many people had died and Elsie stood over him with a whip. I shall try to be quite impartial.' There is no evidence to show that Kipling's daughter stood over Charles Carrington with a [figurative] whip. She would have done so at her peril.

The Society to which she was most attached was the Dickens Fellowship. She disapproved of the revelations about Dickens and the actress Ellen Ternan which the actor Felix Aylmer published to the world. Angela and all her family had known about it for years. 'It was simply a family affair which was known about but not broadcast,' she wrote. She spoke to the Fellowship on 'Children in Dickens'. 'A *delightful* society—we all adore Dickens and most of us come from *his* class . . . we are all united in love of him.'

'Lord Cross' and his son 'John-Arthur' first appeared in *Enter Sir Robert*. They reappeared in the next novel, *Never Too Late*. There was, however, a real Lord Cross. To avoid offending him, Hamilton suggested adding an 'e' to the fictional Lord Cross in *Never Too Late*. Earlier there had been the threat of trouble from Lord Norton whose name had been used in several of the novels. Angela raged. 'I *think* with pride that Baron is the *oldest* title of nobility, whereas Your Man is a 3rd Viscount, of whom I say Pouf!' Her Cross, she maintained, pre-ceded the real Lord Cross who, she declared, was a parvenu.

She stood firm. 'I am still Crossly Irate about Cross v Crosse, and cannot think why he should mind . . . It is I, *le moi*, who will look a fool who can't spell a name the same way in two separate books . . . Angela Furiosa.' She added a footnote. 'I believe it [Furiosa] means dippy—not angry.' Hamilton was adamant and Angela gave in. But, as she had predicted, scores of readers wrote to tell her of the mistake. In the following novel, she borrowed a new titled character, Lord William Harcourt, from George du Maurier's *Peter Ibbetson*.

The romance between Lord Cross(e) and Mrs Morland in *Never Too Late* suggests that Angela had in mind the romance between John Cross, the banker, and George Eliot. As we have seen, she had met John Cross, who was twenty years younger than George Eliot. In the novel, Mrs Morland rejects Lord Cross(e). 'She feels she is too old to be bothered with a man about the house.' Angela's attitude to any man whom she attracted was summed up in her remark: 'It's very peaceful with no husbands.' This was quoted by the *Observer* in their 'Sayings of the Week.'.

Colin MacInnes's first book, *To The Victor, The Spoils*, 1950, attracted a good deal of attention. The *Daily Sketch* hailed it as 'Book Find of the Month', and it was recommended by the Book Society. It dealt with the seamy side of army life and Angela did not care for it. Everywhere she went, she was congratulated on Colin's novels and art criticism. Colin was morbidly afraid of becoming known as 'Angela Thirkell's son', especially as he detested his mother's novels, which he described as 'sterile and life-denying'. He soon followed on with other novels. Angela, for her part, was frightened by Colin's books, which dealt with the underworld. Colin admitted that some of the subjects he wrote about had been deliberately chosen because they would disgust his mother. 'I did not like my mother,' he wrote. 'On my productions she preserved a stony silence.'

Colin MacInnes was bi-sexual, had many homosexual friends, and drank heavily. His sexual frankness appalled Angela. In his Australian

novel, *June in Her Spring* he described the reactions of a boy whose
father, a renowned singer, has had a homosexual relationship with a
musician. The musician tells the boy:

> Your mother . . . was no more to him than an episode . . . one of
> many, disastrous all of them to his happiness and career, flights from
> his duty in those awful alcoholic fits that made him a savage monster
> . . . I see him standing now . . . with the first choir and orchestra of
> Europe massed behind him, swaying with dark eyes like a fallen
> angel, missing the beat from the conductor and coming in blindly—
> late behind the music—a *catastrophe* . . . because he'd drunken like a
> beast and all his thoughts were centred for a while upon some worth-
> less woman . . . Some men are born . . . who are not fit for women
> . . . You are so like your father . . .

The thinly-veiled autobiographical passages in this novel horrified
Angela. To make matters worse, in the novel the boy's father had been
not only a singer, a drunkard and a homosexual, but a hero who had
fought at Gallipoli and Gaba Têpe, thus telescoping the lives of
Colin's father and stepfather.

In 1955 Colin was in trouble with the police; Angela paid the
lawyers' fees. 'He is 41—too old to make a fool of himself,' she wrote.
Probably the trouble was a sexual misdemeanour, and she was immediately concerned lest his behaviour should damage the reputation and the
careers of her other two sons. Colin came, drunk, to Shawfield Street
and made a scene. At the time Angela reacted calmly. 'Probably I
ought to have had hysterics on the spot—but one just doesn't,' she said
to Margaret Bird. 'I don't think I shall ever recover; one's mind can
reason, but one's body reacts automatically.' Colin's behaviour inevitably reminded her of James McInnes, and a complete estrangement
followed. She wrote to Haight, 'A woman's tender care *can* cease
toward the child she bears . . . and mine has ceased. In the middle
forties one does *not* behave like a drink-sodden fiend—even to a mother.'
The effects of this quarrel were long-lasting and she was never able to
understand what Colin's particular hate of her was all about. When
Colin's books were mentioned, she immediately changed the subject.
And when she made her will, Colin was excluded.

Angela occasionally spent weekends with Carola Oman, the historian and novelist, at Bride Hall, a splendid and perfectly preserved
Elizabethan manor house near Welwyn. Like Angela, Miss Oman

(Lady Lenanton) was a Council Member of the Royal Society of Literature. Countess Reventlow, a neighbour and friend, who was wife of the Danish Minister at the Court of St James, and since 1947, Ambassador, expressed a wish to meet Angela. She was a great reader of her novels, and Carola Oman invited her to luncheon over the week-end that Angela was there. At luncheon, Angela hinted broadly that she was in need of a holiday. She had never been to Denmark, she said. A polite invitation to spend a fortnight with the Reventlows soon followed, although Angela made it clear that she hoped to be invited for the whole winter. She described the holiday to Haight:

> I was on her big estate in the island of Fynen for a fortnight and saw Patriarchal life combined with wealth in a fascinating way. Huge house, almost castle, with the church as part of it; magnificent rooms all opening out of the other, crammed with *boiseries*, old portraits, gilding, carpets, tapestries; lovely ballroom with glittering chande-liers, octagon rooms with enchanting views; a lake, a chinese bridge.

She loved the splendour of it all. But more than that, she enjoyed the delicious meals. Habits of frugality—her cupboard was always bare —combined with the dreariness of living alone, had made her under-nourished. A fortnight in Denmark more than adjusted the balance. 'I burst right out of my one good suit while there.' There were evening parties in the old style, *grandes toilettes*, glitter and romance in the great chateau, and dancing. 'Wonderful! Wonderful!' she wrote wistfully in September when she had again begun 'starving hard and also miserably beginning *T 1955* with the moral consciousness that I am played out and done for'.

'I am 66,' she wrote in January 1956. 'I feel more like 666.'

St Valentine's Day 1956 was the date of the delivery of her next novel, *A Double Affair*. 'It is very beautiful in places,' she wrote, 'and I cried several times while correcting it . . . Love from an Exhausted Authoress.'

She was weeping from self-pity and loneliness. In *A Double Affair*, she 'married off' two lonely middle-aged women. She reached out herself repeatedly to people she had known in her youth. She even wrote to strangers.

Her memory was stirred one evening when she heard a talk on the radio about an Edwardian childhood. The speaker was the Earl of Lytton, the son of Neville Lytton, the painter to whom she had sat in her youth. She wrote to Lord Lytton, telling him that she had known his father. They met for an Italian meal in a restaurant in the King's Road and talked about books, paintings, families, and London in those glorious Edwardian days.

She was an indefatigable correspondent, and usually replied by return of post. One American wished her to write a thesis on 'the use of dialogue in A.T.'s novels'. In answer to a touching letter from a young man who said he was poor and loved Greek, she sent a copy of one of her father's books. There were endless letters from fans, and so involved with her characters did some readers become, that they suggested what should happen next and who should marry whom. From a teetotaller came a complaint that one of her characters drank too much. Another objected to Angela's description in *A Duke's Daughter* of a spaniel 'rolling its eyes like a negress'. One correspondent wrote angrily to say that the Church of England, unlike the Roman Catholic Church, had no real head. Angela replied crisply, 'His Most Gracious Majesty is our Head.' A clergyman who shared 'Tony Morland's' passion for trains wrote to tell her he had adopted her fictitious Barsetshire place-names for his model railway, and to prove it sent her an article he had published.*

Angela had been friendly with the *Observer*'s film critic C. A. Lejeune during and since the war, when they had both been in Beaconsfield. The Thirkell novels were Caroline Lejeune's favourite bedside reading, and when the two women met, they 'went to Barsetshire'. In an instant, Angela could, and did, enter her fantasy world.

1 Shawfield Street was always cold. Coal had to be brought up a great many steps and stairs. Angela's visitors invariably kept their coats on. So much of her social life was spent outside the house that she kept little food in it. Her guests were not allowed to help. 'No, don't,' she would say, 'I like to pretend I'm a lady.' Her favourite supper when she was alone was a bowl of porridge. To keep warm, she wrapped herself in rugs and furs and drank sherry. To the sherry, she added rum. 'One can't always get Myers's which I think much the most lady-like,' she wrote.

She was writing in bed: 'I have every gas and electric fire on and the old nursery lamp . . . lovely patterns of light on the nursery ceiling . . . I am wearing an old pair of my Mother's red woollen combinations, a woollen nightgown, a shawl and bedsocks. I have an electric pad to my shoulders or stomach, and a hot water bottle to my feet; over me two

* D. Sherwin Bailey. *Model Railway News*. January 1959.

blankets, one thin eiderdown, one brand new very thick ditto and anything in the way of rugs or shawls that are about, and the gas fire on all
night.'

In September 1956 she put her writing aside and went to stay with
some friends at Millom in Cumberland. She walked as much as she
could about the wild fell country, which never failed to move her. 'I
feel like Man Friday whose word of wonder and worship was simply O.
I say Oh! all day long . . . *How* lovely every bit of this part of the world
is.'

She returned to London, and on the morning of 25 September
opened *The Times*, to find her name leaping out at her from the fourth
leader. 'It is not everyone who has the luck to be brought up next door
to a public house.' The quotation was from *Three Houses*. Angela
immediately took up her pen, opening her letter to *The Times* with a
quotation from Byron: 'I woke up one morning and found myself
famous.' *The Times* was also rebuked, the writer of the leader had called
her 'Miss Angela Thirkell'; 'But there appears to be a curious belief
that any woman who writes a book is unmarried. They ordered things
better in Victorian days when Mrs Humphry Ward and many other
writers were always known by their married names.'

Guy Fawkes Day found her hard at work on the next novel. '*T
1957* rolls its slow length along . . . still I *do* enjoy finding out what my
old friends are doing and trying *not* to invent new ones as there are
already *far* too many people in Barsetshire.'

Several people suggested that she should write her memoirs. She
steadfastly declined. 'I said all I had to say in *Three Houses*,' she replied.
'And though my career has been chequered there have been no *lovers* or
Lesbians in it. A great deal of hard work as wife, mother, nurse, cook,
housemaid, parlourmaid, journalist and broadcaster . . . and now as
grandmother.'

To her grandchildren, Angela was a rather alarming figure. She
repeatedly read to them the stories in *The Grateful Sparrow*. When she
took them shopping, she bought them what she wanted them to have
rather than what they chose, even though it was something as small as
a pencil-sharpener.

She planned to go again to USA and Canada at the end of April 1957,
but she was increasingly unwell and the doctor advised against it. The
nature of her illness had not been diagnosed; only the symptoms of
general fatigue had been noticed. Her limp was due to the fall when she
moved into Shawfield Street. 'Still it is quite distinguished to be an

Elderly Author with Limp and I must make the best of it. The only thing to do is to A C T the part and I now stump about with very large umbrella ... People now give me seats in buses, and the bus waits while the Poor Old Lady hirples along (I hope your Scotch blood knows this excellent word).' And she embellished the letter to Hamilton with a pen-and-ink sketch of herself in a tailor-made suit, hat and stick, captioned, 'Very Old Mrs T with stick hobbling along.'

She went to the Royal Albion Hotel at Brighton—'Doctor Brighton' she called it—and from there saw many friends. She would go over to Rottingdean, and suddenly appear at North End House. Enid Bagnold was usually welcoming.

Angela was still in demand and still indefatigable. Macy's, the American publishers, were reissuing Trollope's novels and she had been asked to write introductions to *The Warden* and *Barchester Towers*. In addition, she was asked by the Royal Society of Literature for an article on Gilbert Murray, who had recently died. 'I was 7 when he came into my life ... I have no Greek and think poorly of his League of Nations. But he wrote the funniest skit on it that I have ever met,' she wrote.

During the war she had regularly given ten copies of her books to the Red Cross. Now they wrote to her to ask her to donate copies of her books for prizes at their annual ball. There were other begging letters— from strangers claiming kinship and from fans who wished for a spare wrapper of *A Double Affair* so they could have her photograph. And the National Portrait Gallery wrote to ask her to be specially photographed for the National Record of Distinguished Persons.

Towards the end of 1957, Angela began *T 1958*, and when she was not writing, she was re-reading her earlier novels, 'and I find *much* pleasure in them,' she wrote. In particular she liked *Ankle Deep*, her first novel. 'Very fair comment,' was her judgement. 'Lord! What a lot of books I have written.'

T 1958 was *Close Quarters*. The hero was one of her most endearing parsons, 'Tubby' Fewling. In her later novels she introduced a heroine 'Edith Graham', who shared many of the characteristics of the young Angela: spoiled, difficult, demanding. 'Lord Pomfret' remarks about Edith: 'What that girl needs is someone who will beat her'. 'Lady Emily' likens her to 'an ice-maiden', and 'an Undine ... an enchanting creature without a soul'.

She had a surprise visit from her old friend, Lady Glenconner's son Stephen Tennant. 'Always affectionate with the three generation background,' he appeared in his new Rolls Royce and whisked her off to the Carlton Grill for lunch.

She was frumpily dressed now and, apart from occasional visits to her beautician and hairdresser, she neglected her appearance. She constantly wore the same shabby tweed suit which was more than twenty years old and threadbare in places. Angela darned the material where her bony knees had worn the skirt thin. She described it herself as 'like a sieve—a disgrace'. But she still made an effort for an evening engagement. 'I shall wear my mantilla,' she would tell her beautician, Mrs Wyn-Reeves.

She walked with some difficulty. 'Luckily I have my grandmother's umbrella with long handle and crook at the top which makes a nice crutch,' she wrote.

In September 1958, 'I am angrily beginning *T 1959* knowing (as I have done with *every* book) that I have nothing to say and can't say it'. It was to be her thirty-second work of fiction. 'I would sooner *die*,' she wrote. 'Rum is the only thing that keeps me alive.'

Graham and his family were in London. He was Deputy High Commissioner for Canada. 'They judge *everything* by Ottawa standards and think very poorly of us—especially me because I live in a small house without central heating and haven't a car.'

The relationship between Angela and Graham had grown more difficult over the years. He wrote of her, 'She was not able to "give" ... Hers was the tragedy of the inarticulate heart. The one she had was deeply buried.' In her novels, she betrayed her mistrust and fear of the slightest physical contact, and even expressed the view, which few psychiatrists would agree with, that 'nothing makes children more ashamed of their parents than to see them both freely expressing their feelings'. Her two elder sons disagreed with her political and social conservatism, which they thought too narrow. For Angela, however, the old ways were the best, and she would not, and indeed could not, change.

At her son's diplomatic parties, she sat slightly apart, because it was too tiring for her to stand, and Joan McInnes brought people to her whom she thought her mother-in-law would like to meet. On one of these occasions, she met the London liaison officer of the National Library of Australia at Canberra. She told him, to his surprise, that she had written an Australian novel. He asked if she could spare a copy for the library.

At Shawfield Street, Angela found a spare copy of *Trooper to the*

Southern Cross. She posted it to Canberra with a letter describing how it came to be written. 'If this book can find a place among Australian war archives I shall feel honoured, 'she wrote. 'It is offered as a token of my regard for that country and its people and with it comes a true affection for a land where I lived for ten years, knowing good and evil days and making friendships that still endure.'

In the letter of thanks, the National Library of Australia wrote, 'We think of you as an Australian writer.' When *Marling Hall* was reissued in Australia, a critic wrote: 'The book might well have been written by a broad-minded Australian looking at the rural aristocracy in England with mixed affection and amusement.'

In 1958, while she was writing *Love at All Ages*, her creativity weakened; it was something that had never happened before. 'It is like pushing a garden-roller up hill,' she wrote. She was struggling to accomplish her daily ten pages. A first part was sent to Margaret Bird who was obliged to tell her that it was full of inaccuracies and repetitions. Angela scrapped it and prepared to start afresh. 'I might idealize or rationalize myself as Mrs Morland and let her do the work for me!' she wrote. The novel was not going at all well and she felt constrained to write and tell her publisher that she had serious doubts whether it would really be in time. 'What I want is a *protector*, who will say, "Now, little woman, don't trouble your little head about your books, I will take you to Cannes" (or Majorca, or New York, or Timbuctoo) "and you must just forget everything." But with a Back and a Leg, I don't think Protectors will be forthcoming . . . As soon as I find any signs of Life or Hope I'll let you know.' Her sales fell again. 'I *cannot* expect to go on earning as much as I used to,' she wrote.

But in spite of her leg, the cold, fatigue, and general depression, she managed to finish and deliver *Love At All Ages*.

She was not, to her chagrin, included in the Queen's Birthday Honours List for 1959, and reacted characteristically. '*How* I should dislike to be an MBE (and even more a DBE) . . . if Her Majesty offered me a title I should ask for brevet rank as the wife of a younger son of a Duke. To be Lady George, or Lady William, seems to me the *very* smartest thing.'

After her sixty-ninth birthday luncheon hosted by Hamilton, her condition rapidly deteriorated. 'I am still miles behindhand with the next book,' she told Margaret Bird. It was provisionally called *The Vicar's Daughter.* 'I feel rather like Tom in *The Water Babies* when he came during his travels to a place called *stop*.'

Epilogue
The Solitary-hearted

During the early summer of 1960 she was taken to St Thomas's Hospital in south-east London, suffering from aplastic anaemia. She wrote to Margaret Bird, 'It is just what an old friend used to call "a bad patch".' St Thomas's was an old Victorian building with public wards of thirty or forty beds. 'Never alone, never a dull moment, and after lights out, Matron and Staff sitting round a table making their plans for next day, all very Rembrandtesque.'

From St Thomas's, she was transferred to Hyde-Stile, a convalescent home near Godalming, where she was less happy, and later still, to Birtley House, Bramley, in Surrey. Almost every two weeks she had a complete blood-transfusion which drastically altered her appearance. 'You would laugh at me,' she told Lance, 'as I do myself when I look in the glass—a Large, Red face . . . bursting with fat!'

The nursing home was a large, comfortable house full of old people, mostly confined to single rooms, set in beautiful country. 'Leaves hardly falling yet, *such* lovely golden weather with every tree gilded,' she wrote to Lance. She was excessively bored. She devoured Gibbon and Proust. 'I can just bear to stay here a bit longer (say a week),' she declared, and then exploded, '*they* have put all Gibbon upside down while tidying the room!'

The room was adequately heated, but she constantly felt cold. 'As I haven't got a scarf with me I have tied a silk stocking over my ears to keep the draught out and pretend it is a small hat or bonnet.'

As the weeks grew into months she became increasingly unhappy. 'I don't want to finish my days here *at all*.' She longed to return to the conviviality and comradeship of the public ward at St Thomas's. 'I am *Raging* to get out of here . . . at least you are not lonely,' she told Lance. 'I have just a little boy in me that's saying "Look Mummy! I'm dead".'

More than the loneliness, more than the cold, more than the need for company, was the desperate, urgent need for rum. 'It is an eternal purgatory . . . If you do come for God's sake bring me a large, or two small bottles of *rum* or post them if you can't . . . I would give anything for Drink—rum is my tipple . . . *Please.*' She stumped, leaning on her silver-topped stick, further than she had ever done before, as far as the cottages on a main road, in search of a public house for some rum. 'None. Sickening place.' She was driven in on herself. 'Claustration,' she called it. 'I hate everyone who sent me here,' she wrote.

Her only comfort was Gibbon and Proust, to whom she added Stendhal. The autumn's splendours were followed by a rainy November. 'A very queer sky over this valley today, all in whites and greys, very soft and vaporous—no blue . . . the huge fat clouds low-down are magnificent—a fleet of Great San Phillips—but no Little Revenge.'

A week before Christmas her condition worsened. Her lawyers, Joseph Burrell and Matthew Farrer, went to see her. They told Lance that 'her memory was bad about things which happened a few minutes ago . . . She quoted from Gilbert and Sullivan.' She was dying, but she was still able to quote.

'What I should *like* to do when I leave is to tell *everyone* here exactly what I think of them,' she wrote. A friend sent her a book of Pre-Raphaelite memoirs which aroused thoughts of Burne-Jones, Kensington, Rottingdean . . . 'Yes', she reflected, 'a very happy childhood—I haven't a single complaint or criticism to make of my early years.'

Bibliography

GENERAL

ASQUITH, Cynthia *The Queen*. Hutchinson, 1937.
— *Haply I may Remember*. James Barrie, 1950.
— *Remember and be Glad*. James Barrie, 1952.
— *Diaries 1915–1918*. Hutchinson, 1968.
BALDWIN, A. W. *The Macdonald Sisters*. Peter Davies, 1960.
BALDWIN, Monica *I Leap Over the Wall*. Hamish Hamilton, 1948.
BURNE-JONES, Georgiana *Memorials of Edward Burne-Jones*. Macmillan, 1904.
BUTTERWORTH, George *Diaries and Letters*. Privately published, 1918.
ELWES, Winefride & Gervase *The Story of his Life*. Privately published, 1935.
HAIGHT, Gordon C. *George Eliot. A Biography*. OUP, 1968.
HORNER, Frances *Time Remembered*. Heinemann, 1933.
KNOX, Ronald *Barchester Pilgrimage*. Sheed and Ward. 1935.
LAGO, Mary M. *A Golden Age Revisited*. Apollo Magazine, November 1975.
LEGGE, Robin *Music in the XIXth century*. Grant Richards, 1902.
MacINNES, Colin *June in her Spring*. MacGibbon & Kee, 1956.
— *Mum's the Word*, New Statesman, 7 June, 1963.
— *A Pre-Raphaelite Memory*. The Spectator, 11 October 1963.
McINNES, Graham *The Road to Gundagai*. Hamish Hamilton, 1965.
— *Humping My Bluey*. Hamish Hamilton, 1966.
— *Finding a Father*. Hamish Hamilton, 1967
ORMOND, Richard *John Singer Sargent*. Phaidon, 1970.
PINKHAM, Roger *Catalogue of Pottery of William de Morgan*. Victoria & Albert Museum, 1973.
ROBERTSON, W. Graham *Time Was*. Hamish Hamilton, 1931.
— *Letters to Frances White Emerson*. Privately published, 1950.
TROLLOPE, Anthony *An Autobiography*. Williams and Norgate, 1883.
VAUGHAN-WILLIAMS, Ralph *Heirs and Rebels*. OUP, 1959.
WEMYSS, Countess of *A Family Memoir*. Privately published, 1935.
WOOD (afterwards Williams), Adeline *R.V.W. A Biography*. OUP, 1965.

Three Houses	OUP, 1931. Parkfield Mill, Leeds 1970
Ankle Deep	Hamish Hamilton, 1933; 1966
High Rising	Hamish Hamilton, 1933; 1966
Wild Strawberries	Hamish Hamilton, 1934; 1966
Trooper to the Southern Cross	Faber & Faber, 1934
The Demon in the House	Hamish Hamilton, 1934
O, These Men, These Men!	Hamish Hamilton, 1935
The Grateful Sparrow	Hamish Hamilton, 1935
The Fortunes of Harriette	Hamish Hamilton, 1936
August Folly	Hamish Hamilton, 1936; 1967
Coronation Summer	OUP, 1937
Summer Half	Hamish Hamilton, 1937; 1967
Pomfret Towers	Hamish Hamilton, 1938; 1967
The Brandons	Hamish Hamilton, 1939; 1968
Before Lunch	Hamish Hamilton, 1939; 1968
Cheerfulness Breaks In	Hamish Hamilton, 1940; 1968
Northbridge Rectory	Hamish Hamilton, 1941
Marling Hall	Hamish Hamilton, 1942; 1974
Growing Up	Hamish Hamilton, 1943
The Headmistress	Hamish Hamilton, 1944. Stacey, 1971
Miss Bunting	Hamish Hamilton, 1945; 1974
Peace Breaks Out	Hamish Hamilton, 1946
Private Enterprise	Hamish Hamilton, 1947
Love Among the Ruins	Hamish Hamilton, 1948. Stacey, 1973
The Old Bank House	Hamish Hamilton, 1949. Stacey, 1972
County Chronicle	Hamish Hamilton, 1950
The Duke's Daughter	Hamish Hamilton, 1951
Happy Returns	Hamish Hamilton, 1952
Jutland Cottage	Hamish Hamilton, 1953
What did it Mean?	Hamish Hamilton, 1954
Enter Sir Robert	Hamish Hamilton, 1955
Never Too Late	Hamish Hamilton, 1956
A Double Affair	Hamish Hamilton, 1957
Close Quarters	Hamish Hamilton, 1958
Love At All Ages	Hamish Hamilton, 1959
Three Score and Ten	Hamish Hamilton, 1961 (with Lejeune)

Index